True Tales from the Edgar Cayce Archives

True Tales from the Edgar Cayce Archives

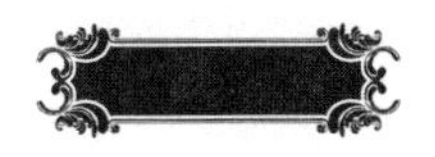

Lives Touched and Lessons Learned from the Sleeping Prophet

Sidney Kirkpatrick and
Nancy Kirkpatrick

A.R.E. Press • Virginia Beach • Virginia

1st Printing, May 2015

Printed in the U.S.A.

A.R.E. Press
215 67th Street
Virginia Beach, VA 23451-2061

ISBN 13: 978-0-87604-826-9

Source Notes

Unless otherwise indicated in the text, this book is based entirely on interviews conducted by Sidney and Nancy Kirkpatrick, primary source material collected by them, and Edgar Cayce's personal papers and correspondence, which can be found in the archives of the Edgar Cayce Foundation (ECF) and the library of the Association for Research and Enlightenment (A.R.E.) in Virginia Beach, Va. Extracts from the Cayce readings come directly from typed transcriptions housed in the A.R.E. library or found on the Official Edgar Cayce Readings DVD-ROM. Additional access to the entire readings database is available to A.R.E. members at EdgarCayce.org/members.

Most photos are courtesy of the Edgar Cayce Foundation Archives or www.commons.wikimedia.org

Cover design by Christine Fulcher

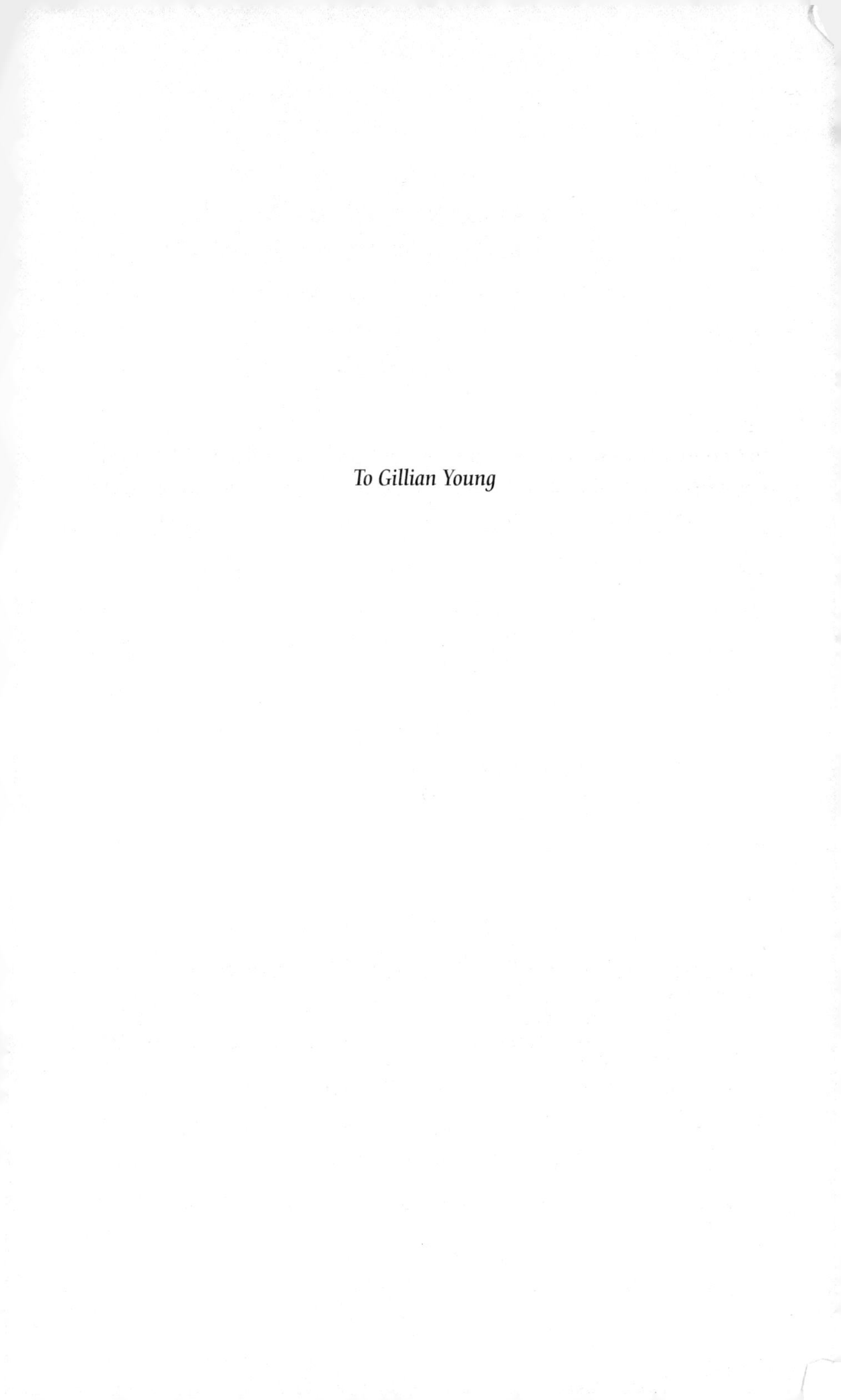

To Gillian Young

Hear now my words: If there be a prophet among you,
I the Lord will make myself known unto him in a vision,
and will speak unto him in a dream.

Numbers 12:6

Contents

Acknowledgments

The authors wish to acknowledge the substantial contribution to this book by A.R.E. archive assistant Karen Davis, who carries on the commitment and dedication to the Cayce archives begun by Gladys Davis.

We also want to express our appreciation for the talent, hard work and patience of our editor Stephanie Pope, and both Cassie McQuagge and Cathy Merchand of A.R.E. Press.

And many thanks are due to Kevin Todeschi, Jennie Taylor Martin. Susan Lendvay, Alison Ray, Alison Hendrick Parker, Claire Gardner, Pat Belisle and all the staff, board members and volunteers at the A.R.E., the Edgar Cayce Foundation and the A.R.E. Press for their commitment to carrying on the Cayce work, and for the help and support they have, without fail, always granted us.

Edgar Cayce (March 18, 1877-January 3, 1945).

Introduction

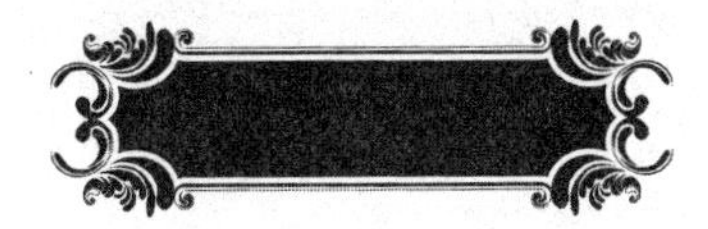

Why Edgar Cayce?

Like many journalists, I once arrogantly believed that psychic phenomena was a subject unworthy of serious study and that anyone who put his faith in a trance medium was either fooling himself or the unwitting victim of fraud. Then along came Nancy Webster, who would become my writing partner and wife. "Edgar Cayce is going to be the subject of your next book," Nancy prophetically declared. Not wishing to be rude or condescending, I politely declined further discussion. But Nancy, a dedicated student of Cayce's work since she had been in high school, was unrelenting. Books and articles about the so-called "sleeping prophet" of Virginia Beach appeared in my mail box with such regularity that to finally put the matter to rest, I read one.

To say that the Cayce story challenged my imagination is an understatement. A backwoods Kentucky farm boy with an eighth grade education, he allegedly had the ability to enter into a deep hypnotic trance from which he could diagnose illness, witness events in the distant past, preview the future, and converse with angels. No subject was off limits, regardless of how simple or complex the question—whether it was help finding a lost pocket watch, how to perform a surgical procedure, or what to expect in the hereafter. Cayce would lie down on a couch, fold his hands over this stomach, seemingly drift off to sleep, and miraculously answer any question put to him. Rarely, if ever, was he proven wrong.

In the course of his forty-one year career, Cayce reportedly saved hundreds of people from intractable diseases and crippling injuries. A hospital dedicated to his healing arts was built in Virginia Beach where patients received his trance readings, and specialty technology, years ahead of its time, was used to treat them. He guided the business interests of Detroit auto-parts manufacturers and helped New York stockbrokers along with Texas oilmen become millionaires. He identified the location of buried treasure, solved a murder, and dictated trance-induced Hollywood screenplays. Yet Cayce and his family led lives of constant struggle and hardship, moving from home to home often under threat of being persecuted for fortunetelling or practicing medicine without a license. He didn't profit from giving trance counsel nor did he promote himself. For much of his life he earned his livelihood as a portrait photographer and was a much-admired husband, father, and church deacon.

Cayce's story was altogether too incredible to be true. This was why, I suspected, fifty years had elapsed since a comprehensive biography of Cayce had been written. No serious writer or journalist would devote time to making a rigorous examination of the facts because they wouldn't stand up to scrutiny. Dig deeper and Cayce's story was sure to unravel. Or so I supposed.

Always a step ahead of me, Nancy would send me transcripts of Cayce's trance readings. Accompanying them were physician's reports and convincing first-person testimony of how his recommended health treatments—frequently dismissed in his lifetime as the fanciful products of his imagination—had later become fully accepted by the mainstream medical community. Trance discourses he gave on such subjects as foods for health and healing, hydrotherapy, massage, and the intimate connection between psychological and physical health would earn Cayce distinction as the undisputed father of today's holistic health movement. Information he gave on world history, physics, electrical engineering, and earth sciences also proved uncannily accurate. And though he died decades before widespread popular interest in paranormal phenomenon, Cayce's trance readings on subjects such as remote viewing, life after death, reincarnation, the secret of the Sphinx, and the lost continent of Atlantis would set the standard by which nearly all metaphysical information has subsequently been judged. He was to the world of psychics and mediums what Babe Ruth was to the world of baseball.

Most compelling, Cayce didn't speak in vague, ambiguous terms that were open for interpretation but used precise medical and scientific terminology well beyond his education and training. Further, he didn't perform these superhuman feats a few hundred times in the course of his career. He gave well over sixteen thousand trance readings, each one different, and some lasting thirty minutes to an hour. On many occasions professors from Ivy League universities, notable church leaders, bank presidents, historians, physicians, inventors, and scientists attended his trance session. Master magician Harry Houdini, having dedicated himself to exposing the fraudulent practices of hundreds of occult mediums and spiritualists, failed to debunk or explain the Cayce phenomenon, as did Hugo Münsterberg of the Harvard Medical School.

Even this, however, was not what made the Cayce material most relevant. As his trance readings make clear, their ultimate purpose was not simply to provide diagnostic insights to aid physicians, bring about miraculous cures, locate lost treasure, or to excite the intellect. They were provided to help individuals to understand and accept the truth of the multidimensional world in which we live. Cayce had provided incontrovertible evidence for the existence of a consciousness beyond our five senses. His work was an open door into another dimension through which we can more fully understand ourselves and our place in the universe.

The question that I was soon asking myself was not whether Cayce did what he was alleged to have done—the evidence was overwhelming—but how he did it. Thus began our study of Edgar Cayce, and along with it, a partnership was formed between myself, a nonbeliever, and Nancy, whose faith in Cayce never faltered. Together we would research Cayce's life and work as it had never been conducted before, producing his definitive biography, *Edgar Cayce, An American*

Prophet; authoring numerous articles; contributing to movie and television projects; and most important, endeavoring to apply his trance guidance into our everyday lives and those of our four children.

A trip to Virginia Beach, Virginia, was our starting point. Here, at the Association for Research and Enlightenment (A.R.E.) are housed the Edgar Cayce archives, which consist of an estimated half-million pages of trance readings, correspondence, family papers, and photographs. As Cayce primarily gave readings for particular individuals who requested his help and follow-up biographical research had been conducted to determine the effectiveness of his advice, we had a massive collection of additional reference material which we would use to track down the people who received the readings and judge the truth for ourselves. The vast majority of names of these individuals meant little or nothing to us at the onset of our research, for they had led otherwise undistinguished lives as farmers, housewives, building contractors, musicians, students, and nurses—even an Alabama tombstone cutter. Children and adults from nearly any profession one can name came to Cayce for advice.

However, among these individuals were names that we instantly recognized. Composer George Gershwin and Hollywood film pioneer Jesse Lasky had readings, as had inventors Thomas Edison and Nikola Tesla, electrical engineers at RCA and NBC, and the president and founder of Goodyear Tire and Rubber Company. Readings were conducted for the mother of Ernest Hemingway, on behalf of the husband of aviator Amelia Earhart, and though shrouded in secrecy, for President Woodrow Wilson. This aspect of Cayce's work had not heretofore been called attention to because Cayce had never promoted himself. He didn't trade on the names of the rich and famous who consulted with him for the same reason he didn't charge a fee for giving readings. He believed that his gift was from God and not to be used for selfish or self-serving purposes, but for the brotherhood of man; what the readings say is our collective purpose or soul's destiny.

In Hopkinsville, Kentucky, where Cayce lived and worked for the first half of his career, Nancy and I camped at the edge of a farmer's field, walked the woods where Cayce played as a youth, and visited the tobacco barn where he had first begun communicating with the spirit world. In Selma, Alabama, we visited the First Christian Church, in whose archive we read the minutes once kept by its church secretary, Edgar Cayce. In Cleburne, Texas, we met the son of a newspaper reporter who had worked with Cayce to develop the Desdemona oil fields, one of the largest petroleum and natural gas deposits ever found. In Dayton, Ohio, we interviewed a man whose employer's dream was to build the hospital dedicated to Cayce's healing arts. Many others who knew Cayce personally or had received readings came forward with stories that had previously gone unrecorded. As we would discover, their enthusiasm for Cayce went beyond the trance counsel he provided. They enjoyed his company—whether he was teaching Bible study, working alongside them in the photo studio, or joining him at his favorite fishing hole. A humble, kind, and affectionate man, he preferred the company of children, friends, and co-workers over and above his many rich and famous acquaintances. He touched their lives, and they touched his.

Herein lies the theme of this book. Edgar Cayce could not do what he did alone. Deep in a hypnotic trance, he had no conscious memory of anything that was said. He needed someone—more often than not his wife, Gertrude—to guide him into trance and put questions to him. He also needed someone to record and transcribe what he said, a task which would ultimately fall to his devoted secretary, Gladys Davis. He needed plenty of others—physicians, nurses, physical therapists, scientists, engineers, and biblical scholars, even an Alabama tombstone cutter—to help recipients of the readings make the most of the advice that was provided. Most important, he needed someone who genuinely wanted his help. The more deeply felt and true the desire for that help, the longer, more detailed and often more profound was the information that came through. He needed a team, just as the trance readings tell us that all of us need a team or partners with whom, and by design, we are to share life's experience.

Now, more than two decades after first entering the Cayce vault in Virginia Beach, it is not just Edgar that keeps us coming back for further research and study, but the many people whose lives gave shape and meaning to his trance readings. Understanding their challenges, triumphs, failures, and desires is to understand the higher purpose of our own life's journey. This is what is meant by "Cayce's work." It's not just *his* work, but *our* work, too.

Lulu Boyd Cayce:

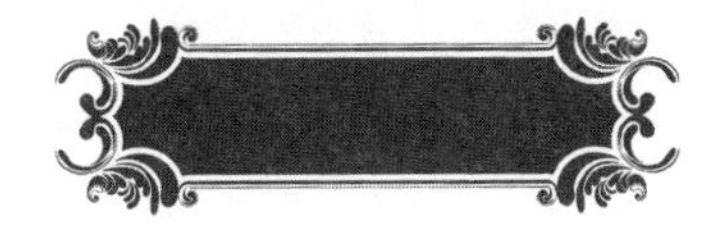

Angels and Demons

Edgar Cayce's first reported spirit encounter was with his dead grandfather Tom Cayce, who was killed in 1881 after being thrown from a horse on the family's Beverly, Kentucky, tobacco farm. The matter didn't worry Edgar's mother Carrie, who believed her four-year-old son simply had a vivid imagination. Edgar's father, Leslie, a failed farmer and heavy drinker, was gone from the house for weeks on end and may not have noticed his son's increasingly strange behavior. The family member most concerned was Edgar's twenty-four-year-old aunt, Lulu Boyd Cayce, who recommended that Little Eddy ought to be taken to a doctor. It was either that or to a priest. "He's got the Devil in him," Lulu told Edgar's parents. "No good can come of this."

Lulu and her extended family members knew how close Little Eddy had been with this grandfather. The child had often napped in Tom's arms and was never happier than when he was wrapped in Tom's long overcoat. Tom had taught him to fish, ride on horseback, and tend to the garden. He even helped Edgar build playhouses out of the tall brush that grew along the banks of the Little River, a meandering stream that cut through the Cayce property.

The Lulu Boyd and Clinton Cayce family of Beverly, Kentucky, c. 1882. L. to R.: Maud (with doll); Lulu Boyd; Florence (center); Clinton Cayce; Granville

Edgar had been riding behind Tom on his favorite mare when the tragic accident had occurred. As eyewitnesses told the story, Tom was heading back from the tobacco fields when they stopped at a pond to water the horse. Tom had let Edgar down from the saddle to play in the shallows, his favorite pastime. Moments later the horse was startled by what may have been a water moccasin. The horse reared up, pitching Tom into the water. From shore, Edgar watched as the horse brought its hoofs down on Tom's chest. A physician who lived nearby was called for help, but Tom was dead before Lulu Boyd's husband, Clinton, pulled Tom out of the water.

As Lulu soon noticed, Little Eddy seemed undisturbed by the tragedy. Not long after the funeral, she found him standing alone in the tobacco barn. When asked what he was doing, Edgar matter-of-factly declared he was talking with Grandpa. According to Eddy, often times Grandpa was out in the fields too, whispering to farmhands to remind them of chores or how to fix farm machinery. But Grandpa, he said, could sometimes be hard to see. He appeared in "beams of light." If Edgar looked really hard, he could see right through him.

Edgar's grandfather Thomas Jefferson Cayce, c. 1875.

The pond where he was thrown from a horse and died in 1881.

Grandpa's favorite place to sit, Edgar confided, was under the rafters in the barn. Edgar wanted to show Lulu the spot, but she sternly declined. This was strange behavior indeed. But what really frightened her were the stories Edgar said his grandfather had been telling him about the Cayce family's pre-Civil War past in Virginia. These stories were not the kind easily produced by the vivid imagination of a youngster, but authentic accounts of the Cayce family before coming to Kentucky. Only Tom's generation would know these things.

Lulu counseled Edgar not to tell anyone about his visions and encouraged Leslie and Carrie to seek help for the child. Further, Edgar continued to exhibit other strange and unnerving behaviors which unsettled the family. Among them was an incident which occurred in 1882, after Edgar's mother gave birth to a second child, whom the family named Thomas in honor of his deceased grandfather. There is no record if Carrie carried the newborn to term, nor are there any details known about the circumstances of his delivery, only that Thomas was born on November 19, lived for ten days, and was buried in the Cayce family plot. Edgar's father Leslie, for reasons not now known, disappeared for several weeks, leaving Carrie and Edgar alone in the cabin to care for themselves.

Grave of infant Thomas Cayce.

Carrie took to bed for three and four days at a time, most likely suffering from post-partum depression and grief over the death of her child. Her anguish left an indelible impression on Edgar, and he often referred to this period in his family's life as a particularly troubling one. Neither then, nor later, would Thomas' name be spoken or appear in family correspondence. But for Edgar would ultimately come a life-affirming insight out of this experience.

Edgar and his mother were alone in the cabin when she unexpectedly burst into tears and collapsed onto the dirt floor. This was remarkable for Edgar because it was the first time he had seen his mother cry. When he tried to comfort her, she pulled him down to his knees, and she, rising up on her knees, cupped her hands over his and began to pray. This, too, was something new for Edgar as he hadn't seen anyone pray before. Lulu and her husband Clinton were dedicated Christians and members of Liberty Church, Beverly's only house of worship, but this was not the case with the Leslie Cayce family.

As Carrie prayed—earnestly asking the Lord for His blessings and His help in her time of need—Edgar experienced what researchers today call clairaudience or the ability to hear and perceive sounds that are beyond the normal human audio range. Though no one was playing an instrument and he and his mother were alone in the room, Edgar heard music. "Her prayers were like musical notes," he later described the experience.

Edgar spent many years pondering the relationship between prayer and music, but it was not until he was an adult that he articulated what he believed in a public lecture. He compared a single person praying to a musical note, rising toward heaven. Two people praying together could create a chord or harmonic, and a roomful of people praying together could create a divine symphony. He would further refer to Jesus as the Master Musician.

Exactly what Lulu thought of his experience is anyone's guess. A pinched and humorless woman, as described by some, she and her husband, a third generation farmer and Beverly's postmaster, were also deeply empathetic. When Carrie and Leslie were unable to care for Edgar, Lulu and Clinton took Edgar in and briefly saw to his edu-

Edgar at the Beverly School, (back row, 3rd from left, in front of a window).

cation, something which proved quite challenging.

As more than one of his teachers would note, the most frightening thing about Edgar was his ability to press his head against a book, close his eyes, and somehow know the book's entire contents, right down to where on a page a particular word or paragraph could be found. The same was true with unopened letters. He had only to handle an envelope to know what was inside—a talent that soon earned him a nickname, the Freak. These were especially strange abilities for a young boy who had difficulty learning to read or paying attention in class.

Like other accounts of his strange abilities, skeptics would dismiss such stories as fabrications intended to burnish what later became legend. The historical record, however, provides startling evidence otherwise. As a young teen, encouraged by his father who wished to show off his son's talents, Edgar performed in front of audiences of forty or more people, including the mayor of nearby Hopkinsville and a U.S. Congressman. Edgar recited, verbatim, a 110-page congressional speech.

Reading the Bible soon became the only subject that interested Eddy. This was triggered by a conversation that Edgar had had with a black woodcutter who lived on his grandfather's old farm. People in Beverly called him "Crazy Bill" because he was, as Edgar himself later said, "not quite right in the head." They happened to meet on his way home from school one day when Bill was clearing a tree that had fallen across the road. "I'm feeling as strong as Samson," Bill declared, swinging his ax. As Edgar didn't know who Samson was, Bill recounted the Old Testament stories of how the heroic Samson, invested by God with superhuman strength, pulled a temple down with his bare hands and subdued a lion.

Edgar now wanted to know all about the Bible. His mother and father didn't own one, but Lulu did. She was especially pleased to let him handle her Bible and then to accompany him to Liberty Church where she said people studied it. That prayer was part of the equation excited him all the more.

Lulu's Bible, handed down through her family, was quite large and heavily illustrated. She showed him woodcuts of the divinely inspired Samson pulling down the pillars of the temple and holding open the gaping jaws of a ferocious lion with his bare hands. Also among the illustrations was one of Archangel Michael with wings spread. Edgar soon asked for a Bible of his own, which was presented to him by Elijah Hopper of Hopper Brothers Bookstore in Hopkinsville where Edgar would one day work.

Edgar immediately tried to read the Bible. At first he couldn't pronounce the names and had to have Lulu and then his mother follow along with him. Reading sessions would always end with a prayer. By early the following year Edgar could read many passages without help. He was especially drawn to the Old Testament stories of what today are considered supernatural or psychic phenomena. From age ten onwards, a Bible was seldom out of his reach, and he would read it cover to cover once each year of his life. He carried it with him so often that his mother sewed what he called a "hind pocket" on his overalls in which to protect it on his way back and forth to school or on long walks into the woods.

Edgar soon joined Liberty Church, part of the immensely popular Kentucky-based Disciples of Christ, which rejected all "man-made" creeds and accepted the Bible alone as its full and final authority. Aunt Lulu and Uncle Clinton, and other Cayces, would witness his baptism by immersion into the Little River at age twelve.

Lulu, no doubt, was relieved that he should take to church the way he did. He sat through the two-hour services, attended meetings of the church elders, and became the church's sexton—a position that had never before or since been held by a child. He could also quote long passages and interpret scripture. Like his experience at school, however, his entry into the church presented unexpected challenges. The miracles of the prophets, he declared, were still possible. He knew because God had spoken to him through an angel.

The angelic encounter took place in his bedroom, after Edgar had spent a long day reading his Bible and asking how he could be of service to the Lord. He had eaten dinner with the family and had gone to bed at sundown as usual. His three younger sisters were fast asleep in the bed beside him when he suddenly awoke and saw what he described as a powerful light coming through the doorway.

> I felt as if I were being lifted up. A glorious light, as of the rising

> morning sun, seemed to fill the whole room, and a figure appeared at the foot of my bed. I was sure it was my mother and called [out], but she didn't answer. For the moment I was frightened, climbed out of bed, and went to my mother's room. No, she hadn't called. Almost immediately, after I returned to my couch, the figure came again. Then it seemed all gloriously bright—an angel, or what, I knew not, but gently, patiently, it said: 'Thy prayers are heard. You will have your wish. Remain faithful. Be true to yourself. Help the sick, the afflicted.'

Edgar couldn't go back to sleep. He instead walked outside and sat beneath his favorite willow tree, where he often went to read his Bible. He knelt, thanking God for answering his prayers and providing direction in his life. What he would do and how he was to prepare himself were questions he hadn't thought to ask.

Three years would elapse before he summoned the courage to tell anyone about the angel's visit. To have done so would surely have further upset Lulu and the rest of the family, and even if he had felt up to facing an interrogation at home and the one that would inevitably have followed at church, he didn't feel he had the skills to convey the intensity of his vision or to avoid public mockery. "I had no way of knowing which was more real," he later confessed, "the vision of the lady or the pillow I rested my head upon."

Many more years would pass before he was able to understand his vision in the broader context of his childhood experiences. Edgar concluded that he had been born with special abilities and that as a youth he frequently experienced a reality that existed beyond his five senses. That the angel who appeared in his bedroom was strikingly similar to an illustration in his aunt's Bible didn't invalidate the experience, nor did seeing his dead grandfather dressed in the same long coat he wore out into the fields. Such visualizations were the only means by which a psychically gifted adolescent could interpret what he would, as an adult, experience when he entered a hypnotic trance.

Did his Aunt Lulu become convinced that her nephew's visions were a gift from God and not the work of the Devil? Unfortunately, about this—the earliest documented long-term relationship Edgar had with someone besides his mother and father—few intimate details are now known. All that can be said with certainty is that Lulu and the vast majority of the Cayces in Beverly were loath to discuss or even say what later became of Eddy when he moved from Beverly. Even decades later some extended family members believed that Edgar and his trance readings had sullied the family name. Parishioners at Liberty Church, well into the 1950s, were reluctant to acknowledge that he had once been the sextant.

Lulu's role in the Cayce story, however, would be substantively different from that of her other Beverly relatives or the Cayce family's neighbors. In January 1893, when Edgar's father, Leslie, had lost his share of the family inheritance and moved his wife and their three daughters to Hopkinsville, sixteen-year-old Edgar remained behind in Beverly. That he chose to live with Lulu and Clinton and work their farm for the next nine months is indicative of the love and trust that existed between them. Lulu's side of the family was also the first to accept what they referred to as his "calling." Lulu's sister was the first of the extended Cayce family members to receive a dedicated trance reading, followed by Lulu's husband, Clinton, and eventually Lulu herself at age sixty-five.

Bedridden, she had contracted a life-threatening congestive condition and couldn't stop coughing. Her nephew, then living in Virginia Beach, went into trance, immediately diagnosed her condition, and recommended a unique blend of medicinal herbs, hot packs, and spinal adjustments. Days later she was back on her feet, and in two months she was cured. Though she personally didn't write to thank Edgar or reference to friends and neighbors that she had had a reading, Clinton did so on her behalf. Further, after Lulu and Clinton retired and moved to Hopkinsville, they would always invite Edgar to stay with them on his yearly visits back to Kentucky. As she and Clinton finally acknowledged by welcoming him home, God works in mysterious ways.

Anna and Barnett Seay:

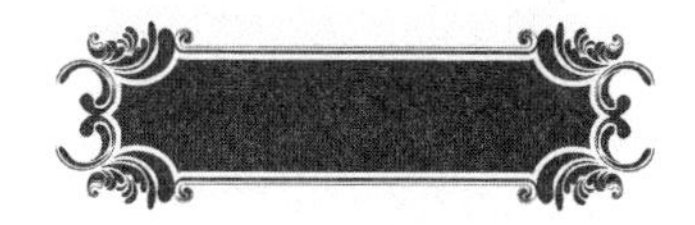

Together Again

The ghostly appearance of Tom Cayce was the start of a revolving door of spirit entities in Edgar's life. His first childhood playmates were the "make-believe" kind—so his parents believed. Only the "Little Folk," as Eddy referred to them, were not your usual imaginary friends. They had names, distinct personalities, and they told him stories about Egypt and Persia—subjects not ordinarily discussed by rural farm children in Beverly. The only things that troubled Eddy were the facts that the Little Folk never seemed to get wet when it rained and they didn't like being seen by other people. They would disappear. Troubled by their precocious child's overly vivid imagination, Edgar's parents were relieved when Eddy made friends with neighbor Barnett Seay's daughter. Hallie, a petite dark-haired girl a year older than Edgar, was called "Little Anna" because she shared the same first name as her mother.

Little Anna and Eddy were always together. In the winter they would run through the fields trying to catch snowflakes and play under a covered bridge. Their summer activities included chasing dragonflies and picking flowers, playing on the banks of Little River, or watching the farmers at work. As Edgar later told the story, the Little Folk liked Anna as much as he did—only she got to know them better because she was always asking them questions.

Edgar and Anna's favorite hideout was in the rafters of a neighbor's barn, where they hollowed out a space for themselves in a haystack and played house together. Anna was his wife, he was her husband, and the Little Folk were their children.

On one occasion they borrowed a neighbor's flat-bottomed skiff and drifted downstream on Little River, where they came upon a small island near a fork in the river. Here, too, they were joined by the Little Folk. But as Edgar later related the story, they were also joined by creatures that were not much larger than insects. He called them "sprites" as they gave off unusual sparkling colors. He and Anna didn't get to visit with them long because they didn't like to play with children or, for that matter, any other humans.

Little River in Beverly, Kentucky, where Edgar and Little Anna played together.

Edgar's family naturally dismissed the notion of sprites, but Edgar never did. Like the vision of the angel and the Little Folk, they were all part of the multifaceted spirit dimension. Only sprites, Cayce came to believe, were "energy forms" which lived in and among plants and trees and played an integral role in their growth process. Just as the Little Folk appeared to him as children, the sprites appeared to him as twinkling stars, which was how he, an adolescent, could best understand or decode what he observed in his mind's eye. That Edgar shared the experience with another, Little Anna, made it all the more real to him.

The eighteen months Edgar spent with Little Anna were the happiest of his childhood. They ended when Leslie sold the cabin where they were living and moved into a hunting lodge several miles from the Seay homestead. He and Little Anna's separation was made permanent when she contracted and died of pneumonia. Edgar was reported to have walked six-and-a-half miles through deep snow to be with his friend when the end came, only to arrive too late to say goodbye. She was buried in a small coffin near her home in Beverly, where she was joined a month later by her father, Barnett Seay, who is believed to have died from pneumonia contracted while nursing her. The remaining members of the Seay family eventually sold the Beverly farm, and their descendants settled in Virginia and California.

This story, however, does not end with a bereft young boy and the tragic death of his only friend. As with Edgar's grandfather, Little Anna, too, would make another appearance, only not as a delicate brown-haired young girl with whom he had explored Little River.

Nearly five decades after Little Anna died, Edgar Cayce received a letter from a twenty-nine-year-old bookkeeper, Beatrice Coffing, from Altadena, California. She had read an article about Cayce's medical clairvoyance in "Miracle Man of Virginia Beach," which had run in the popular *Coronet Magazine*. She sought and then received trance advice from Cayce on behalf of her fiancé, Richmond, a violinist and music teacher, suffering from a blinding case of cataracts.

Edgar, then sixty-two years old and living in Virginia Beach, provided a remarkable medical diagnosis. He described her fiancé's condition as stemming from an injury his mother had sustained in pregnancy, which had resulted in his premature birth—information which had not been provided to Cayce, but was later confirmed as true. Further, Cayce said that Richmond's cataracts could be cured and recommended a treatment comprising of specific osteopathic spinal adjustments in his upper dorsal and cervical area and his taking Codiron, a health supplement composed of cod liver oil and iron with vitamins A, B, C, and G.

Beatrice Coffing's fiancé, Richmond Seay.

After undergoing these and other recommended treatments, his condition rapidly improved. As Beatrice and her fiancé reported several months later, for the first time in nearly half a decade he could read the notes on a page of sheet music. Before the New Year his cure was complete. So successful was the experience that Beatrice wrote to Edgar to request readings for herself and to say that she and her fiancé would be driving from California to Virginia, a distance of nearly three-thousand miles, with her fiancé behind the wheel, to thank Edgar in person.

The information that came through in Beatrice's reading was quite a surprise to the Cayce family for rarely did a trance session speak directly to events and karmic connections with Edgar's childhood in Beverly. Beatrice, age twenty-nine, hadn't even been born when Edgar, in 1893, had moved from Beverly to Hopkinsville.

Edgar Cayce and Beatrice Coffing in Virginia Beach.

Reincarnation, at this point in Cayce's career, was not a new subject. In addition to upwards of nearly ten thousand medical readings, he had given several hundred "Life Readings," in which a soul's previous incarnations were identified and descriptions were given that would help the recipients of the reading understand how their behaviors and relationships in previous lifetimes impacted their present lifetime. In Beatrice's case, many of those relationships in her previous lifetimes had been with Edgar.

Something highly unusual during the Life Reading happened when the reading began with the curious statement, "This isn't the name! [But] yes, we have the records here of that entity now called Beatrice Coffing."

Then, the reading continued:

> In the present, then, we find that the entity is one of those that may indeed be said to be the consistent thinker and exponent of *all for one*, and *one for all*, in those things in which it has enjoined itself in active service. These attitudes make for hardships at times in the material experience in the present. But in those activities in which there may be the outlet for the greater home building, and the expression of same, may the entity find the greater field of service, the greater harmony, the greater outlook for peace and joy in the experience of this entity.

In other words, she would find her greatest fulfillment at home and in the life she would share with others. In terms of previous lives, the reading would further reveal that she and Edgar had been together as recently as Edgar's present incarnation in a rural farming community in Kentucky through which flowed the Little River. And yet, in the correspondence Edgar sent to Beatrice with her Life Reading, he remained unusually circumspect about sharing with her how they had known one another, only that they had.

It was not until he met Beatrice in person that Edgar let the "secret slip out." He had to "see the truth" for himself before he could, as he later said, "be absolutely certain." That day, when Beatrice and her fiancé arrived in front of the Cayce's Virginia Beach home, Edgar stood on the porch, unable to move. He couldn't even speak to her as she had exited the car and raised her hand to greet him. Tears began to pour down his cheeks. He could barely put together more than two words. "Little Anna . . . Little Anna," he repeated. "It's true."

Before coming to Virginia Beach, Beatrice had read everything she could about Edgar, and though she believed him to be a "kindred spirit," she was not prepared for the curious way he addressed her. Who was Little Anna? Why the tears? Edgar's wife Gertrude and secretary Gladys Davis were equally mystified. They, too, had never heard of Little Anna nor could guess why Edgar was moved to tears.

When Edgar and Beatrice sat down in his study and talked together, she began to understand what seeing her meant to him. She also gained a startling insight into the greater message that came through in the readings. She had not only known Edgar in her previous incarnation as Little Anna, but she had also known her fiancé, Richmond Seay, whom she had cared for during his years-long ordeal with cataracts. He was none other than Anna's father, Barnett Seay, who had cared for her when she contracted pneumonia. Little Anna and her father Barnett Seay, who had both died of pneumonia in Kentucky in 1887, were now in 1941 Beatrice and Richmond Seay, soon to be husband and wife.

Beatrice cared for Richmond in his hour of need as he had once cared for her. That's how karma, which is so fundamental to the process of reincarnation, often worked out in the cycles of reincarnation described in the Cayce readings. Mothers in a previous incarnation often became daughters or sisters in the next. And invariably there was at least one family member who returned within the same family, as Edgar's grandfather, Tom Cayce, eventually returned as Edgar's grandson, Charles Thomas Cayce.

What was begun in one lifetime was continued in the next, bringing forth lessons and learning experiences crucial to what the readings described as the essence of human evolution—the development or growth of a soul preparing to meet or return to its maker. Family members could be construed as team members working together in this life and the next.

Once Beatrice and Edgar began to compare notes about their present lives, they realized how much they had in common. Both loved gardening and frequently spoke to their plants. Like Edgar's childhood in Beverly, she had spent her formative years in Attica, Indiana, playing alone in the woods and conversing with "imaginary" playmates. Their respective spiritual paths, though very different, had also brought them to the same deeply rooted belief in Christianity.

Edgar and Beatrice would become fast and devoted friends. She and Richmond, who soon became her husband, would move to Blackstone, Virginia, and became active leaders in the fledgling A.R.E.—

Edgar with son Hugh Lynn, Beatrice and Richmond Seay, and secretary Gladys Davis in Virginia Beach.

the association that would carry the Cayce work to future generations. They never referred to one another as Edgar and Beatrice, but simply as Eddy and Anna.

Beatrice frequently poured out her affection to Edgar in letters:

> I have a great many things to be thankful for, Eddy, but I think you are one of the greatest and deepest of those things that I am thankful for, so I'm always so very grateful to you for giving us some of your time and blessedness," she wrote. "I've just finished reading through and pondering all of your letters since first you addressed me . . . Although at that time I had no idea that "Little Anna" or "Little Eddy" ever existed—something flickered even then. And what a wonderful revelation and what beautiful things have come out of finding a certain Mr. Edgar Cayce.

Later, Beatrice would write: "The beauty and wonder of it! I could not understand what pulled and tugged at my heart and soul from the moment I heard of you and your work, until little by little you have told me of experiences that have helped me to understand . . . It seemed as though you were part of my heart and soul."

Edgar felt likewise.

> [For me] you stand between the living and the dead, and the plague of doubt in my own mind is stayed . . . when [I] am with you . . . All doubt slips away, and when I allow myself to slip back to days long since gone, a part of the whole business of living, [I] am just transported into another world. A world that one cannot help but see, feel, hear the goodness and the love of God. I now am never able to put into words what I feel, but it is there, and [I] know I am better able to at least try and serve others better when I have been with you.

Three years after meeting Beatrice, Edgar suffered a stroke which resulted in complete paralysis of the entire left side of his body. He was sent to Roanoke, Virginia, to recover. Knowing the end was approaching and wishing to die in the company of friends and family, he asked to be driven home. But on the drive back to Virginia Beach he requested the ambulance take a detour to Blackstone. He wished to see Little Anna one last time.

Beatrice and Richmond Seay were not home when Edgar's ambulance arrived in their driveway. They, too, had sensed that the end was near and had driven to Virginia Beach in hopes of seeing him for one last time. They had left for Virginia Beach while the ambulance was driving to Blackstone.

Beatrice never got to say goodbye to her beloved Edgar, just as, some forty-years earlier, Eddy had been too late to say goodbye to Little Anna.

Dwight Moody:

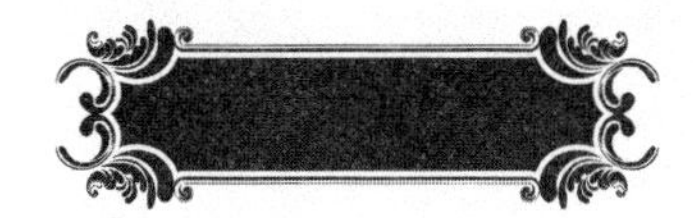

A Pastor in This Life and the Next

The Union Tabernacle was the place to be on weekend nights in Hopkinsville, the county seat. With stadium seating for two-thousand, the block-long civic auditorium played host to vice-presidential candidate Theodore Roosevelt, African-American educator Booker T. Washington, temperance leader Carrie Nation, orator William Jennings Bryan, and bandleader John Phillip Sousa.

Eighteen-year-old Edgar Cayce, a frequent visitor, came to hear the evangelists. There was the "soul saving" and "eternal optimist" former baseball star Billy Sunday; the advocate of Christian education George Stuart, the feisty and always humorous Sam Jones, and Mordecai Ham, the preacher who later converted Billy Graham at a revival meeting in North Carolina. Edgar eagerly awaited the arrival of the immensely popular and charismatic Dwight L. Moody, known simply as "D.L.," who sometimes drew ten and twelve thousand people to hear his sermons.

Edgar Cayce, c. 1890s.

Dwight Moody, c. 1890.

On the morning before Moody was scheduled to speak, April 5, 1898, Edgar was living with his family in a white clapboard home on the corner of 7th and Young Streets, a short walk from the tabernacle. He had grown to be quite tall, standing just over six-foot two with tousled brown hair he cut short, which accentuated his high forehead, deep-set, blue-gray eyes, and receding chin. As his father was still unemployed since leaving Beverly two years earlier, Edgar's salary as a clerk in Hopper Brothers Bookstore was now his family's sole means of support. Still, Edgar had chores to perform. Among his responsibilities was to milk the family cow, which that Tuesday morning had gone missing.

Edgar followed the cow's tracks through an open gate at the back of the house, across a meadow, down a riverbank, and along a creek that ran through the middle of town. After he followed the creek some hundred or so yards, he came upon a middle-aged, overweight man seated on a log. He had a great beard, which had begun to turn white, like his hair. Edgar couldn't help but notice that he held a Bible in his hands.

"Good morning, young man," the stranger said. "I'll venture you are seeking this cow here just behind me. She must have come up this way from the path you came over."

Edgar asked him how he knew he was looking for the cow. Dressed in a suit jacket and vest, he didn't think he still looked like a farm boy. It was the anxiety in his face that gave him away, Dwight Moody replied, and he then introduced himself.

They got to talking and their conversation inevitably turned to the Bible, the bookstore, and Edgar's desire to become a preacher. Moody then invited him, as his guest, to attend his revival at the tabernacle, which was scheduled to run an entire week.

Edgar showed up that night and was very impressed. He sat in the front row amidst a standing-room-only crowd. The text Moody read was from the Gospel of Luke, 10:25, the parable of the Good Samaritan. Edgar had read it many times and heard various interpretations, but he had never heard it treated in quite the same way as Moody presented the subject. Edgar communicated his excitement to Moody the next morning when he found the evangelist waiting for him at the same place he had found him the day before. He and "D.L." continued to meet by the river for Moody's entire visit to town.

Revival Meeting, c. 1890s.

Edgar would ask Moody the same question that he had put to many different pastors. Had God ever spoken directly to him? Asked what had prompted the young man to pose such a question, Edgar told Moody the stories of his early childhood. As Edgar's own reading of the Bible revealed to him and Lulu had drawn to his attention, the

Devil often spoke through spirits. How could one be sure?

"You can tell a tree by its fruit," Moody reminded Edgar, then shared stories with him of people, many of them children, who had received messages from God. Moody also shared his own experience on a trip to Cleveland to hold a revival meeting.

The planned visit was to last a few weeks and a large audience was expected. But no sooner did he arrive than he had a dream in which he was told to close his meeting at once and go to London, England. As Moody had never been to England and could hardly afford doing so, he was reluctant. However, as he believed his dream to be a genuine expression of the will of God, he prematurely ended the Cleveland revival and at the risk of stalling a promising career, set off for England where no one knew who he was.

Moody felt like a stranger in London and began doubting that his vision had been authentic. Then one afternoon, when he was wandering the streets in a poor section of the city, he came upon a window box on a nearby tenement in which a geranium bloomed. This was his favorite color and flower. Stepping closer to take a closer look, he heard an angelic voice singing a favorite hymn. He followed the voice inside a tenement and up the stairs to an open door. Inside was a young crippled girl.

"Oh, Mr. Moody," she said, looking up at him. "I knew God would answer my prayer and send you here."

The experience left Moody convinced that his coming to the child's apartment had been God's plan. He resumed his ministry with a prayer meeting in that same room and eventually touched the lives of a quarter of a million or more people in England. "I know it was God who spoke to me," Moody told Edgar.

Edgar would cherish his conversations with Moody as much as he did the evangelist's Union Tabernacle revival meetings. In each new sermon, Edgar would find what seemed like a special message intended just for him. Simply listening to Moody, Edgar said, sent chills up his spine. What he remembered most was the last morning they met.

Edgar had arrived before sunrise and found Moody holding a stick and making marks in the soil, just as the Book of John reported Jesus having done. Moody asked Edgar what he was going to do with his life. Edgar confessed that he wished to be a minister, like him. Moody advised him to be true to the spirit of that vision but to know that there were many different ways to serve God besides from the pulpit. He could be a missionary or teach Bible study. He would know the right path when the time came.

For many years to come, long after Moody had died, Edgar would reflect on how special their meetings had been. And though he never again spoke personally with him in the flesh and blood, Moody would appear in both his dreams and trance-induced visions.

In one trance vision, Edgar was on a moving passenger train riding in an ornate white and gold Pullman with plush club chairs. Outside he could hear the noise of the wheels rolling on the tracks and the blasts of the train whistle. His fellow passengers were preachers dressed in white robes, many of whom Edgar had heard preach as a youth in Hopkinsville. Though long since dead, they appeared to Edgar as they did at the height of their careers. Conversing with them, Edgar learned that they were on their way to attend a revival meeting in which John the Disciple was to speak. Edgar was along for the ride.

Among the passengers was Sam Jones, who was making jokes and chewing tobacco just as he did when he was a circuit riding revivalist. When Jones spit out the tobacco juice, Edgar was taken aback, surprised at the preacher's lack of decorum in such a fine Pullman. As Edgar himself wanted a cigarette, he queried Jones: "Sam, aren't you afraid you will get the tobacco juice on the cushions? Jones didn't think anything of it. In Edgar's dream, life went on as normal in the afterlife as it did when he was in the flesh and blood.

Another passenger was Dwight Moody, whom Edgar was especially pleased to meet again after so many years. He asked Moody if he remembered meeting him in Hopkinsville. "Oh, yes," Moody said. I remember you and I remember the tale I told you about the little girl."

As they got to talking, Moody said that Edgar was not in the same place as himself or the others on the train. "You are on this same train with us right now, but don't forget you have to go back and don't you get too far away."

The other passengers, pleased to be together, were discussing sermons they had given and what had been their experience in the afterlife. One preacher said that he thought he had gotten it right when he was in the pulpit, while others didn't think that they had.

Jones said, "Well, things are quite a bit different from what I preached or imagined they were." Then he turned to George Stuart and said, "George, don't you find it that way?"

George said that things were indeed quite different. "We are . . . still going to meetings; the only difference is that we are being preached to instead of preaching, for we have found that we didn't know it all."

At another point in the dream all of the preachers turned to Moody to find out what he thought. "D. L., how do you find it?" Jones asked.

Moody replied: "Well, it isn't so different. You know what we called human nature is still human nature. It isn't so different."

Edgar had the impression that these men were having just as good a time in the afterlife as they did when they were alive. He wanted to continue the journey with them to hear Disciple John speak but was counseled to disembark before they reached a tunnel that lay ahead.

"You must get off before it goes too far," Cayce was warned.

In similar visions he experienced in trance, Cayce always had to get off the train. However, there was one dream he had in 1942 in which he arrived at his destination. The dream made such an impact on him that he wrote it down for later study and reflection:

> I was sitting alone in the front room [of my Virginia Beach house] playing solitaire when there was a knock at the front door. When I went to the door a gentleman whom I did not recognize said, 'Cayce, I want you to go with me to a meeting this evening.' At first I said, 'But I seldom go out in the evening . . . ' He insisted I should go with him and I did. As I went out I realized that another person was waiting for us in the street. We walked . . . on as if into the air, up and up, until we came to where there seemed to be a large circus tent . . . We approached the flap of the tent, and as he pulled the flap back, I for the first time, realized that the two men with whom I had been walking were the evangelists Dwight L. Moody and Sam Jones.

In Cayce's dream, they entered the tent, which was filled to overflowing with inspirational religious leaders, some of whom Edgar recognized, and some he did not. And then, Cayce remembered:

> It seemed that there was . . . lightning in the distance. With the

lightning there was a noise, not of thunder but of wind, yet nothing seemed to stir . . . When I asked one of my companions what it was, I was told 'The Lord our God will speak to us.' Then a voice, clear and strong, came as from out of the cloud and the lightning and said, 'Who will warn my children?' Then from out of the throng before the throne came the Master . . . He spoke saying, 'I will warn My brethren.' The answer came back, 'No, the time is not yet fulfilled for you to return . . . " Then Mr. Moody spoke and said . . . 'send Cayce, he is there now.' Then the Master said, 'Father, Cayce will warn My brethren.'

Here the dream ended. But the message for Cayce remained.

Gertrude Evans, c. 1897.

GERTRUDE EVANS:

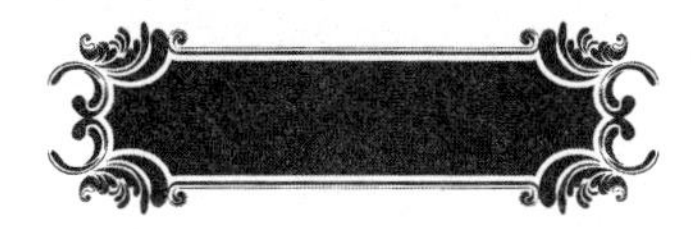

THE YOUNG LADY FROM THE HILL

Edgar was working at Hopper Brothers Bookstore when he met his former Beverly school teacher Ethel Duke. She recognized him immediately, and after they got to talking, she invited him to a party. It was to be hosted by her cousins, the Salters of Hopkinsville, who routinely held "moonlights" in which their grand antebellum home, known throughout Hopkinsville as "The Hill," was lit with colorful Chinese lanterns. Guests, mostly young people and students from Hopkinsville's South Kentucky College, would stroll about the property under the moonlight and stars.

Excited as Edgar was to attend, he was also worried. As he later admitted, he thought the guests would find him "uncouth and uneducated." The decision, however, was out of his hands. Leslie forbade him to visit the Salter home, if only because its occupants were known liberals. They openly espoused such radical notions as a woman's right to vote and hold public office. Everyone in Hopkinsville had heard at least one story of how the three older Salter sisters—Elizabeth, Kate, and Caroline—virtually ran "The Hill" and how their dinner guests included Jews, blacks, Hindus, and Native Americans. Leslie may have suspected that all kinds of "subversive" things occurred at The Hill and wanted Edgar to have no part of it.

Edgar abided by his father's decision. However, this didn't keep him from finding out more about life at The Hill from his employer Harry Hopper's girlfriend. Mary Greene, a teacher from South Kentucky College, knew the Salters well and had attended many a moonlight. Among other intriguing things she had to tell him were stories of the family patriarch, seventy-three-year-old Sam Salter, a respected civil engineer, architect, and non-practicing physician from Philadelphia. Since coming to Hopkinsville, he had overseen the construction of the city's largest building projects, such as South Kentucky College and the Western Kentucky Lunatic Asylum and later became that hospital's chief building superintendent. He was the radical thinker who set the tone at The Hill. But it was the Salter girls who were in charge. In addition to adding to the family's extensive personal library and growing their own crops, medicinal herbs, and livestock, all of the Salter children and grandchildren were sent to college, studied foreign languages and music, and were taught the business and professional skills to carry the Salter legacy into the future.

Elizabeth, or Lizzie, the eldest Salter girl, was extremely bright and well read. She married Sam Evans, the owner of the Hopkinsville coal yard and eventually had three children: Hugh, Lynn, and Gertrude, the youngest. The children were still infants when their father died suddenly from a burst appendix, and Lizzie had used the income from selling the coal yard to build a cottage immediately adjacent to The Hill. Though they lived next door, everyone dined together in the larger house and pitched in with chores.

Kate Salter Smith, the next in line, was a gifted musician and could be counted on to entertain at the piano or read poetry. She was also quite the reader, kept up the family library, and was active in theatrical performances at her church. Also thanks to her, the family moonlights included such guests as visiting pastors and distinguished lecturers and musicians who came to speak or perform at the Union Tabernacle or Holland's Opera House.

Caroline, known as Carrie, was the youngest and most beautiful. A buyer for Anderson's Department Store, who volunteered part-time as an art teacher at the Hopkinsville asylum, she was not as outspoken as Lizzie and could not write poetry or play music as well as Kate, but she had inherited the full range of Sam Salter's talents and his fierce sense of independence. Edgar knew Carrie and some of her young cousins because they frequently stopped at the bookstore for college supplies.

The more Edgar learned about the family, the more he regretted not taking Ethel Duke up on her invitation. Thus, when she stepped into the store the following month and issued a second invitation to attend a party at The Hill, Edgar immediately agreed. On this occasion he also caught a glimpse of Ethel's best friend and second cousin, Gertrude, who sat in a carriage outside. Few words were exchanged that day, but Edgar had the distinct impression that Gertrude, the petite brunette in the back of the buggy, and not Ethel, was issuing the second invitation and was perhaps responsible for the first. His suspicions were confirmed when, disregarding his father's edict, Edgar polished his shoes, oiled his hair, and attended the party the following Friday at The Hill.

While making bookstore deliveries, Edgar had been inside several of Hopkinsville's finest homes. They had been built by the wealthy tobacco planters and traders. These homes were more grand and imposing, had more land, and were more conveniently located near the city center. The Hill, however, built by Sam Salter himself, impressed him more than any other. Inside, Edgar was confronted by a rainbow of colors. There were deep purples and blues in the oriental carpets and Chinese porcelains, gold leaf on the picture frames, flaming red window sashes, and velvety greens and browns in the brocade upholstery. But what most captured his attention was the scent of perfume: lavender, primrose, chamomile, and honeysuckle. For a country farm boy, who had grown up in a cabin with a dirt floor, stepping into The Hill was like entering a new, exciting, and distinctly female environment.

Ethel Duke took him by the hand and introduced him to the grey-haired Sam and his wife Sarah, and then to the ladies who ruled The Hill.

Thirty-five-year-old Lizzie, Gertrude's mother, was as petite and dark-haired as her daughter. She supervised the planting and harvesting of the vegetable gardens and the orchard in addition to seeing that

Edgar Cayce, c. 1890s.

the home was always full of flowers and color. She was also chiefly responsible for The Hill being a forum for political discussion. Elected or aspiring policy makers were always welcome at her frequent salons and dinner parties.

Then there was Kate, a fat-cheeked woman with fine hands. He recognized her from Hopper Brothers, and her contribution to the house was everywhere evident in the library, where could also be found the piano which she played so well.

Twenty-year-old Carrie was surrounded by adoring young male suitors. That she hadn't yet married, Edgar quickly realized, wasn't for lack of proposals. She simply had hadn't found the right man and wasn't willing to settle for second best because she was no longer a teenager. She, too, was a striking contrast to Edgar's own familiar experience where a woman wasn't welcome to express an opinion of her own, freely mingle with unmarried men, or use perfume.

Mingling, as Edgar soon realized, was what the moonlight was about. In a matter of minutes he was introduced to clergymen from the Methodist church, railroad engineers, and practically the entire junior class from South Kentucky College. He couldn't easily enter into the conversation, but he was a good listener, and Ethel Duke filled in gaps in their conversation. All too soon, though, she disappeared, leaving him on the lawn in front of a table with small sandwiches, cookies, and a punchbowl of lemonade. Young people sat on benches and chairs or lay on the ground looking up at the moon. Almost miraculously, Edgar found himself face to face with Gertrude, who took his hand and led him down the carriage path to see her rose garden.

Edgar couldn't take his eyes off of her. Fifteen-years-old, standing just five-feet tall and weighing eighty pounds, she had silky brunette hair, large brown eyes, an oval face, porcelain white skin with fine, delicate features. This evening she wore an embroidered ankle-length gingham dress that her aunt Carrie had purchased in Springfield for her. "A mere slip of girl" was the way Edgar described her. "Petite, winsome, and graceful" another would say.

How much time Edgar spent inspecting Gertrude's rose garden, or the full moon overhead, is anyone's guess. However, in the years to come, he always associated her beauty with roses. He brought her a rose when they later went out on dates and would never plant a garden in any of the homes they lived that didn't feature at least one rose bush which was produced from stock originating from Gertrude's plot at The Hill. Today at the A.R.E.'s Virginia Beach headquarters roses from this same stock still grow.

To Edgar's relief, Gertrude did the lion's share of talking that night. A romantic, she encouraged him to listen to the sound of tree limbs swaying in the wind. "The souls of lovers, who were cruelly parted," she is reported to have told him. Eventually she got him to talk about himself and flattered him by suggesting that he was probably so good as a clerk that he would someday own a bookstore himself. A great reader herself, she knew the Hopper Brothers' inventory nearly as well as he. Clergyman and fiction writer E.P. Roe was her particularly favorite author, something Edgar would note on her next birthday.

Edgar left The Hill that night convinced of two things: that she was most certainly behind Ethel Duke's invitation and that she knew considerably more about him than he did her. This, too, would soon be confirmed. Thanks to Ethel Duke, who had been a substitute teacher at

With a chaperone on a date to Pilot Rock, Gertrude is at far right, c. 1902.

the Beverly School, and Gertrude's aunt Carrie, who knew Edgar's sister Anne from Anderson's Department Store, Gertrude had been told all about the stories of his ghostly encounters and strange abilities. That Gertrude knew this in advance and was still interested in pursuing a relationship made him all the more enamored of her.

No sooner had Edgar attended the party at The Hill than he received numerous other invitations to parties and social gatherings which, by no coincidence, Gertrude was also invited. Still, he remained painfully shy around her, mostly because he couldn't fathom why a beautiful young woman like Gertrude, from a well-off and well-educated family such as hers, could be interested in a mere bookstore clerk with an eighth-grade education. He wasn't certain she actually liked him until he accompanied her and Ethel Duke on a picnic to Pilot Rock, a massive limestone outcropping nestled into the Christian County foothills.

They set out from Hopkinsville by wagon with baskets of fried chicken, beaten biscuits, fresh tomatoes, and cake. Outside of town they parked at the foot of the towering rock formation and made the rest of the journey up Pilot Rock on foot. As was customary on this day, and on the many dates they would have in the future, they were accompanied by a chaperone. Their Pilot Rock picnic was followed by a more adventurous trip to a mineral spring (boys and girls bathed separately) and then an exploration, by lantern light, of an abandoned mine.

Edgar and Gertrude soon became a couple, joining one another at parties, church socials, presentations at the Union Tabernacle, and shows at Holland's Opera House. Both greatly enjoyed sitting in the bleachers whenever the Hopkinsville Moguls took the baseball field. Gertrude's brother, Lynn Evans, played shortstop. Sunday mornings were devoted to church—Edgar attending the Christian Church and Gertrude the Methodist Church. Afterwards, Edgar would ride his bicycle to The Hill, and they would sit together on the large veranda or in the parlor playing games or reading out loud from books that he had brought from Hopper Brothers.

As a future in-law would later write, theirs was an appeal of opposites. "He [was] excitable, earnest, born of extremes, a social outsider; and she—calm inquisitive, practical, an embodiment of southern gentility. He became charismatic and extroverted [as their relationship developed]; she kept her own counsel. Their immediate rapport held their relationship intact through one crisis after another."

The first crisis was the disapproval of the senior Salters. Edgar wasn't educated, had no refinement, and most important couldn't raise a family working as a bookstore clerk. Even when, several months into the courtship, Edgar received a substantial raise at the bookstore, he was still having difficulty supporting his parents. Leslie hadn't yet found a job, and Edgar's mother earned money taking in laundry and working as a seamstress. His sisters helped out as well, but Edgar was the primary breadwinner.

The younger Salter generation—Ethel, Hugh, Lynn, and others—however, embraced Edgar as a brother. They truly enjoyed his company as he did theirs. Hugh and Lynn also engaged him in ways that few others dared. They challenged him to psychically read a deck of playing cards face down (which he did without apparent difficulty). They also tested his uncanny ability to find lost objects (which he

Edgar and Gertrude at the house known as The Hill, c. 1902.

invariably was able to do) and to read unopened letters. To them, he wasn't a freak, but a wonder to behold.

Gertrude's aunt Carrie wasn't interested in these activities, but she, too, appreciated his unique abilities. She was more fascinated by his experience with the angel, and how, when praying, he sometimes heard heavenly music. Feeling secure in her company, he shared aspects of himself he had kept hidden. Among other things, he revealed that he could sometimes see colors or patterns of colors around people when the person was feeling strong emotions.

Gertrude didn't embrace this part of Edgar's life. Concerned, she discussed the matter with one of her college professors. He told her in no uncertain terms that Edgar would become mentally unstable if he continued to experiment and indulge in psychic-related activities. Likely he would one day have to be committed to the Hopkinsville asylum. This was a particularly difficult thing for Gertrude to put out of her mind. She had only to step out on the veranda of her house to see the asylum's spires, built by her grandfather, on the horizon. They became a constant reminder of what might be. Unable to remain silent on the matter, she finally discussed the subject with Edgar. He told her the truth. He didn't like or understand the strange abilities he seemed to possess and wanted nothing more than to live a normal life. He also promised not to engage in further experimentation.

Two incidents, however, left Gertrude frightened. One Sunday evening, when Edgar was nodding off on the sofa in the family's parlor, Gertrude told him to "go to sleep." Edgar immediately went to sleep and couldn't be woken up that night or the following morning and afternoon. Not until a frantic and frightened Gertrude shouted, "Edgar, wake up!" did he instantly open his eyes, acting as if minutes, not an entire day, had passed. Somehow or another, Edgar's unconscious self had responded to her words as a command. It was as if her voice had a hypnotic effect upon him.

Another curious incident took place at the Cayce's home on Seventh Street. On a particularly cold winter night, Edgar and a friend from out of town were returning from a revival meeting at the Tabernacle. The plan was for his friend to spend the night with Edgar in his bedroom. But when they walked into the Cayce house, they were surprised that extended family had unexpectedly dropped in from Beverly. Leslie had requisitioned Edgar's bedroom, and there was no place for him or his friend to sleep. Edgar was steaming mad. This was his bedroom. Further, he was paying the rent on the house. While Edgar and his father exchanged angry words, Edgar's friend bid a hasty retreat.

Edgar, fully dressed, went to sleep on the sofa in the living room. As he later told the story, which was corroborated by family members, at some point after everyone had gone to bed, the sofa upon which Edgar slept burst into flames. He ran outside and rolled in the snow, putting out his burning clothes. By this time everyone else in the house had awakened and helped to haul the burning sofa out the front door as well. As Edgar had not been smoking, the lamps were extinguished, and the sofa had not been near the stove, the cause of the fire remained a mystery. However, evidence suggested that the fire had started in Edgar's clothes before spreading to the sofa and that somehow or another, the incident was directly connected with Edgar's state of mind.

But as he and the Cayce family, and Gertrude too, would one day experience when they entered the photography business, fires had a strange way of igniting under unusual circumstances when Edgar was angry. Two of Cayce's four photo studios would burn down, and a third suffered serious fire damage. In later years, special efforts would be made to fireproof the various storerooms which housed the Cayce trance readings.

The impact that such incidents had on Gertrude were more profound than commonly thought. She would be the last of her family members to receive or witness a trance reading. For the first eighteen months of their courtship and for years to come, she and Edgar would not talk about or discuss anything related to his psychic gifts. This was how she wanted it, and it may have been a condition when Edgar, on March 7, 1897, days before his twentieth birthday, proposed to seventeen-year-old Gertrude.

"It's true that I love you," she told him. "But I will have to think about it."

Edgar naturally wanted to know when he would have an answer, and a part of him still believed she wouldn't accept his proposal. There were times when Gertrude looked at him, he said, as if he were "a strange fish that ought to be thrown back."

Perhaps, even in their relative youth, both suspected that theirs would never be a normal life together. They would never simply be Edgar and Gertrude. There would always be a third unseen "other," what in years to come would simply be called "the Source." It seemed at times to threaten to end their relationship and as events would unfold, was ultimately what held them together.

On the evening Edgar proposed to her, however, Gertrude was holding her ground for a different reason. One of her aunts had counseled reserve in matters of the heart. She shouldn't seem too eager. Gertrude went to a calendar in the parlor, closed her eyes, and put her finger on a date. "I'll tell you on the twelfth."

Five days later, in a driving rain, Edgar arrived back at The Hill on horseback. Gertrude, after giving the matter consideration, said she would marry him. As Edgar later related the story, he didn't know what to do next. She was standing in front of him, waiting for him to kiss her. When she asked him why he hesitated, he explained that he had never kissed a woman before. Gertrude showed him how.

The matter of how her voice, in particular, had a profound effect upon him, and other psychic matters, was forgotten for the moment. Like her, he envisioned a day, not long in the future, in which he and she would stroll through the park on a Sunday afternoon, taking turns pushing a stroller, and greeting friends they met along the way. He believed, if he tried hard enough, he could put the strange incidents of his past behind him.

Gertrude and Edgar portrait, c. 1903.

AL LAYNE:

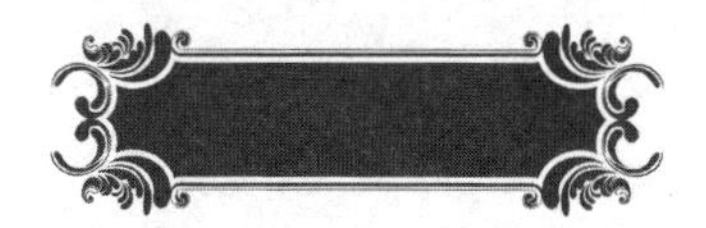

INTRODUCING THE PSYCHIC DIAGNOSTICIAN

Hypnosis is widely regarded as an effective therapeutic technique to relieve pain, overcome bad habits, and recall past events. Less understood is its ability to enhance psychic ability. People who are hypnotized routinely perform better in laboratory tests of clairvoyance, telepathy, and precognition. This was the case for twenty-four-year-old Cayce who, with the help of self-taught hypnotist and osteopath Al Layne, produced his first trance reading on March 31, 1901.

Putting Edgar into trance was more difficult than one might suppose for a young man who had already displayed a wide range of other talents. The first attempt to hypnotize him was made by Stanley "The Laugh King" Hart, who invited Edgar onto center stage at Holland's Opera House shortly after Edgar and his family had moved to Hopkinsville. Although Hart was an ardent spokesman for the alleged powers of hypnotism to cure headaches, treat alcoholism, and eliminate self-destructive behaviors, it was comedy that drew crowds to his performances. He invited members of the audience onto the stage, put them into a hypnotic trance, and ordered them to do embarrassing things. Hart swore just by looking at Edgar that he would make the ideal hypnotic subject, but to everyone's disappointment, Hart was unable to put Edgar into a trance, and he was asked to leave the stage.

Four years later "Herman the Great" made a second attempt. While

OPERA HOUSE

One week, commencing Monday, MAY 22.

The Greatest Organization of its kind in existence,

HART,

The LAUGH KING COMPANY.

In their remarkable hypnotic performances. Endorsed and attended by Clergymen and society people everywhere. Entire change of program nightly.

Prices: 50, 35, 25 and 15 Cents.

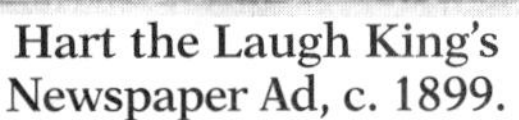

Hart the Laugh King's Newspaper Ad, c. 1899.

Holland's Opera House.

visiting the Louisville printing company where Edgar was then working as a clerk—Edgar needed a greater income if he was to marry Gertrude and raise a family—Herman declared the young man would make an ideal subject for hypnotism and asked permission to put him "under." Edgar agreed to be hypnotized but advised Herman of the previous attempt. The hypnotist was not put off. He told Edgar that the more often a person was hypnotized, the easier it was to put him under, and the deeper he could go.

Herman had Edgar concentrate on some object that was held up in front of him while Herman repeatedly made suggestions that he relax and go to sleep. The next thing Edgar remembered was that he was lying on a countertop surrounded by co-workers. He had not only gone under but had done everything that the hypnotist told him to do. Edgar laughed about the experience and promptly forgot about it until a year later when he was hypnotized in Madisonville, Kentucky, while on a business trip with his father, Leslie.

Edgar and Leslie had been in Madisonville only a few hours when state health officials arrived at their hotel and ordered its doors closed. The hotel was being quarantined due to an outbreak of smallpox. No one could come or go for three days. By coincidence, a fellow guest at the hotel was a stage hypnotist who volunteered to provide entertainment.

Like Herman the Great, the hypnotist succeeded in putting Edgar into a trance. Again, Edgar had no memory of what happened because he lost consciousness the moment the hypnotist put him "under." Edgar knew only what Leslie and the other hotel guests told him when he woke up. According to them, the hypnotist suggested that Edgar play the piano.

Leslie had expected Edgar to simply bang away at the keys like a child pretending to make music. After all, he had never had a single lesson. Only Edgar took the hypnotist's suggestion literally, exhibiting a skill far beyond what even the hypnotist believed possible. Edgar played beautiful music. The hypnotist, no doubt, believed that he had helped Edgar to discover a latent ability. The truth, however, was more astonishing. Edgar was capable of doing extraordinary things when under trance—the likes of which no one could have imagined.

The incident which led to Al Layne's entry into the story came in the winter of 1900 when Edgar, on a business trip to Elkton, Kentucky, was prescribed too strong a sedative to treat a migraine headache. Several hours after taking the drug, Edgar was found wandering semi-conscious in the Elkton railroad yard and was brought home to Hopkinsville. Physicians didn't know how to help, so they put him to bed. He seemed to be fine the next morning. The only problem was that his throat was dry and scratchy, and his voice thin and raspy.

Days passed, then weeks, and eventually months, and his condition became more severe. Unable to communicate, Edgar lost his job as a salesman. Eventually he took a position, arranged for by friends, working in a darkroom in a Hopkinsville photo lab. It would be here where he learned the trade that would lead him to become a professional studio photographer. Here, too, he bemoaned the fact that he was now unsuitable to be a husband and father. In a moment of self-loathing and pity, he begged Gertrude to release him from what had now become their year-long engagement. She deserved more from a potential husband than he could deliver. Gertrude would hear none of it.

After nearly a full year without any improvement, everyone in Hopkinsville knew about Edgar's condition. Friends urged him to pay a return visit to Stanley Hart, who was scheduled to appear at

Edgar, thin as a rail after a year of laryngitis.

Holland's Opera House. Hart was certain he could affect a cure and was undoubtedly pleased at the prospect of proving himself in front of a paying audience.

On the night of his performance, Hart invited Edgar onto the stage. When the oil burning footlights were dimmed, Hart stood directly in front of Edgar and told him to concentrate on an object which he dangled in front of Edgar's eyes. Edgar slipped easily into a trance.

No record exists of what words Edgar spoke, only that he did. His laryngitis was gone. The audience gasped, then began to cheer wildly. Hart had performed his magic.

Or had he? Once Edgar was released from Hart's hypnotic suggestion, his voice once again became a whisper.

After the show had ended, Hart took Edgar and Gertrude backstage and explained the problem. Edgar could not go deep enough into a trance to take "post-hypnotic suggestions." More trance sessions would be necessary.

Assured that he could affect a permanent cure, Hart promised that for $200 he would keep trying until Edgar had completely regained his voice. Edgar and his parents, and likely Gertrude, too, agreed to the arrangement even though they hadn't the money to pay his exorbitant fee. The problem was apparently solved when the editors of the *Kentucky New Era* newspaper stepped forward. They met with Hart and a Hopkinsville throat specialist who agreed to examine Cayce both before and after the hypnotic sessions. In return for an exclusive, they would see that Hart was adequately compensated.

The sessions did not go as expected. Hart could easily put Edgar into a trance, but the moment Edgar was commanded to wake up, he lost his voice again. Given future events, it is reasonable to conclude that Hart's appraisal of Edgar's condition was correct. Edgar's laryngitis was psychosomatic, a condition which could be helped with hypnosis. However, his condition was also partly physiological. His vocal chords were constricted when he was in a waking state. This was perhaps because Edgar, in a waking state, was trying so hard to suppress his psychic gifts. With his desire to please Gertrude, earn a better income, and lead a normal life, he had strayed far from the promise he had made to the angel of his youth. The "voice" within him was trying to be heard, and the only way to suppress it was to constrict his vocal chords. This condition, too, may also have been treated with hypnosis, but Hart didn't know how to put the correct suggestion to Edgar when he was under. When hypnotized, Edgar had powers over his own body that were far beyond what Hart, or anyone else, could imagine.

Hart gave up on Edgar. But others took up where he left off. College professor William Girao, who had been in the audience at the Opera House, wrote to John Quackenboss in New York, who was considered one of the foremost experts in hypnotism. The fact that he was also an ardent believer that illness could be healed by a person learning to marshal the forces of the unconscious mind would prove to be most helpful.

Quackenboss took the case on and made repeated visits to Hopkinsville. Before he began his experiments, he questioned Edgar and his parents at length, listened to Leslie's account of Edgar's childhood experiences, and took copious notes.

In one experiment, when Edgar was asked to sleep for twenty-four hours, he immediately closed his eyes and went to sleep. Not just this,

Edgar appeared to be comatose. He didn't awaken for twenty-four hours—precisely to the minute. This was a modest breakthrough, as it showed that when Edgar was put into a deep trance, he truly did what was asked of him. However, it didn't cure his condition.

After Quackenboss gave up, Girao continued to experiment and engaged the help of Al Layne, the only person he knew in Hopkinsville who had training in hypnotism. A delicate middle-aged man with a pencil-thin gray mustache and a prominent bald spot on the top of his head, Layne weighed less than 120 pounds, in contrast to his wife, Ada, a heavy, large-breasted, robust woman. As would soon prove helpful, Layne was predisposed to assist Girao because he knew Edgar personally. Layne's wife, Ada, employed Edgar's younger sister Anne Cayce and Gertrude's aunt Carrie Salter at Anderson's Department Store.

Though Layne called himself both a hypnotist and physician and operated a small office at the back of Anderson's Department Store, he had little formal training. The extent of his certification was a correspondence course. Still, he had a modest following of dedicated clients, many of them people such as himself, who suffered stomach ailments and who had found no relief from standard allopathic medicine. Like Professor Girao, he was an ardent believer in a popular slogan of the day, "Every man his own doctor," and was part of a groundswell of popular interest in what today would be called holistic health. Hypnotism was merely one aspect of a medical treatment that also included osteopathy, the science of

Al Layne, taken from a newspaper article, c. 1906.

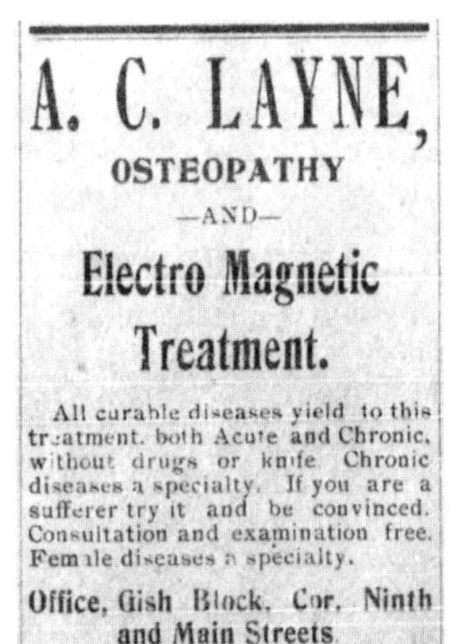

A. C. LAYNE,
OSTEOPATHY
—AND—
Electro Magnetic
Treatment.

All curable diseases yield to this treatment, both Acute and Chronic, without drugs or knife. Chronic diseases a specialty. If you are a sufferer try it and be convinced. Consultation and examination free. Female diseases a specialty.

Office, Gish Block, Cor. Ninth and Main Streets.

Al Layne's newspaper ad, c. 1902.

manipulating or realigning human vertebrae to permit the body to heal itself, and homeopathy, a treatment based on the use of natural remedies to trigger the body's own immune response.

Edgar, as Layne concluded, was in desperate need of both osteopathy and homeopathy, but it was hypnotism that he and Girao applied first. As in the earlier experimentation with Quackenboss, Edgar went into trance easily and would speak in a normal voice. But as soon as Edgar came out of trance, the laryngitis returned. The only thing new they learned from their efforts was the observation that Edgar was unusually talkative in his trance state. Layne could actually carry on a conversation with him. Edgar would stop talking only when the suggestion was made that he go into a deeper trance, at which point communication would cease altogether.

Layne and Girao put their findings into a letter to Quackenboss. In response, the New York hypnotist said that he had observed a similar tendency when working with Edgar. He noted a particular point in the hypnosis process when Edgar's unconscious self seemed to "take charge." An avenue to explore, Quackenboss suggested, was to put Edgar "under" and ask Edgar's unconscious self what he thought should be done to restore his voice.

Edgar's parents were reluctant to let their son be hypnotized yet again. He had lost sixty pounds and as Edgar himself admitted, was a "nervous wreck." Now, along with his Bible, he carried a pencil and pad, which was the only way he could communicate with the outside world.

Gertrude, too, had suffered. Already thin, she now looked anorexic. She had dropped out of college and rarely ventured into public to attend the many social and church gatherings around which her life had previously revolved. She also hadn't attended Edgar's hypnotic sessions with Quackenboss, Girao, and Layne. Edgar's public embarrassment on the Holland's Opera House stage was humiliation enough.

With Edgar's blessing, Layne convinced Leslie and Carrie to let him try one more experiment. On Sunday afternoon, March 31, 1901, less than two weeks after his twenty-fourth birthday, he and Layne retreated to the Cayce's upstairs parlor. Edgar lay down on the family's horsehair sofa, and Layne pulled up a chair to sit next to him. Edgar's mother stood alongside Layne. Leslie was seated in a chair across from his son.

Edgar put himself into trance, as he had learned to do from having undergone so many previous experiments. Just as Edgar's pupils began to dilate and his eyelashes fluttered and when he looked as if he was going "under," Layne made his first suggestion.

"You are now asleep and will be able to tell us what we want to know," Layne said. "You have before you the body of Edgar Cayce. Describe his condition and tell us what is wrong."

Edgar began to mumble, then his throat cleared and he spoke. "Yes," he said. "We can see the body."

Layne told Edgar's father to write down what was being said. Leslie scrambled to do so but was so disconcerted by what was happening to realize that a pad and paper were within easy reach. He instead ran into the kitchen and retrieved the pencil that was tied to the grocery list. Even so, he was too flustered to write anything coherent down on the paper. What Edgar said is today pieced together from the recollections of Edgar's mother and Layne.

> *In* the normal physical state this body is unable to speak due to partial paralysis of the inferior muscles of the vocal cords, produced by nerve strain. This is a psychological condition producing a physical effect and may be removed by increasing the circulation to the affected parts by suggestion while in this unconscious condition. That is the only thing that will do it.

Layne would note the curious way that Edgar was addressing himself in the third person. He also spoke more slowly than he normally would in a conscious state, enunciating each individual consonant and vowel as if he were translating from some foreign language.

"Increase the circulation to the affected parts," Layne then commanded.

Edgar replied: "The circulation is beginning to increase. It is increasing."

Layne leaned over to look at Edgar. Just as the "sleeping" Cayce had said, the circulation to his throat actually appeared to increase. He could see his neck begin swelling with blood to the point that Leslie was compelled to lean over and unbutton his son's shirt collar. The upper portion of his chest, then throat, slowly turned pink. The pink deepened to become a fire-engine red. A full twenty minutes elapsed before Edgar cleared his throat and spoke again.

"It's all right now," Cayce said, still in trance. "The condition is removed.

The vocal chords are perfectly normal now. Make the suggestion that the circulation return to normal, and that after that the body awaken."

Layne did as instructed. "The circulation will return to normal. After that the body will awaken."

The red around Edgar's neck faded to rose and then to pink. He woke up a few minutes later, sat up, reached for his handkerchief, coughed, and spat out blood. The blood that came out was not just a drop or two, but enough to soak the thin cotton cloth.

"Hello," he said, in a clear voice. "Hey, I can talk."

Edgar's mother cried with relief. Leslie pumped Layne's hand. Edgar's sisters, Anne and Mary, who had been eavesdropping through the keyhole, also found "brother's experience," as they called it, "quite exciting!"

Edgar had no memory of the experience. He repeatedly asked to be told every detail of what had happened. What had Layne said? What did I say? How did I look? Unbelievable as the story sounded, his shirt collar was open at his neck, his handkerchief was bloodstained, and he could once again speak in a normal voice.

Mrs. Elizabeth E. Evans
requests your presence
at the marriage of her daughter
Gertrude Salter
to
Mr. Edgar Cayce Jr.
Wednesday afternoon, June seventeenth,
nineteen hundred and three,
at four thirty o'clock,
at home,
Hopkinsville, Kentucky.

At Home
after June twentieth,
Bowling Green, Ky.

With his voice restored, Edgar and Gertrude finally set their wedding date!

Layne had conducted Cayce's first trance reading. He also made the observation which would result in the second. "If you can do this for yourself," he told Edgar, "I don't see any reason you can't do it for others."

Edgar and Gertrude married on June 17th, 1903.

Carrie House:

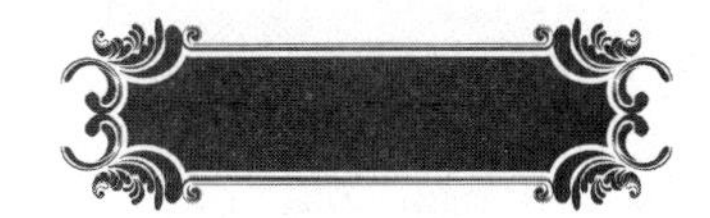

Her Dying Infant

Edgar and Gertrude were married on Wednesday, June 17, 1903, in a small ceremony held in the bride's rose garden. Among those present was Carrie Salter, herself recently married to the debonair Dr. Thomas House—a rising star in the Kentucky medical community. And it was she, not Gertrude, who championed Cayce's psychic gifts when Edgar partnered with Al Layne, and she who steadfastly remained at his side and encouraged him to continue providing medical advice when Layne, under investigation by the board of the American Medical Association, left Hopkinsville to pursue a formal medical degree.

In contrast to Carrie, Gertrude was frightened by Edgar's strange trance abilities. Better that her husband risk losing his voice than his sanity, she believed. She was also concerned about sharing Edgar with what became a growing number of physician researchers who, in secret, were experimenting with her husband and treating him as if he were some strange and exotic specimen, not a flesh and blood human being. Nor did she want this third other—the Source—interfering in their lives. She couldn't very well have a fairy-tale marriage when her mate might suddenly drift off into a coma-like sleep and become some other person or worse still, might not wake from that sleep. And what of their children? Would they inherit this weird ability?

Carrie had no such concerns. She believed that Edgar was touched by the Divine and that a heavenly spirit spoke in and through him when he was in a trance. Her faith in him had also proven its value. In what may have been his earliest trance reading for a female, conducted by Al Layne, the Source advised Carrie not to undergo an abdominal surgery recommended by her doctors, which indeed turned out to be unnecessary. After Carrie's marriage to Dr. House, the chief physician at the Hopkinsville's mental asylum, the Source had also predicted that she would become pregnant, something that Dr. House and two specialists had said was physically impossible. Further, the Source had accurately foretold the date of birth and said she would deliver a boy. And the spiritual message that had accompanied Cayce's prophetic trance discourses—that God's love and forgiveness must be foremost in her heart—had inspired her to give up her position at Anderson's Department Store and minister to the patients at the asylum as an RN working alongside her husband.

Most compelling of all was a reading Edgar subsequently gave to three-month-old Thomas House Jr. in November 1909. As Cayce had suggested in a previous trance session, the child's delivery might be difficult with complications setting in. This turned out to be the case. Born prematurely, her child suffered from severe infantile spasms, nausea, and vomiting. His condition had deteriorated to a critical point when Carrie sent word to fetch Edgar in Bowling Green, Kentucky, where he and Gertrude were operating a photography studio. Little Tommy Jr. was too weak from malnutrition to nurse from Carrie's bosom or to even wrap his tiny hands around her fingers. She needed Edgar as never before.

Carrie's husband, Dr. House, and two other physicians—Dr. Jackson, a general practitioner in Hopkinsville and Dr. Haggard, a pediatric specialist from Nashville, who had been attending the child since birth—believed that Thomas House Jr. had little or no chance of living through the night. Carrie wasn't sure Edgar or anyone else could help her son—no more than Edgar himself was—but she wanted him to try.

Like most physicians in Hopkinsville, Dr. Haggard wanted no part

Caroline (Carrie Salter)
House, c. 1907.

Edith
Estella
Smith,
(Gertrude's
cousin),
old Salter
home place.

Western State Kentucky Hospital (the Lunatic Asylum built by Gertrude's grandfather) where Dr. and Carrie House worked and where Gertrude feared Edgar might one day become a patient.

of what he deemed "trickery." Dr. Jackson shared his colleague's skepticism, but as the family's longtime physician, he had seen the inexplicable. Cayce, with Al Layne's help, had provided trance advice that had helped a child recover from whooping cough and had correctly diagnosed a case of scarlet fever.

In what was deemed to be an even more startling trance discourse, Cayce had detailed the location of blood clots in a patient's lung. And along with more routinely recommended treatments, he advised the use of state-of-the-art electromagnetic therapy. Physicians hadn't followed up; such therapy had never been used before in Kentucky and was considered experimental at best. Jackson had been left wondering if the treatment might have helped. But it was too late now. The patient had died.

Dr. House also didn't believe that Edgar or anyone else could diagnose illness in his sleep, but he, like Jackson, knew Cayce too intimately to believe that he was a charlatan. His in-law didn't charge for his services, seek publicity, or encourage anyone to obtain trance readings. After Al Layne had left for medical school in 1904, people found their way to Cayce's Bowling Green photo studio by word of mouth. House believed that the people who came to Cayce were predisposed that Cayce could help, and hence the people heard what they wanted to hear. Physicians working with Edgar did the rest.

Only a dying child, such as Tommy Jr., was another matter altogether. The child was beyond help. The only reason that Dr. House reluctantly agreed to wire Cayce in Bowling Green was to indulge headstrong Carrie, who to his mind was overcome with fear and unwilling to accept what he deemed to be the inevitable.

Edgar arrived by train to Hopkinsville in the midst of a rainstorm. Gertrude's brother Lynn picked him up at the station and drove him the mile and a quarter to the house. Both were drenched head to foot when they stepped into the house. Carrie, holding her infant son, was seated in the parlor by the fireplace, surrounded by family members. There were no pleasantries, only an awkward silence as Dr. Haggard, disgruntled that Cayce was to be consulted, packed his bags and left. He encouraged Dr. Jackson to do the same lest he was investigated as had been Layne. "Let the child die in peace" was the message he conveyed to House family, whether he spoke the words or not.

Carrie asked if Edgar wanted to examine Tommy. Edgar demurred. In his conscious state he could no more diagnose the child's condition than he could speak a foreign language or play a musical instrument. Besides, he was anguished to see Carrie and her child in such distress. Gertrude likely hadn't accompanied Edgar to The Hill that night for this same reason. Perhaps, too, she was protesting the fact that Edgar, despite his promise to her, was back experimenting with his gifts.

Dr. House, accompanied by Jackson, conducted the session in the master bedroom adjoining the parlor. The process, previously developed by Layne, was for him to read from a small leather-bound pocket notebook. He had only to sit beside Edgar as he went into trance, watching for his in-law's eyelashes to flutter, before putting the suggestions to him.

Similar to the routine he practiced with Layne and would do without significant variation for the next thirty-six years, Edgar took off his jacket and shoes, removed his tie and collar, and lay down on a large oak bed. He pulled a down comforter over his stocking feet, adjusted himself on his back. Then, with feet together and finger tips at his temples, Edgar concentrated on a spot on the ceiling. When he felt himself about to drift off to sleep, he slowly lowered his hands and crossed them over his chest.

With the rain pounding on the roof and the weak cries of the dying child in the next room, Edgar's breathing deepened and his eyelashes fluttered.

"You have before you the body of Thomas House Jr. of Hopkinsville, Kentucky," Dr. House said, inserting his son's name into the paragraph he read from the pocket notebook. "Diagnose his illness and recommend a cure."

Edgar looked fast asleep, only Dr. House knew better. He had once seen his in-law go into a trance so deep that fellow physicians, conducting an experiment, had removed one of Cayce's fingernails, and another had stuck a hypodermic needle into his foot. Edgar hadn't so much as stirred. Yet the "sleeping" Cayce answered questions as if he were fully conscious.

Edgar began to speak in his normal voice. Here, and in many instances to come, his first words were garbled, almost a hum, as if a musical instrument were being tuned. Then his voice cleared and his words became well-modulated and easy to understand. "Yes, we have the body and mind of Thomas House Jr. here," he said.

Cayce proceeded to recite the infant's temperature and blood pressure. As House and Jackson would note, the information was correct. They had taken Tommy's vitals a few minutes before Edgar's arrival at The Hill. Only Edgar had not examined the child. How would he know?

Cayce—in trance—next described the condition of Tommy's organs, doing so in such a detailed and detached manner that House and

Jackson were left with the impression that he was a physician conducting an autopsy. In this case, however, the physician looked to be asleep and his patient was cradled in his mother's arms in the next room. This information, too, appeared to be correct or to conform to what House and Jackson supposed. Only there was no way to know such things for certain. Was Edgar somehow reading their minds, picking up on what the two physicians were thinking?

House and Jackson soon dismissed this possibility when Cayce described an epileptic condition which he declared was causing the child's severe infantile spasms, nausea, and vomiting. Further, Cayce explained that this condition was the outcome of the child's premature birth, which in turn had been the result of his mother's poor physical condition during the early months of her pregnancy. In conclusion, Cayce recommended that the child be given a measured dose of belladonna, administered orally, to be followed by wrapping his body in a steaming hot poultice made from the bark of a peach tree.

The session ended as mysteriously as it had begun. "We are through for the present."

Reading from the same notebook, House instructed Cayce to regain consciousness. Cayce dutifully followed the command and awoke.

In the few minutes that it took Edgar to regain consciousness, stretch his arms and legs, and then sit up from the bed, the two physicians had already left the room. Edgar was alone. Worried that the trance session had been a failure and wondering whether the reading was successful, he walked across the room and peered through the partially open door. House and Jackson were in the parlor, deep in discussion and obviously agitated.

The two physicians both agreed that the diagnosis sounded reasonable. The recommended cure was what upset them. Belladonna, a toxic form of deadly nightshade, could be lethal. Even if the peach-tree poultice could somehow leach the poison out of the child's system, administering a large dose of the drug to an infant in little Tommy's condition was murder. Jackson made his feeling clear to Carrie: "You'll kill little Tommy for sure."

Dr. House concurred. Homeopathic belladonna could be used to treat lung and kidney ailments, but pure belladonna, as Cayce had recommended, was used only in topical ointments.

Edgar joined the others in the parlor but couldn't contribute to the ensuing discussion. He didn't remember anything that he had said in trance. One minute he was wide awake, the next he was fast asleep. That's how he perceived what always took place. As Al Layne liked to remark, Edgar was the only one who never got to experience one of his own readings.

Anxiety became fear when Edgar finally understood the full import of the information that had come through. His sessions with Al Layne and others had been experiments. No one could get hurt. Now he had to face the horrific possibility that the treatment he recommended could—and likely would, according to House and Jackson—result in Tommy's death. A family member and mere child, no less!

Carrie had more faith in the trance advice than Edgar himself. She believed the sleeping Cayce was an instrument of God's divine love and compassion. This night God was reaching out to her and her child. If Cayce—in trance—told her to poison her son in order to save his life, she would act on the information.

Dr. House could not say the same. Common sense, along with decades of medical training, taught him that Cayce couldn't possibly be doing what he appeared to have done. Until now, he had looked at what Edgar was doing as mere entertainment—parlor tricks at best.

Carrie demanded that he prepare the belladonna. Despite his very great reservations and a threat from Dr. Jackson that he would lose his medical license and possibly be brought up on charges of manslaughter, he retrieved the drug from his doctor's bag. He loved Carrie too deeply to act otherwise. And regardless of how this might end his promising career, he could at least console himself by knowing that his son would surely die if nothing else were done. He would be putting little Tommy out of his misery.

Lynn Evans led Edgar outside to collect the ingredients for the poultice that had been recommended in the treatment. Edgar climbed a peach tree in the orchard behind the barn, opened his pocket knife, and cut the bark away from the freshest growth. He handed the bark down to Lynn, and they took it into the kitchen at the rear of the house where Carrie's sister Kate had put a kettle on the stove to boil.

Kate prepared the hot poultice and then carried it into the parlor where the others were waiting at the child's side. Dr. House dissolved the white powder into a spoonful of water. Carrie then opened Tommy's mouth, poured the liquid inside, and massaged his neck until he swallowed. Then she wrapped the naked child in the steaming hot towels dipped in peach-tree solution.

Edgar remained outside, standing on the veranda in the rain. He didn't join the others in the parlor because as he later said, he "couldn't stand the thought of seeing Tommy House die in his mother's arms." Gertrude had been right in not coming. He understood this now.

He heard no cries coming from inside the parlor. As the others described what happened, Tommy instantly fell asleep. Dr. House, in his later report, noted that this was the child's first deep and uninterrupted rest since birth. Tommy awoke hours later, drenched in sweat, cheeks pink, breathing steadily, and nursed at Carrie's breast. He never had a convulsion again.

The "miracle," as Carrie and Dr. House would forever describe Tommy's recovery, impacted the lives of everyone at The Hill that night and many thousands of others to come.

Thomas House Jr., c. 1911.

Carrie and her family would receive over two hundred readings in the three decades ahead. She not only continued to champion and defend Edgar but also encourage others to seek his counsel. She became one of the most adept students of the life-transforming messages of love and hope she found in the Cayce readings. She would later join Edgar and

Both seated, Edgar and Dr. House (with Gertrude's cousin Raymond Smith).

Gertrude when they left for Virginia Beach, and she would become chief of the nursing department at the Cayce hospital. In addition to her capacity as an RN, she would help to explain the readings to those who sought Cayce's counsel, most notably young mothers.

Dr. Thomas House underwent a personal crisis. What he had witnessed at The Hill that night made it impossible for him to return to practicing medicine as he had been taught. A rising star in the medical community, once under consideration to become head of the American Medical Association, he left his practice at the Hopkinsville asylum, turned his back on standard allopathic medicine as practiced by his colleagues, and embraced a type of holistic treatment put forth in the trance readings. Along with his wife, he moved to Virginia Beach where he became the Cayce hospital's chief physician.

Tommy House Jr. would grow healthy and strong and also make his home in Virginia Beach. A gifted engine mechanic and repairman, he personally built the health equipment recommended in the readings. Today, patients still use the batteries he first assembled for the electromagnetic therapy prescribed to treat a wide variety of illness, including conditions that were similar to his own at birth. Often times, at great personal expense, he would drive hundreds of miles to deliver

Carrie House, Gertrude, Gladys Davis, Hugh Lynn, Edgar Evans, and Tommy House in Dayton, Ohio, 1924.

readings and medical equipment to patients unable to come in person to receive Cayce's help.

Equally profound was the impact Tommy House Jr.'s reading had on Edgar. He had proven to himself and others the life-saving potential of his work. Regardless of how unusual and sometimes altogether unbelievable the information that came through in his readings, he would never again doubt the good that could result. From this day forward he would dedicate a portion of his time each day to giving readings. No one who genuinely needed and wanted help would be refused. And though it would still be several years before Gertrude herself would become his partner in what he was now beginning to call the work, thanks to Carrie's courage and example, she would conduct more readings than anyone else.

Wesley Ketchum:

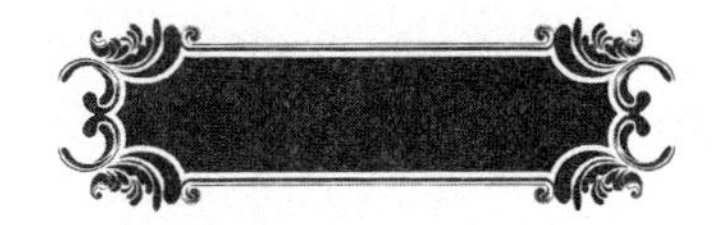

The Psychic Partnership

As news of the success of the Tommy House reading circulated through Hopkinsville, ever greater numbers of ill and dying people turned to Edgar for help. Among them was Gordon Putnam paralyzed from the waist down. Cayce—in trance—recommended osteopathic treatments which were able to effect a cure. There followed successful readings for a woman suffering from glaucoma and a young girl with a throat inflammation. The only readings which were judged by Edgar to be a failure were those given to Joe Dickey who was intent on using trance advice to lay bets at the Latonia Race Track. Edgar correctly picked the winning horses but in the process suffered severe migraine headaches and temporarily lost his ability to go into trance. Only by trial and error would he discover how the readings were to be used or what, in fact, the rules were.

Just as more patients came to him for help, so did several Hopkinsville physicians. Among them was Dr. Wesley Ketchum, a short, thickly built, well-groomed thirty-one-year-old homeopath from Ohio. Ketchum was not only better educated than any others

Cayce had worked with but despite the criticism and veiled threats he received from colleagues, was fearless in applying the recommended therapies. And while a few other physicians also consulted Cayce, Ketchum was the only one willing to admit it and seemed to actually enjoy the controversy this created. He told his patients that he was consulting Cayce and would deliver lectures at medical conferences in which he described the trance process in detail. It was one of these lectures, delivered to the American Association of Clinical Research that would result in a front page *New York Times* article which turned Cayce into an overnight sensation.

ILLITERATE MAN BECOMES A DOCTOR WHEN HYPNOTIZED

Strange Power Shown by Edgar Cayce Puzzles Physicians.

The *New York Times*, October 9, 1910.

The first reading Cayce provided to Ketchum was for a boy who had suffered a venomous bite from a brown recluse spider. The reading advised using "oil of smoke." Thinking this was a commercial preparation, Ketchum did not ask where the product might be found. A search of the local drugstores didn't turn it up, nor could it be found

Wesley Ketchum was fearless in applying Cayce's readings.

in pharmaceutical catalogs. A second reading was taken to determine where to find it. Cayce named a Louisville drugstore. But when Ketchum wired the drugstore, the manager informed him they did not know what he was talking about. In a third reading, Cayce described the back room of the same Louisville drugstore and identified the shelf where the product could be found. Ketchum wired the instructions to the manager of the drugstore. "Found it," came the reply.

The reading that most convinced Ketchum of the potential of the Cayce readings was for George Dalton, the wealthy owner of Hopkinsville's brickworks. Dalton—who weighed well over two hundred pounds—had broken his right leg both below and above the knee. Hopkinsville's other doctors said that Dalton would never walk again and that amputation would be necessary. But Ketchum—on trance advice from Cayce—said that the knee could be healed.

The subsequent reading recommended that Ketchum bore holes in the kneecap and leg bones, insert nails into them, and put Dalton in traction. Ketchum was dubious, at best. Inserting metal screws or nails into bone was a procedure that had never before been performed in

Kentucky or anywhere else in the United States. However, there was no harm in trying the procedure. The worst case scenario was that Dalton would lose his leg, which is what the other physicians anticipated from the start. Ketchum had nails made to Cayce's specifications. Assisted by another doctor and two nurses, he bore holes in the knee and leg bones and then inserted the nails. Two months later Dalton was back on his feet. The nails were still in his leg seventeen years later when he died.

Ketchum described these and other radical procedures in his lectures. With the eventual front page article about their work in *The New York Times*, celebrities began to seek Edgar's counsel. Among them was inventor Thomas Edison and electrical genius Nikola Tesla, who consulted Cayce in Bowling Green. Unfortunately this was years before Cayce had a dedicated stenographer to record the readings and save copies for later study. Like an eventual reading that was given for President Woodrow Wilson, documentation on what came through is scant, and hearsay at best. However, almost overnight, everyone wanted a Cayce reading. Ketchum and Cayce would have more patients than they could possibly accommodate.

Ketchum thus proposed a formal partnership. Cayce would provide trance counsel, Edgar's father would conduct the readings, and Albert Noe, the manager and later owner of the Hopkinsville's Latham Hotel, would provide the financing. The idea seemed to be a good one: patients would make an appointment to consult Ketchum, who would then charge a fee for his services. Along with those services would come a trance reading performed by Edgar. Half the income generated by the partnership was to go to the Cayces. The other half would go to Ketchum and Noe, who would pay the partnership's overhead expenses. In addition, it would finance a move to bring Cayce and his family from Bowling Green and establish a photography studio in Hopkinsville. The only caveat, and one that was critically important to Edgar, was that Ketchum had to solemnly promise that readings were to be given "for sick people only" and that no one in desperate need would be turned away. The racetrack readings with Joe Dickey had taught him all he wanted to know about using his gifts otherwise.

Gertrude, a young mother at this point, wasn't keen on the idea. She was dubious of any business in which Leslie was a partner, as

Edgar's father had proven himself to be unreliable. She was equally concerned about the freewheeling Ketchum, who had a reputation as a gambler and was rumored to be having an affair with his office receptionist. For all of Ketchum's talk of unleashing Cayce's incredible potential, the good doctor's primary interest was in gaining social prominence and power, and as he himself later admitted, availing himself of personal information he had obtained through Cayce in trance to further his cause.

Knowing in advance that Gertrude would not approve, Edgar went

Gertrude with first born, Hugh Lynn Cayce, 1907.

ahead with the plan. He believed that in time Gertrude would come to realize that the business of giving psychic readings had to be accorded the same degree of professionalism as his photography business. He needed an established place patients could go to, preferably close to home in Hopkinsville. Moreover, after an unexplained fire had destroyed his Bowling Green photo studio in December 1906 and with the birth of his son Hugh Lynn the following year, he desperately needed the income that the partnership would provide. The arrangement permitted him to both earn a living as a photographer and give readings for people in need.

Having increasingly learned to put his trust in the readings, he volunteered to let the Source itself make the decision if this partnership was a good idea or not. The message that came through was decidedly positive. The Source indicated that "the work" should be supported by those who benefited from the readings and the credibility that the readings generated. The more people believed in the value of the information, the more Cayce and his partners would gain materially from it. But the most important aspect of this reading was the suggestion that the ultimate purpose of the work was not to provide diagnostic insights. Rather, as Carrie House had long ago said, they were to help people "open" their minds and accept the truth of the "ethereal" or "spiritual world." The Source would then offer an important clue to the future success or failure of the work. "The minute we gain credence and give credit to ourselves," came the message, "we lose it."

Edgar, Leslie, Noe, and Ketchum chose to make their headquarters in a suite of rooms on the top floor of Hopkinsville's Thompson Building, a large redbrick building adjacent to the Hopper Brothers Bookstore. A long-running joke was that Edgar Cayce had finally moved up in the world since leaving the Hopper Brothers Bookstore. Upstairs, that is.

A sign reading the Cayce Photo Studio was posted outside on the street. In the hallway at the top of the stairs, another sign marked the entrance to Edgar's three-room photo studio, which was outfitted with the most modern photographic equipment. A few yards further down the hall was a third sign, written in smaller letters, reading: "Psychic Diagnostician." Here the door opened into a suite of offices that were connected through the back to the photo studio. However, patients were not normally invited into these offices and rarely got to meet Edgar Cayce in person. Those who desired to come to Hopkinsville for a reading and be examined by a physician would meet with Ketchum at his office. Personal contact between Edgar and his patients was viewed as an unnecessary interference in Edgar's personal life and unnecessary to the business of conducting daily trance sessions. It didn't matter where a patient resided for Cayce to give an accurate reading.

Due to the unique nature of their proposed partnership and before their formal five-year contract was signed, several prominent Hopkinsville judges, among them John T. Hanberry, were invited to witness a reading to give their honest opinion as to whether or not laws would be broken by conducting their business. Judge Hanberry, who had previously received his own medical reading, concurred with the others in giving his blessing. He was so impressed by the demonstration that he offered to purchase Cayce's contract from Noe and Ketchum, which they declined.

Readings were begun the same day that the documents were signed. Before the end of the first week, nine patients had received and paid for readings. Mrs. Eleanor Sledge, who received a reading three weeks

Waiting room in Dr. Ketchum's office, c. 1910.

later, came to Ketchum suffering from debilitating migraine headaches. Cayce—in trance—suggested that the problem was the result of a lesion that had grown on her spine, which could be removed through osteopathic manipulation. Her eventual cure, less than two months later, was considered nothing short of miraculous.

In the process of studying the larger body of readings, Ketchum became aware of the Source as a distinct personality or being with many human characteristics. However "all knowing" the Source might be, it could also be abrupt, disliked what it considered inane questions, and demonstrated what could only be characterized as a wry sense of humor. This became more evident in the years to come. Asked how a person should overcome worrying, the Source simply said, "Quit worrying!" A woman, wanting to know if wearing glasses, as Cayce had recommended, was really necessary, was told, "The body really needs glasses, else we wouldn't have said it!" When a patient asked if a medication should be rubbed on the outside, he was simply told: "You can't rub it on the inside!"

The Source sounded so "human" to Ketchum that the physician concluded that the voice speaking through Cayce was not a separate entity but Edgar's higher unconscious self. He disputed what Carrie House believed—that a heavenly presence took over when Cayce went into trance—maintaining that Cayce's spirit was free to communicate with other spirits when he lost consciousness. Although subsequent readings suggested that there was clearly much truth in this theory, Ketchum himself later admitted that whatever happened was far more complicated than Cayce's spirit reaching out into the universe. This was, however, a good starting point.

Ketchum also suspected that Cayce's subconscious mind could travel to the physical location of the patient. During one reading, Cayce remarked on the color of a patient's pajamas and on another occasion mentioned a particularly handsome tree in her yard.

There were, however, limits to what Cayce could do. The Source, for example, would sometimes come right out and say that this information wasn't to be shared, while at other times Cayce seemed to be able to peer at will right inside a person without interference. From this, Ketchum suspected that the individuals receiving the readings could somehow block Cayce's examination of their bodies. Motivation on the part of the patient requesting the reading clearly factored into the equation, as Ketchum obtained the best results when a person genuinely wanted help for the reasons that he had stated. Moreover, information that would hurt or harm someone would simply not be given. Further, and all the more extraordinary, the Source would only make recommendations that a person was capable of undertaking given their logistical or financial means. If a trip to the Mayo Brothers Hospital in Minnesota was out of the question, the Source seemed to find a solution closer to home, even if it meant having to instruct a local physician on how to perform the treatment.

Just as the number of readings grew, Edgar himself was slowly beginning to understand some of the dynamics involved in giving them. He also began to take an interest in the medical side of the business. He seemed to genuinely want to know how the recommended treatments worked, though he and Ketchum, too, at times, were a long way from understanding them. However, as both Cayce and Ketchum discovered, the challenge was not obtaining helpful information from the Source but in finding medical practitioners willing to apply the treatments. All too often a patient's personal physician simply dismissed a reading as beneath his consideration. Ketchum could treat the patients coming to Hopkinsville, but the vast majority lived outside of Kentucky and couldn't reasonably be expected to take up residence in Hopkinsville while the treatments—sometimes lasting months—were conducted. This realization was foremost on his mind when Frank Mohr, a successful businessman whose three-and-a-half-year-old niece was cured of polio, offered to build a hospital where the treatments could be performed exactly as recommended.

Noe and Ketchum also liked the idea. However, they believed they should be compensated for "developing" and "publicizing" Edgar's abilities. Their general understanding with Mohr, agreed to in principle, stipulated that Noe and Ketchum would receive a modest share of all proceeds from the hospital and that Noe would receive compensation from patients or their families taking long-term residence in the hotel.

Based on their verbal understanding, Mohr surveyed and cleared land in Nortonville, Kentucky, and a team of laborers poured the foundation for the hospital. Problems, however, soon arose. Noe and Ketchum kept coming up with one reason after another for not signing a formal contract. They had apparently decided to stall negotiations, holding out for a greater share of profits, or so it appeared to Mohr. Then, in the midst of heated arguments on the matter, Mohr injured his back. Edgar gave an emergency diagnosis. His health could be restored, the Source indicated, but unless certain corrective measures were taken, injury to his spine would gradually produce uric acid poisoning and would result in blindness.

Mohr and his doctors believed the diagnosis to be absurd. Ketchum, either not wishing to appear foolish to his peers or secretly desiring to drive a wedge between Mohr and Cayce, laughed along with Mohr's doctors. How could a curvature of the spine cause blindness? Mohr didn't know whom to trust. Suspecting some kind of fraud, he went to court, and the hospital project never progressed beyond the foundation, still visible today. He also eventually went blind.

Adding to the stress weighing on Edgar and Gertrude's shoulders, she gave birth to another child, Milton Porter, on March 28, 1911. Edgar was so preoccupied with Noe and Ketchum and two separate civil suits which would arise from the falling out between Mohr and Ketchum that he did not pay close enough attention to the situation at home. Milton Porter was not receiving enough nourishment from his mother's milk. A wet nurse was brought in, but by this time the child was ill with whooping cough and then colitis. Edgar gave a reading as he had done for Tommy House Jr., but the Source held out no hope for a recovery. Milton Porter's death certificate states that he died on May 17, one month and twenty days after his birth.

The stress nearly ended the Cayce marriage. Edgar faulted himself for not giving a reading sooner. Part of the reason was that he had indeed had been too preoccupied with his business affairs. However, it

Gravestone of 1½ month old Milton Porter Cayce.

was also true that Gertrude was still upset with him giving readings, and as he also admitted, she hadn't wanted him to give readings for their immediate family members. Gertrude, too, must have felt responsible for not having taken proper care of the child.

Just as had been the case when Edgar suffered from laryngitis, Gertrude stopped eating and took to bed. She might well have been suffering from depression similar to Edgar's own mother on the birth and subsequent death of her second child. But also true, the following July, she began coughing up blood. The diagnosis was tuberculosis, which at that time was considered incurable.

Edgar volunteered to give a reading immediately, but Gertrude was still resisting. Despite the help Edgar had provided to her nephew Tommy House, Gertrude still didn't like the business of his giving readings and didn't want their lives to revolve around them. To her way of thinking, the only way to make her point was to stand her ground by asserting what little control she had over the situation.

Edgar tried and failed to convince her to have a reading. Ketchum, too, made an attempt, but his pleas for her to receive trance counsel were ineffectual, perhaps even aggravating an already tense situation. Gertrude may also have considered him one of the root causes to Milton Porter's death. Had her husband not been preoccupied by the court battle with Mohr and the discord among the partners, her husband would have been on hand to help.

Edgar wasn't about to sit back and watch Gertrude die as Milton Porter had. Who intervened is not clear. Edgar may have prevailed in speaking with her. Carrie may have demanded she have a reading. No doubt Dr. House also encouraged her, as he was one of two of her consulting physicians. All that is known is that she finally agreed to have a reading after both her physicians and a tuberculosis specialist brought in from Louisville declared her to be on her deathbed.

Edgar lay down in bed beside her and with Ketchum conducting, began the reading. Outside on the porch and in the street were gathered those who loved Gertrude and prayed for her recovery. Her pastor had called his congregation together, and hand in hand with others who loved and supported Gertrude, they formed what was described a human chain around the front of the house while the reading was given.

Cayce—in trance—outlined treatments that included osteopathic adjustments for her back, inhalation of spirits from a charred oak keg to relieve the congestion in her lungs, heroin to shock the her system, other drugs and laxatives to help cleanse the blood and various organs, and a diet high in iron supplements and raw vegetables. When Cayce woke up, Ketchum and the other doctors were pacing the room. As with the Tommy House reading, the diagnosis was considered excellent. The concern was the treatment.

The recommended osteopathic adjustments were judged not be harmful, nor the laxatives. What alarmed the physicians was the inhalation of apple brandy fumes from a charred oak keg, which might further congest or weaken her lung capacity. Then there were the drugs. Cayce had recommended that she take a combination of heroin, eucalyptol, turpentine, and creosote, which were to be mixed into a liquid and placed in a capsule made from crystallized phosphates of soda. The shock to her system might put her into a coma from which she would never regain consciousness.

Edgar wouldn't listen to their concerns. With Ketchum's help, he was prepared to act immediately, which they did.

The effect on Gertrude was dramatic and made all the more miraculous because no one before—not in a trance reading or a laboratory—had ever come up with a cure for tuberculosis. There were treatments to prolong a person's life, but no cure. After taking the first capsule, Gertrude stopped hemorrhaging. The fumes of the apple brandy reduced the congestion in her lungs. Days later her fever broke. A month into the treatments she was decidedly gaining strength.

Gertrude Cayce, c. 1921.

Ironically, it was in the midst of Gertrude's recovery—in what might be viewed as Ketchum and Cayce's most spectacular success—that the year-old partnership would come under the most intense scrutiny, criticism, and investigation by the medical profession. Such would be the case many more times in Cayce's life to come, though in different cities and with other physicians. That Cayce's trance readings recommended treatments which helped the patients who came to him was beside the point.

In November 1911, while Gertrude was still in bed recovering and Edgar had once again begun suffering from migraine headaches and throat problems, Ketchum was informed by a neighbor that he and Cayce were being investigated by the Christian County Medical Society. A resolution had been passed demanding that a committee of concerned physicians visit the governor and the attorney general to revoke Ketchum's medical license, end the partnership, and put a stop to what they deemed to be a mockery of medical science.

Knowing that there would be upward of forty-five doctors in the county attending the next medical society meeting, Ketchum considered bringing eyewitnesses and patients whom he and Cayce had helped, along with affidavits. However, the resourceful and wily Ketchum concocted an altogether different scheme. He withdrew a thousand dollars from his bank account. This was all he took with him into the packed meeting which would decide his and in turn, Edgar's future.

Ketchum entered the crowded meeting room and took a seat in the back. After the session was called to order and the names of the committee members were selected to go to Frankfort to see the governor and attorney general, Ketchum asked that he be permitted to briefly address fellow society members. He walked to the front of the room and put the cash on top of the secretary's table, where everyone could see it. Then he delivered a short, previously prepared speech. Here, in his own words, is part of what he said:

> I'm sorry to have brought this on the doctors of Christian County. But you were born and raised here [and] I came here on the encouragement of quite a number of your top citizens. If you gentlemen want to get the real meat of the bull, I want your help.

> Of course, if you're just going to kick me out of the profession, that's different. But I have a suggestion to offer you. I'd like you to appoint six men to choose one of his most complex cases, then have Cayce lie down and go to sleep and diagnose each of the six cases. If the diagnoses are not absolutely correct, I will turn this money over to any charity you name in Christian County.

A hush fell over the room after Ketchum sat down. Eventually, a physician in the back of the room made a motion that there should be further investigation before their committee visited the attorney general. Ketchum would hear nothing more from the medical society.

Ketchum did, however, engineer a meeting with the attorney general at a gathering of the regional bar association. The meeting was to be held at the Hotel Latham, and Cayce was scheduled to put on a demonstration of his psychic abilities. Ketchum never revealed whose idea the presentation was, but given the presence of the attorney general at the head table, Ketchum's handiwork was much in evidence.

On the night of the event, Ketchum invited the assembled attorneys to write out questions which he would have Cayce answer. More than a dozen lawyers participated. Ketchum then had Cayce come into the room, lie down on a table, and guided him into trance. Cayce reportedly answered each question. In some cases he provided lengthy, comprehensive responses; in other instances said "yes" or "no."

The performance made for quite a sensation as the attorneys marveled at Cayce's uncanny abilities. As Ketchum anticipated, the attorney general pulled him aside after the performance. He had heard about the trouble that Ketchum and Cayce had had with the local medical society. He now understood why.

"I'll tell you," the attorney general said, gesturing with his hands. "It's not far from here to over there. I think this fellow [Cayce] falls through."

This was all the attorney general said, and all that Ketchum believed he needed to hear him say. "[In] some way and somehow," Ketchum replied, "he does fall into another sphere about which we know nothing."

Ketchum had artfully dodged a bullet—not once but twice. His third experience, however, would send him on a one-way cruise to Honolulu.

Dr. Hugo Münsterberg, c. 1908.

HUGO MÜNSTERBERG:

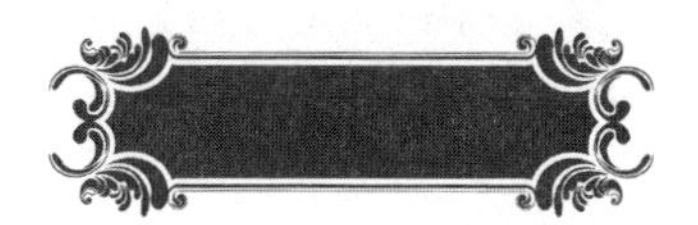

HARVARD COMES TO HOPKINSVILLE

Heightened interest in Edgar Cayce drew the attention and scrutiny of physicians well beyond Hopkinsville. And while Ketchum was proving adept at handling his Kentucky colleagues, he was out of his depth when Dr. Hugo Münsterberg of Harvard University unexpectedly checked into the Latham Hotel and requested to meet with Edgar and his partners.

An imperious and altogether imposing man, who stood six-feet tall and weighed two-hundred-and-fifty pounds, Münsterberg was the most famous academic at the most prestigious institution in the United States. Born and raised in Germany, with an MD from the University of Heidelberg and a PhD from the University of Leipzig, he came to Harvard at the request of William James, the most influential figure in the history of American psychology. He had dined at the White House with two presidents, entertained European royalty in his Boston home, and was the most quoted German intellectual in the world press. He spoke five languages, enjoyed oil painting and portraiture, wrote poetry, played the cello, directed films, authored bestselling books and popular magazine articles, and pioneered technology which would lead to the creation of the modern-day lie detector. Most important to the Cayce story was the joy he took in exposing fraudulent mediums and psychics.

In one highly publicized case in 1909, Münsterberg investigated Eusapia Palladino, an internationally renowned Italian medium who was championed by British psychic researcher Hereward Carrington. Madame Palladino, calling upon her spirit guide John King, could allegedly levitate tables, remotely transport objects from one place to another, spontaneously excite musical instruments to play, and summon otherworldly blasts of wind to blow through rooms with sealed windows and doors. Münsterberg proved otherwise.

Dr. Hugo Münsterberg, seated at center, with his medical students, 1891.

At a séance held in the Manhattan apartment of a wealthy Bostonian, he and two colleagues had joined Palladino around a circular table in a darkened room. At Palladino's direction, he was seated to the left of the medium with his right foot in contact with her left foot and his right hand in contact with her right hand. Similarly, one of Münsterberg's colleagues sat to her right with his left hand and left foot touching her right hand and right foot. According to Palladino, investigators seated in this way could be certain that she didn't move her hands and feet without their knowledge. What Palladino didn't know was that Münsterberg had an accomplice hidden in the room.

After the séance had begun, Münsterberg's accomplice, not spirit guide John King, made his presence known. Palladino was caught having stealthily slipped her bare feet out of her shoes and using her toes to raise the table around which they sat. She had also surreptitiously placed Münsterberg's right hand on top of his colleague's left hand. With her own hands thus liberated, she was then free to move objects and make the instruments play. The mysterious wind, Münsterberg further revealed, was the result of a rubber bladder secreted into the palm of one of her hands which she used to release sudden jets of air to blow through the room.

Eusapia Palladino, Italian medium, 1898.

Münsterberg's success in exposing Palladino and the laudatory press that followed surely contributed to his decision to investigate

Cayce. The event that triggered the professor's departure for Hopkinsville was the presentation of a scholarly paper written by Ketchum delivered at Harvard to the American Association of Clinical Research in 1911. The presentation, attended by upwards of four thousand physicians, clinical researchers, and university scientists, reportedly sent Münsterberg into a blind fury. "I will expose Cayce to the world!" he grandly announced.

Fellow faculty members in Cambridge were not so quick to dismiss Ketchum's report or rally behind their headline-grabbing colleague's efforts to debunk Cayce. They believed that Münsterberg, who was in the process of rewriting the Harvard curriculum, had betrayed the legacy of his now-deceased mentor William James, who had encouraged the open-minded study of paranormal and extrasensory phenomenon and had been a prominent supporter of the Society for Psychical Research in England. In striking contrast to James, Münsterberg denied the existence of the unconscious mind and any supposed powers associated with it. He bridled at the notion that a psychic could correctly diagnose illness in a hypnotic state and was determined to destroy the careers of physicians and scientists entertaining such claims.

Three months after Ketchum's presentation, on January 20 after attending a formal state dinner in Washington D.C., Münsterberg arrived in Hopkinsville by train and checked into Cayce partner Albert Noe's hotel. As Münsterberg's archived correspondence makes clear, he didn't alert the press of his visit because he condescendingly believed that his mere presence in Hopkinsville would give credence to the "humbug" he believed to be psychic phenomenon. Rather, he would catch Cayce in an act of fraud, compile his findings, and go public at a time and place of his own choosing—Harvard's Emerson Hall.

The following day Münsterberg hired a carriage which took him down the Russellville Road to the modest single-bedroom cottage at the furthermost edge of city limits to where the Cayces had now moved. As Münsterberg learned from the carriage driver, Edgar owned no property. Even the cameras in his Hopkinsville photo studio belonged to others in the partnership. Edgar and his wife Gertrude had moved into a cottage near The Hill belonging to his mother-in-law to

The train coming into Hopkinsville.

save money and to make it more convenient for family members to care for bedridden Gertrude recovering from tuberculosis.

Münsterberg's unexpected arrival, his thick German accent, trademark silver-handled cane, and ankle-length beaver coat caught Cayce by surprise. Though taken aback, Edgar was cordial. He invited the forty-eight-year-old professor into his home, introduced him to three-year-old Hugh Lynn, and briefly showed him into the bedroom to meet Gertrude.

The Harvard professor expressed no pleasantries nor excused himself for arriving without an invitation. He immediately asked to see the table, lights, crystal ball, or any of the "modus operandi" that were the accoutrements of psychics such as Palladino. Cayce truthfully said he didn't know what Münsterberg was talking about. He needed no darkened room to go into trance, could not levitate tables, move objects, or conjure unearthly gusts of wind. He described how he could go into trance whether he was lying on the floor in the living room, outside in the yard, or in the middle of the road. He also informed Münsterberg that his readings were now recorded by a stenographer and that typed transcripts were available from Dr. Ketchum for his inspection. He would be pleased to accommodate.

As an example of Cayce's trance-induced diagnoses, Münsterberg was shown a transcript of his latest trance session, a follow-up health reading Edgar had given his wife the previous day. Münsterberg studied the reading and with permission, briefly examined Gertrude. He also heard the dramatic story of how, on her deathbed, the Source had recommended she be given the combination of drugs and charred oak keg filled with apple brandy which had saved her life. Unbelievable as it all seemed, Münsterberg could see for himself that Gertrude was on the path to a full recovery.

After further discussion of Gertrude's case and examining the readings that had been given her, Münsterberg abruptly left without shaking Edgar's hand or saying goodbye. He would, however, return several days later, this time by appointment and accompanied by Dr. Jackson with whom he had discussed Gertrude's medical history and conducted a more thorough physical examination.

Münsterberg's investigation was underway, but it was not Cayce who was being tested. What the Harvard professor hadn't revealed to Edgar and Gertrude was that he had lost family members to tuberculosis. As a highly trained medical professional he knew the disease as only a specialist did. As the bereft stepson of a mother who had died from it, he also knew the agony of those who had contracted it. He had, as a result of his experience, been inspired to found a tuberculosis institute in Berlin. Until he sat at Gertrude's beside, he had never personally examined a patient whose dramatic recovery was so miraculous.

Despite what he had seen and heard at the Cayce household, Münsterberg was unwilling or unable to make the creative leap necessary to take the next step: admit the possibility that Edgar's trance readings had cured his wife of tuberculosis. Pride, not scientific inquiry, was the reason. The same was likely true of Harry Houdini, who would witness and investigate Cayce a decade later in New York. In the case of both men, no evidence would be convincing enough for them to publically call into question assumptions which contributed to their popularity. Houdini would try and fail to prove Cayce a fraud in 1921 at the McAlpin Hotel but would never go on record as having witnessed a Cayce reading, despite evidence otherwise.

Magician Harry Houdini, c. 1905.

The McAlpin Hotel in New York where Houdini performed and Cayce sometimes stayed when in New York.

Unbeknown to Cayce, Münsterberg's undeclared purpose in exposing Cayce as a fraud was to gather ammunition that would remove the last vestiges of James' influence on the Harvard curriculum. A sharp-tongued man with a well-deserved reputation for lashing out at his perceived enemies, Münsterberg knew he would have a mutiny on his hands back in Cambridge if he publically changed his position. And yet, here in front of him was a possible cure for one of the world's most dreaded diseases. He was in a position to save hundreds and thousands of sufferers—perhaps even millions—yet in doing so he would undermine the foundation upon which he had built his career, endanger his Harvard professorship, and expose himself to rebukes from the many colleagues and perceived enemies he had cowed into silence.

Münsterberg was further tested the next day when he met Cayce at his photo studio and witnessed a trance reading. When Edgar arrived in the morning, Cayce's father Leslie, who was conducting the readings at this point, stenographer Katherine Faxon, and Dr. Wesley Ketchum were already at the studio. Edgar had just finished telling them about Münsterberg's unannounced visit to his home when the professor arrived. He was shown into a small sitting room adjacent to where the readings were given. After everyone was gathered, Münsterberg then proceeded to interrogate Edgar, his father, and Ketchum. The partners answered his questions, and he was shown a file of readings and accompanying testimonials from patients.

Eventually, Edgar's morning appointment arrived. August Boehme had come from his home in Newport, Kentucky, and hadn't told Ketchum or anyone at the office why he had requested the reading. Edgar and Boehme chatted for only a few moments before Edgar lay down on the couch, put himself into trance, and proceeded to give a reading. Leslie stood beside the couch while Ketchum and Boehme sat in chairs adjacent to Cayce. Münsterberg chose a seat beside the door where he could best view the proceedings.

Cayce gave a typical reading. He reported on Boehme's body from head to toe, pointing out problem areas—he was suffering from a stomach disorder which resulted in chronic malnutrition—and made suggestions for how his condition could be treated. When Cayce came out of the trance, Münsterberg resumed questioning Edgar and Ketchum, and now Boehme. He asked Boehme about how much Edgar knew of his condition before the reading.

"Nothing whatever," Boehme answered. "I never saw him before in my whole life. I have only read something about him in the paper. I've been a sufferer for a long time with no results, so I came to see him, only arrived this morning."

Münsterberg asked Boehme if he was convinced by the reading. "I certainly am!" Boehme announced.

For the next five days Münsterberg interviewed other recipients of Cayce's readings. Professor Charles Dietrich, who impressed Münsterberg most, was the former Christian County Superintendent of Schools as well as being the best-educated and most-respected resident of Hopkinsville. In 1902, Cayce's trance counsel had cured Dietrich's six-year-old daughter Aime of mental illness. Over tea in the family's house, Dietrich's wife Minnie discussed their daughter's condition and presented Münsterberg with extensive medical records prepared by specialists. Aime herself, who was soon to attend college, may have entertained Münsterberg with a piano recital. Münsterberg also interviewed George Dalton, the wealthy building contractor who had consulted Cayce about his compound leg fracture, and had received the treatment in which nails were used to set the fracture. Dalton not only provided Münsterberg personal witness to the veracity of Cayce's reading, but he also had X-ray proof of the procedure.

Carrie House, now a hospital nurse, related her equally compelling story of how Edgar had saved her son. Three-year-old Tommy House, who played at Münsterberg's feet while Carrie related what had happened, was living proof. She also shared with him the story of how Gertrude had resisted the readings and had done all she could to convince Edgar to stop giving them until, on her death bed, a reading had saved her life. Carrie, and now Gertrude, had absolute confidence in Edgar's ability, though she, and later Gertrude, would confide to Münsterberg that they had doubts about Dr. Ketchum's integrity and others whom, Carrie said, were prone to take advantage of Edgar. His was a gift from God, not to be exploited or traded upon. Yet increasingly, this was what, after Al Layne's departure, physician researchers were doing. If they weren't jabbing needles into Edgar to test that he was, in fact, in trance, they were obtaining horse racing tips and clues to help them find buried treasure. One group had, without permission from the Salter family, dug up the backyard at The Hill. As Edgar couldn't remember a thing he did or said when in trance, he was as the mercy of the conductor of the readings.

A man long regarded for his acute power of observation and who on occasion helped police ferret the truth from criminal suspects by cross-examination, Münsterberg became convinced that Cayce was not a fraud. His investigation, however, unearthed unsettling facts of which Edgar was unaware until he brought them to his attention. While combing through Ketchum's files, Münsterberg had found readings the Hopkinsville physician had conducted for himself. In addition to helping patients who came to him, Ketchum was secretly acquiring race track tips and was making large sums of money doing it. He also discovered several instances in which money was taken for readings that had never been conducted.

Before his departure from Hopkinsville, Münsterberg took Edgar aside and said that believed his gift to be genuine and encouraged him to continue giving readings. "If you never do another case other than the little Dietrich child, your life has not been in vain," he said. "I believe you will go far." With the praise came further advice. He thought that Cayce was "running with the wrong bunch" and showed him evidence of the various frauds he believed Ketchum had committed. If Edgar were to realize his dream of using the readings to heal the sick and inflicted, he needed someone to conduct the trance sessions whom he could trust not to exploit them. He urged Edgar to continue "listening to the voice," as he referred to the Source, but to reconsider the company he kept. "You will hear from me again."

Edgar never did. Nor were Münsterberg's colleagues ever provided a full account of what had taken place on his weeklong investigation. It would not be for many months before he shared any details with a young graduate student whom he was mentoring. He couldn't bring himself to publically admit what he would reveal privately. Perhaps this was one of the many things that weighed on his conscious when, five years after leaving Hopkinsville, he suffered a heart attack as he began what would be his last public appearance. One can only wonder what might have been—both for Cayce and Münsterberg and for tuberculosis patients around the world—had such an important and obviously talented professor publically born witness to what had taken place.

Münsterberg could, however, be thanked for alerting Edgar to the underhanded way that Ketchum was treating him. Ketchum's race track readings were likely the cause of Edgar's migraine headaches. They were also what had apparently provided income for Ketchum to purchase a car—the first ever in Hopkinsville.

Ending the Cayce partnership was more difficult than one might suppose. Not only did Edgar have Ketchum to contend with, but Edgar's photography studio and the equipment in it were the property of others, notably hotelier Albert Noe. A protracted law suit eventually went to court and was heard in front of none other than Judge John Hanberry, who had previously consulted with Edgar on the formation of the partnership and who had once offered to buy Cayce's contract from Ketchum and Noe.

Hanberry's presence as judge in this case was clearly a conflict of interest, and the judgment reflected it. Despite his previous affirmation that no laws had been broken in the formation of the partnership, he ruled that the contract as originally drawn up was illegal. Edgar and his father, Leslie were asked to pay legal fees, return the photography equipment, and pay Noe a settlement. Ketchum avoided the litigation and what promised to be another review of his medical license by leaving town. He abandoned his wife and a young child. Accompanied by his Hopkinsville receptionist, he boarded a train bound for Los Angeles and then a steamer for Hawaii. Edgar didn't know where he had gone until years later.

In a letter Edgar wrote to a business associate, he detailed the drama that unfolded in the Hopkinsville courtroom, and being overcome with anger by the injustice Hanberry handed down. He also described doing something that he had never done before and which he would sincerely regret later. He wrote that something within him made him rise and address the judge, saying, "For the lie you have this day enacted, the worms of your body will eat you up while you are yet alive!"

According to Edgar Cayce, what he had perhaps "willed," was indeed what later happened. Hookworms, or some form of intestinal infestation, brought on anemia and eventually killed Hanberry. Edgar told his friend, "Possibly it was only a coincidence. Possibly it was playing with fire."

Edgar left Hopkinsville, promising himself never to let his anger get the best of him again. He and his family would move to Selma, Alabama, for the simple reason that no one knew him there. He could start over, only this time with Gertrude at his side to conduct the readings.

Edgar, Gertrude, and Hugh Lynn.

I asked the roses as they grew
Richer and lovelier in their
hue
What made their tints so rich
and bright.
They answered—
Looking toward the Light

EC's handwriting

The Cayce Photography Studio's Window Display.

HANG THIS UP

PRICE LIST

FINISHING KODAK PICTURES

Developing any size roll 10c

Developing Film Packs.................. 15c

PRINTING

Any size up to 2 1-4 by 4 1-4........3c each

2 1-4 by 4 1-4 up to 4 1-4 by 6 1-2, 4c each

Post Cards................................ 5c each

Enlargements.............................25c up

Best Results Obtained By
Practical Workmen

"LET US FINISH YOUR SNAPS"

CAYCE
ART COMPANY

21 1-2 Broad St. Selma, Alabama

The company's price list.

Hugh Lynn Cayce:

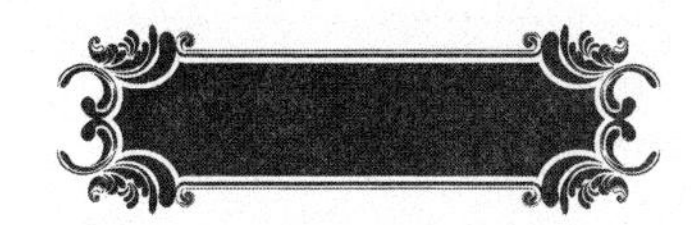

The Psychic's Son

The Cayce family's eleven years in Selma would be the most peace ful and happiest of their lives. Together with Edgar's father Leslie, he and Gertrude took over a photography studio, became active members in their church, and their third child, Edgar Evans, was born to them. More important from the standpoint of the readings, Gertrude took over responsibility as conductor. While she sat beside Edgar guiding him into trance and putting the questions to him, he was assured that his gifts would be used only to heal the sick and injured and as became increasingly evident, to gain greater insight into the human condition. The Cayces' life, however, was not without its frightening moments. The first was an accident that nearly resulted in six-year-old Hugh Lynn losing his eyesight.

By this time Hugh Lynn had already earned a reputation, as friends and neighbors would say, as "a force to be contended with." When he wasn't at school, where he frequently got into wrestling matches with schoolmates, he was rushing up and down the stairs to his family's third floor apartment on his way to play with his buddies, jumping off rocks into his favorite swimming hole, or climbing the tall magnolia trees in nearby Elkdale Park. His innate curiosity, combined with seemingly boundless energy and a particular talent as a prankster, left Gertrude exhausted.

A lover of animals, he was particularly interested when his father was commissioned to photograph squirrels for a newspaper photo spread in January 1914. As it was too difficult to photograph the squirrels in the wild—photography equipment was too cumbersome to easily move from one location to another, and proper exposure necessitated the subject holding still for several seconds—Edgar decided to shoot the photograph in the studio using "flash powder," the turn-of-the-century equivalent of a flash bulb. A cage of squirrels was delivered to the studio, and Edgar, with Hugh Lynn as his assistant, got to work. At some point during the photo shoot a squirrel got loose, creating much havoc. The result was a grainy black and white print of a squirrel in flight as it leaped out of a makeshift enclosure.

After the photo was taken, Edgar absent-mindedly left his box of flash powder on the camera stand. Either that afternoon or the next day, the Cayce family's cleaning lady, a woman nicknamed Bunchie, moved the box onto the floor or within arm's reach of young Hugh Lynn, for reasons that are not now known. Thinking to play a prank on Bunchie, Hugh Lynn poured a scoop of it on the top of the stairs and waited for her approach. The idea was to set it off when she mounted the top step. The problem was that only the tip of the match in his hand broke off when he went to light it. The match head fell into the nearby box of flash powder and exploded in Hugh Lynn's face. The flames set his hair on fire while scorching his nose and face.

Hugh Lynn's screams brought his parents out of their bedroom. Minutes later Edgar was carrying his son, writhing in agony, down the stairs to the street. Hugh Lynn was still kicking and screaming when they arrived, with Gertrude trailing behind, at their physician's office. Dr. Eugene Callaway, an eye specialist, was brought in to consult, but he, like family practitioner Dr. Samuel Gay, could do nothing more than ease the child's pain and treat the burns with salve. The greater problem was Hugh Lynn's eyes. The cornea and retina of the right eye were a blackened mass of burnt tissue; the other burned so badly that Hugh Lynn could barely see light through it.

CHILD BURNED BY POWDER FLASH

Little Hugh Lynn Cayce, son of Mr. and Mrs. Edgar Cayce, was the victim of a bad accident at the studio of Mr. Cayce on Broad street yesterday.

The bright little fellow was in the studio and among some photographic supplies he came across a package of flashlight powder and was playing with it. Afterwards the little fellow struck a match and the head flew off into the powder, causing a quick and dangerous flash of fire, and the flames covered his face and head.

A physician was quickly secured and gave the injured child attention. He stated to Mr. and Mrs. Cayce that one of the eyes would certainly be saved and hopes that the other will also be saved, but cannot say as to the final outcome of the other eye.

Information this afternoon was to the effect that the little fellow was resting well and that hopes are held out for a speddy recovery. Mr. and Mrs. Cayce have many friends in Selma who deeply sympathise with them in this distressing accident.

Hugh Lynn modeling for the Cayce Art Company before the accident.

Hugh Lynn was moved to the hospital where other physicians examined him. The medical consensus held out little hope for his eyesight: Hugh Lynn's right eye couldn't be saved, and his left eye might be permanently damaged as well. Callaway and the others recommended that, to prevent infection, the right eye must immediately be removed. Hugh Lynn had calmed down by this time and was being held in the arms of his Sunday school teacher. He listened to what was said, lifted himself up on one elbow, and demanded that his father conduct an emergency medical reading. In what would become characteristic of Hugh Lynn from this moment forward, he said, "My daddy, when he's asleep, is the best doctor in the world. He'll tell you what to do."

Without hesitation, Edgar and Gertrude returned to the studio. Accompanied by parishioners from their church, including Alfred and Roger Butler, the Cayce's dear friends, and their pastor, Reverend D. P.

Taylor, prayers for Hugh Lynn were said before the reading was conducted. As Edgar would later describe the moment, he felt energy in the room as never before. "Electricity" was how he described it. With Gertrude at his side, Hugh Lynn was begging for help, and loved ones gathered in a circle around him. In this setting the Source was in top form.

Cayce—in trance—declared that Hugh Lynn's sight in both eyes could be saved. The solution that doctors Callaway and Gay had already applied was judged to be correct, except that tannic acid had to be added to the salve. Further, Hugh Lynn was to be kept in an entirely darkened room, and there were precise times, specified in the reading, when his dressings were to be changed. The reading said that after two weeks the mass of burned flesh would drop off and the poisons that pooled around his eyes could be wiped clean, leaving Hugh Lynn's eyes intact.

Hugh Lynn's physicians were willing to give the reading a try, but they were strongly opposed to adding tannic acid to the salve, as it was judged to be far too caustic to be used on the eyes. Edgar and Gertrude were not dissuaded. According to the physicians' own diagnosis, Hugh Lynn's right eye was beyond saving and possibly his left as well. How could tannic acid do more damage than had already been done? And besides, the Source had declared what should be done, and they were going to do it.

The faith Hugh Lynn had in his father never wavered over the next two weeks while he lay in bed in a darkened hospital room, his bandaged eyes constantly bathed in the solution. Just as foretold in the reading, the white mass of burned flesh came loose and fell away, revealing his two brown eyes.

"I can see!" Hugh Lynn shouted.

Follow-up readings were conducted after Hugh Lynn was released from the hospital. Edgar and Gertrude adhered to the recommendations, which described lotions that would not only sooth his skin but would also lessen the likelihood of scar tissue. By the time Hugh Lynn turned eight, not a single scar was evident. Hugh Lynn would suffer mild myopia from his teen years on and would eventually require eye glasses, but the cure was complete.

Hugh Lynn's new challenge was putting up with his classmates, who heard the stories of the strange way in which he had been helped. He was teased unmercifully. "How's that freak father of yours getting along?" classmates would ask. And what trouble is that "son of a freak" going to get into next.

Edgar used lessons from his own childhood to counsel his son. "Don't pay any attention," Edgar said. "Laugh with them. That doesn't hurt me and it doesn't hurt you."

Hugh Lynn didn't pay any attention to the advice, and laughter wasn't on his agenda. "I'd fight every time," he later said. "They'd do it again and I'd fight them again. And they got tired because they knew I'd fight. The more I fought, the better I got."

Hugh Lynn eventually developed a reputation for being able to throw a powerful punch. Edgar stayed out of it, letting his son deal with the situation as he saw fit, even though Hugh Lynn frequently came home with torn clothes and bruises. At school he was a formidable adversary—no one to poke fun at. But at home, he was withdrawn and introspective, trying to reconcile what seemed to be two different worlds—the one his father lived in and the one that he and everyone else seemed to occupy. This, too, would obsess him for years to come.

The power that his father could tap into became abundantly clear one day when Hugh Lynn decided to ditch school and go instead for a swim in the Alabama River, several blocks from the family's apartment. No sooner did he return home than his father told him exactly where he had been and what he had been doing. He even described the tree limb where he had hung his clothes before scrambling down the riverbank into the water. "[At that moment] I knew that I couldn't fool my father," Hugh Lynn later reflected.

Though Hugh Lynn eventually resigned himself that his father could read his mind or somehow watch over him at a distance, he never stopped testing Edgar. His father's readings always proved so accurate that the ones Hugh Lynn came to obsess over were the few his father seemed to get wrong. In these, Hugh Lynn would say, were revealed "the outer limits" of his gifts.

There was one reading in which his father gave health recommendations for a woman whom, as it was later revealed, had died when the trance session was conducted for her. The only explanation that

The Cayce family of Selma, Alabama. Left to Right: Edgar Evans, Gertrude, Edgar, and Hugh Lynn

Hugh Lynn could come up with was a matter of distance. The woman in question hadn't herself asked for the reading, and the only connection between her and Cayce was a six-week-old letter from her son. His father somehow either hadn't been able to find her in trance or was giving a reading linked to when the letter had been written. On another occasion he gave a correct reading but for the wrong man; the other just happened to have the same name and lived in the same town.

Hugh Lynn would also note times when the Source simply said that no information could be given or would mention other occasions, as was the case of buried treasure, when none was found. Hugh Lynn could provide ample testimony to this effect because he himself, as a young adult, spent a fruitless summer with his brother and Tommy House Jr. digging in a swamp trying to locate pirate gold declared by his father to be there. Yet another treasure hunting expedition, generated by a reading for the owner of a Selma pharmacy, led to a small fortune in doubloons. Why one treasure had been found and another wasn't, couldn't be easily explained.

Among the subjects of greatest interest to young Hugh Lynn were ghosts. Once, in his bedroom in the family's Selma apartment, he awoke to see a woman in white standing at the foot of his bed, crying and wringing her hands. Hugh Lynn leapt out of bed, dashed across the hall, and dove into his parents' bed. They told him he was having a bad dream. But a few nights later, the same thing happened. Edgar and Gertrude listened to Hugh Lynn more closely this time, once again reassuring him that it was dream. The third time this happened Edgar asked him for precise details. What did the woman look like? How did she act? Edgar then told him that he would never see her again. Without further explanation, he said he would take care of it, which he did.

Many years passed before Edgar told Hugh Lynn what he had done. According to his father, Hugh Lynn had, in fact, seen an apparition. Edgar knew because he had seen her also and had a conversation with her. She had died in the same building before the Cayces had lived there. What Edgar had done was to explain to the spirit that she did not have to remain in the apartment and could now move on—advice that Edgar would offer many spirits, eventually including that of their cleaning lady, Bunchie, whom he would encounter in Virginia Beach several years after her death. She had come looking for Edgar because she believed herself gravely ill and wanted him to conduct a medical reading. Edgar had to break the news to her that she had already passed on.

Edgar rarely talked about his experiences with ghosts, but Hugh Lynn—perhaps because of the Selma ghost—always wanted to know more. As both a child and later as an adult, he would pester and test his father to learn more, always trying to push the limits of his abilities. No one would ever learn more about his father's gifts nor would treat them with such respect. However, as a result of one final incident in Selma, Hugh Lynn was careful not to let himself become personally involved with the spirit realm. That was his father's business.

The incident that led to Hugh Lynn's healthy appreciation for both the spirit realm and how potentially dangerous it was to journey in that dimension came when a member of Cayce's Bible Study class asked Edgar to try using a Ouija board.

Edgar enlisted the help of Gertrude. Together, they sat down at a table and put their hands on the pointer. Hugh Lynn, who sat beside them, was astonished. "I never saw a piece of wood cavort like that thing did. It was exactly like there was a line of [unseen] people standing up and they could have only three seconds or three minutes to give their little speech and the next one would come on."

The first message to come through was from a student in Edgar's Bible Study class who had subsequently died. He had given Edgar insurance documents which Edgar had put in an envelope in a desk drawer and had promptly forgotten about. After the session, the insurance papers were found and given to the family. Another message was a warning from a deceased former Selma resident who wanted to alert his brother that he would soon die of a heart attack. He wanted Edgar to prepare his brother and his family.

Also compelling was a message from a teen who claimed to have drowned in a nearby pond. His family had thought that he had run away. But according to the deceased, he had gone swimming and hit his head on a submerged tree stump. He described how his body was caught in barbed wire under the water and was still there. The boy's family was subsequently contacted, and they wrote back saying that they had retrieved the body.

To Hugh Lynn's memory, his father had never tried using a Ouija board before and would never use one again. Like the practice of automatic writing or drug-induced hallucinogenic states, Edgar believed that more harm than good would result. Just because one could contact a ghost or spirit didn't mean that the discarnate entity could be trusted, had any more wisdom or insight than it did when it was in the flesh and blood, and could at times be dangerous. "A lot of good stuff has come through Ouija boards and automatic writing," Edgar later said. "But a lot of people have gotten disturbed through it, too. The balance is on the negative side."

David Kahn, c. 1917.

DAVID KAHN:

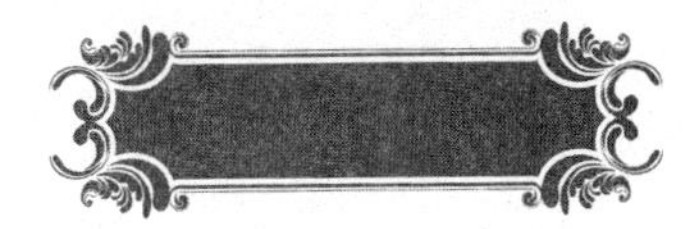

THE JEW FROM LEXINGTON

Edgar's friend during his Selma years, and for the rest of his life, didn't live in Alabama but in Lexington, Kentucky. David Kahn, sixteen years Cayce's junior, would have the distinction of receiving two hundred and fifty personal readings, which was some forty more than Edgar himself and eighty-two more than Gertrude. No one would travel more miles with Cayce, live with him under more unusual circumstances, or do more to promote the work. Even by conservative estimates, Kahn would be responsible for steering an estimated seven hundred people to Cayce for medical or business advice. A gifted salesman, he would talk about Cayce with complete strangers he met on street corners, on buses, and in elevators.

"If Cayce can't help you," he liked to say, "no one else can." If the subject turned to religion, Kahn would always say, "Why Edgar never tries to change anybody's religion! He tries to help you live up to your religion!" No sooner would Kahn bring someone new into the fold than he would excitedly send Edgar a telegram or letter announcing, as he invariably did, "Another 'crusader' for the cause."

Although there is some disagreement about what year Kahn met Cayce—evidence suggests 1913—and in what order subsequent events took place, the circumstances of their meeting are not in dispute. Cayce was scheduled to give a medical reading for Mrs. Lillie DeLaney, who in various accounts is referred to as Amanda Fay DeLaney. The wife of the wealthy owner of a Lexington lumber mill, Mrs. DeLaney had been crippled in an automobile collision. Edgar exchanged letters with her husband, William, who had read about Edgar's work with Ketchum in Hopkinsville, and called Charles Dietrich, the Christian County Superintendent of Schools, who had received help from Cayce for his mentally ill daughter. Dietrich had sung Cayce praises.

Mr. DeLaney arranged for Edgar to come to Lexington by train to examine his wife and give her a reading. Edgar told him that a personal meeting wasn't necessary, but at Mr. DeLaney's insistence, obliged the request. To conduct the reading and facilitate whatever treatment might be necessary, Edgar arranged for Dr. John Blackburn, one of doctors he had worked with in Hopkinsville, to meet him at the Lexington station. But just before Edgar was about to board the train to leave Selma, Blackburn wired him that due to a medical emergency he would be unable to join him. Edgar decided to make the trip regardless and prior to departing, wired Mr. DeLaney to arrange for a physician to be present. He would either teach DeLaney's physician how to conduct the reading or, if need be, Mr. DeLaney himself would conduct.

A carriage was waiting for Cayce when he arrived at the station and took him to Hampton Court, Lexington's wealthiest housing community. After passing under a massive stone archway, he was shown into the finest apartment building he had ever entered, one with a grand stairway as well as separate living and sitting rooms. Mrs. DeLaney, accompanied by her physician, was wheeled in on a stretcher to meet him.

Cayce would later describe her "pitiful" appearance: an immense woman, weighing over two hundred pounds and no taller than five-foot-five; her ankles and joints were so swollen that she couldn't raise her hand to shake his, let alone feed or care for herself. So sensitive was her tightly stretched skin that merely rubbing against bed sheets caused her excruciating pain. Physicians from around the country had all reached the same conclusion. The automobile accident had resulted in severe arthritis, which they were unable to treat. Cayce had serious doubts that anything he said in trance could help her, but he was willing to give his best. As he explained to Mr. DeLaney, several of his own family members who had been on their deathbeds had been saved. Perhaps Lillie DeLaney would be too.

The first hurdle to be overcome was finding someone who would conduct the reading. As Mr. DeLancy didn't have the skill or wherewithal to transcribe medical terminology, Mrs. DeLaney's physician was tasked with this responsibility. Mr. Delaney, however, had to declinc being the conductor on the grounds that he, a Roman Catholic, was forbidden by church doctrine to "conjure" or "call up spirits." The problem was solved by a Jewish neighbor, fifteen-year-old Dave Kahn. Not only would he conduct, but both he and the DeLaney's physician would take notes, increasing the likelihood of correctly getting the information down on paper.

"I not only had no objection," Kahn later said. "I was thrilled. To me it sounded like a great adventure in an area of life which at that time I knew virtually nothing about." Kahn would further relate his first meeting with Cayce:

> He looked like some backwoods Kentucky farmer, but I knew at once that he was much more. He had a kindly face, but it was his eyes that I noticed. They were grayish blue but the tone—even the color—seemed to change. At one moment you might almost think he was dreaming. Then you would feel those eyes seeing right through you. I felt this deep look when we first met. He was fair complexioned, and his face was long and thin. The cheekbones were high. He stood very erect, very slender, and spoke very deliberately. He told me he was in the photography business. His specialties, he said, were children and railroads. He seemed interested in me as a possible subject for future pictures.

Cayce may indeed have been interested in using Kahn as a model in one of the many commercial photo assignments his studio handled: he was that handsome. However, unbeknown to Kahn, there was more to Cayce's interest in the young man. This would be the first time a

Jewish person would conduct a reading. Edgar made a mental note because, a few years earlier when readings were conducted for the Ketchum partnership, the Source had said that one of the people who would figure prominently in the work would be Jewish.

Kahn wasn't the least put off by what Cayce was asking him to do. His mother had an interest in psychic phenomenon, and though neither he nor she had ever heard of anyone doing what Cayce did, he saw no reason not to give conducting a try. Nor was the process difficult. Everything was outlined in Cayce's small black-leather pocket notebook. Kahn had only to look for the moment when Cayce's eyelashes began to flutter and then read from the book, filling in Mrs. Delaney's name where appropriate.

Kahn pulled up a chair and Cayce lay back on the couch. As this proved to be too short for the six-foot-two Cayce, he instead lay down on the floor. As had now become his custom many times before but was new to the others in the room, Cayce proceeded to give a diagnosis.

Though the details that came through were in themselves remarkable—blood pressure, blood count, and other physiological and medical details—it was the "back-story" of her condition that convinced the DeLaneys of its veracity. Cayce referenced an episode approximately seven years before the automobile collision that he said was the root of her distress. The Source said that the family was then living in Fort Thomas, Kentucky, and that Mrs. DeLaney had injured the base of her spine when climbing down from a horse and buggy. The automobile collision was alleged to have compounded or "brought out" the original injury, resulting in her arthritic condition. This was convincing indeed. No one in the room except for the DeLaneys knew that the family had briefly lived in Fort Thomas, where in fact Lillie had been injured in a horse-and-buggy incident.

Another interesting note about this reading was that the Source indicated the recommended treatments were not to be performed by the physician currently caring for Mrs. DeLaney, but by an osteopath named Barbee, whom the readings said had just recently opened his practice in Lexington. In addition to spinal manipulations, she was to be given a variety of prescription medications which were to be taken internally.

Upon waking, Edgar asked what had been recommended. "Everything, including the kitchen sink," Mr. DeLaney announced. "You gave something for every square inch of her body."

Kahn was dispatched to fill the prescriptions while Cayce visited with the DeLaney family and, later that day, dined with the Kahn family. Cayce would not hear from David again for several weeks, and this time by phone. Mrs. DeLaney had broken out in a rash from head to foot. The family physician had apparently warned the DeLaneys of this eventuality but said he could do nothing because he had no way of knowing which of the Cayce remedies had caused the rash.

Cayce went back into trance and reported that an important ingredient, black sulfur, had been left out of her medication. Kahn investigated and discovered that Cayce was right. The Lexington pharmacist had used standard prescription sulfur because he hadn't heard of black sulfur, nor did it appear in his pharmacopeia. Kahn was soon back on the phone with Cayce, and yet another reading was conducted. He was told the same as he had before, only this time the Source identified the pharmaceutical company in Detroit that produced the product. Black sulfur was obtained, put into the formulation, and Mrs. DeLaney's rash disappeared.

Kahn became a convert. "I had met a miracle man," he later wrote. "I was convinced that when Cayce in his hypnotic sleep made a statement it could be relied on. His answer to a question would be a right answer."

As Edgar would tell David on this occasion and would repeat many times over the years under similar circumstances, "If I ever find out that I give wrong information, or hurt anybody, or it doesn't work out, I'll never give another reading. But so far, I've been doing it . . . and experiences with my family have taught me that if they can't be cured [by treatments in a reading] they can be helped."

A month after the DeLaney readings, Cayce returned to Lexington and was astonished by what he saw. Mrs. DeLaney was no longer confined to bed, but was sitting in an arm chair. The swelling had decreased to the point where, with assistance, she was mobile. She could both feed herself and comb her hair. "It has been five years since I even attempted to raise my hands high enough to do up my own hair," she proudly told him.

Edgar visited her once again as a guest at her birthday party. Accompanied by David, who deservedly shared some of the credit for her recovery, they watched her walk across the room. Though Mrs. DeLaney was never totally cured, she eventually was driving a car, shopping by her herself, and would live in relative comfort for the next fifteen years before her death in Daytona Beach, Florida, in 1930.

Edgar continued to make trips to Lexington, but it was not to visit the DeLaneys. Edgar and David had begun to develop a close personal friendship. David would come to describe Edgar as "full of pep and promise," referring to him in later years as "Judge," the result of Edgar having defused a potentially explosive argument between two drunken men at a Selma bachelor party.

Along with David, Edgar came to know and give readings to the greater Kahn family. He would frequently sit next to the grand fireplace in the Kahn's large yellow-brick home, "holding court" as David described it, during which he entertained David along with his nine brothers and sisters with stories. Edgar would recount many of his childhood experiences in sessions that ran well into the night. Dave's mother, Fannie, a statuesque woman whom Edgar affectionately came to call "Mother Kahn," would receive readings that would cure her of neuritis and extend her life for fifteen years after she had contracted breast cancer.

Dave's father, Sol, had serious reservations about his son's relationship with Edgar and tried to convince his son to have nothing to do with the work. A scholar of the Talmud, he cited the example of Saul from the Old Testament, who had called up the spirit of Samuel through the witch of Endor. Saul would pay a heavy price for having disturbed Samuel. After being wounded and seeing his army destroyed, Saul would commit suicide. Edgar rose to his own and David's defense by explaining that he wasn't calling up ghosts when he was guided into trance. He was tapping into some form of a universal consciousness in which both he and the recipient of the reading participated. Ultimately Sol gave his son his blessing to continue the work but would himself decline receiving a trance reading. Doing so might have saved his life; Sol died in 1918 from complications due to an enlarged spleen.

The fate of David's infant brother Leon, suffering from epilepsy, was perhaps more tragic than Sol's. David requested and then received a reading on his behalf. As was the case for Mrs. DeLaney, a remedy was provided, but in Leon's case it required total cooperation of the physician called in to perform the treatments. Although both David and his mother were convinced that the reading was correct and could help Leon, the family found no physicians willing to do what was specified in the readings. Leon died before his second birthday. Having learned this lesson, it was not repeated when Dave's sister, Eleanor, contracted scarlet fever. The treatments were given exactly as recommended, and Eleanor recovered.

The most interesting of their early readings was a request for how the Kahns could expand or grow their family's grocery business. David posed the question, "How do we improve business?" The subsequent reading may have been the first of what would become eight hundred dedicated business readings that would be conducted for a myriad of different kinds of businessmen over the next three decades. A fair portion of these—upwards of over a hundred—would be conducted for Kahn himself as he moved from the grocery business into the garment industry and eventually into the furniture business where he became highly successful.

In response to David's initial question, the Source described how the large schools and universities in central Kentucky—which had to feed anywhere from 150 to 200 students a day—bought their canned goods in pound containers. As mechanical openers weren't yet on the market, each can had to be opened by hand, creating much inefficiency and wasted expense. The Source directed David to Chicago where gallon cans of the same products could be purchased.

Just as the reading had detailed, Dave located the wholesale warehouse referenced and arranged to buy the gallon-sized cans. Further, he made arrangements to become the company's Lexington sales representative. Before the end of the year, the Kahn grocery chain was the leading canned food distributor to the central Kentucky schools.

Kahn was soon asking other kinds of questions as well. He wanted to know if the Source thought he should take over the family grocery business as a lifelong career. The answer was "no," which gave rise to yet another type of reading devoted to vocation. This type of reading would become known as Mental and Spiritual Readings. Cayce would ultimately deliver over four hundred of them.

Among these readings were those for an infant which was later born to David and Lucille, the woman who became his wife. One-month-old David Kahn Jr. was advised to pursue a medical career. "The entity would make a great physician," the Source announced in 1929. Indeed David Jr. became a doctor, a decision he never regretted. Though he wasn't keen on following the strict Cayce dietary or health treatments that his parents demanded of him, he acknowledged that the Cayce advice contributed much to his living a long and highly productive life.

The same was true of his father. In his teenage years during David's first vocational reading, presumed to have been conducted in 1916, he was not only advised that he shouldn't make a career of the grocery business but that there would be "a mighty change" taking place in the nation. The Source indicated that Kahn would be forced to leave home and ultimately find his career path in a field in which he had not been trained. Moreover, his family wouldn't be supportive of what he did. As a final note, Cayce said that he would have to "leave the flock" and go into uniform. Kahn would "go in honor" and "return in honor."

The response seemed strange indeed to Kahn, as it did to his parents. No Kentucky-born Kahn, to their knowledge, had been a police or fireman, and David had no interest in becoming one. Little did they realize that the Source was alluding to World War I.

NEW YORK JOURNAL

House by a Vote of 373 to 50 Passes Joint Resolution

WAR IS DECLARED BY U. S.

Interned German Ships Seized by Customs Authorities

CZAR SUPPLIANT FOR PENSION TO DUMA

April 6, 1917 the U.S. declares war.

Kahn proudly served in uniform, enlisting in the U.S. Army. At each step of his journey, he requested and received guidance from Cayce. Upon handing in his application for a commission as a second lieutenant, which the readings indicated would be made available to him, his commanding officer was mystified how he could possibly have obtained information considered privileged. Kahn much enjoyed later telling the story of the incident, which actually did result in him being made a second lieutenant.

"In a more security-minded age, I might have spent the next few days undergoing interrogations and possible arrest," Kahn said. That was why he remained silent. "I could hardly tell the commanding officer the real truth without probably compromising myself as possible army officer material."

Ethlyne on the cover of the *NY Times Mid-Week Pictorial.*

Ethlyne Clair:

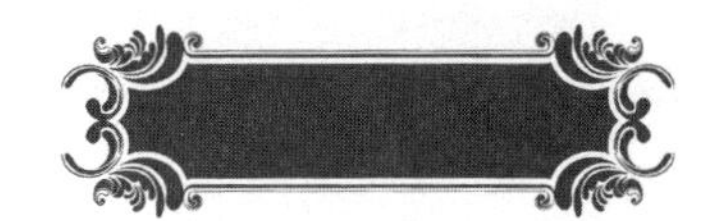

Hollywood Bound

Among Hugh Lynn's friends in Selma were the Williamson children, Ethlyne and Malcolm, whom the Cayces knew from church. Playing "motion picture" was the children's favorite pastime. Ethlyne, age twelve, was the starlet; her older brother Malcolm played supporting roles, and Hugh Lynn, then nine years old, was the director and cameraman. Thanks to a scheme concocted by the children's father, Edwin Williamson, Edgar was to enter the game as a psychic screenwriter. Only it became far more than playacting. Their efforts would result in a two-decade long saga in which Edgar delivered three complete screenplays while in trance. He would eventually rub shoulders with legendary film moguls at both Universal and Paramount Studios, to whom he would give health and business readings, and young Ethlyne—under the pseudonym Ethlyne Clair—would have a shot at Hollywood stardom.

Having successfully conducted medical and business readings, it only stood to reason that Edgar—in trance—could offer script advice as well. Such was the conclusion of Ethlyne and Malcolm's father, who discussed the matter with Edgar after Bible Study class one night in 1916. Thirty-nine-year-old Williamson wasn't so much interested in helping his daughter or son break into the motion picture business. He wanted to write and produce his own movies. The freight agent for

Carl Laemmle of Universal Studios.

the city's Southern Railroad, Williamson had sold several stories and articles to Hollywood fan magazines and believed obtaining a trance reading might help him develop script plots. Edgar decided to give it a try, thinking that it would be a fun experiment and also highly entertaining for Hugh Lynn and Ethlyne, who urged him on.

Unbeknown to Cayce, there was more to the request than the senior Williamson let on. Without Edgar's permission or knowledge, on December 13 Edwin had written to Carl Laemmle, the founding partner and chief of Universal Pictures in Los Angeles. Williamson had described himself as the "spiritual business manager" of Edgar Cayce, the "great psychic." He told how his friend was able to go to sleep and in that state, diagnose many diseases, find lost articles, and perform other amazing feats. "If you are interested, and will write me, name a date and the hour, allowing for the difference in time, stating the name of the party who you have in mind to take the lead in a photoplay, and tell me the street and the house number where the party will be," Williamson wrote. "I think I can surprise you."

Laemmle was intrigued by the promotional possibilities of having a psychic develop a script and called in his New York publicity director, Nat Rothstein, who decided that the right actress for the photoplay would be Miss Violet Mersereau, a performer Universal Studios believed to be poised for stardom. A former child actor with numerous Broadway stage credits to her name, twenty-four-year-old Mersereau had appeared in upwards of fifty shorts and feature productions, most notably as the innocent blonde ingénue in *The Spitfire* and *Angel in the Attic*. Publicist Rothstein, who was looking to help develop an actress that might garner the box office appeal of Mary Pickford, arranged for a party at Churchill's, a swank New York nightclub on Broadway and 49th Street. Amidst the festivities Williamson would wire a "psychic scenario" delivered by Cayce in Selma.

Churchill's Night Club, Broadway & 49th New York.

Among the many journalists and newspapermen invited to attend the event were reporters from *Variety* and *Motion Picture News*. Featured guests included Dr. William E. Young, a reported authority on the subject of hypnotism and mental telepathy, who would give a brief lecture on the powers of mental suggestion as part of the performance. Eustace Ball, a director and screenwriter currently writing movie serials for Universal, was to be the master of ceremonies.

Churchill's Night Club, Interior.

On the night of the event, February 8, 1917, all the tables except one were pushed away from the center of the dance floor. Miss Mersereau placed a single sheet of paper face down on the middle of the table. On this paper, unseen by anyone else, she had written a few lines outlining the type of story she wanted to use in her next film. The lecture by Dr. Young was then given, followed by dancing and champagne.

While guests enjoyed themselves in New York, Edgar Cayce was giving the reading in Selma. Its contents, amounting to approximately 450 words, were then wired to Churchill's. The title was "Through the Subliminal." Reports from the newspapermen were as favorable as their review of Miss Mersereau's dancing ability. One account read:

> His psychic self, traveling more than twelve hundred miles on a space-annihilating train of thought . . . the first psycho-scenario writer of record transmitted from Selma, Alabama, to New York, a five-reel scenario for Miss Violet.

Violet Mersereau, c. 1917.

Universal Discovers Psychoscenario Writer

Edgar Cayce Sends Spirit Five Reel Scenario for Violet Mersereau to her order at Churchill's Restaurant

Article on Edgar Cayce, "Psychoscenario Writer" in *Moving Picture Weekly.*

Unfortunately for all concerned "Through the Subliminal" was not made into a movie; Mersereau never dazzled film audiences as did Mary Pickford; Williamson didn't get the big break he was hoping for, and the Cayce script was subsequently lost. However, a seed had been planted. Thanks to Williamson's efforts, Edgar would go into trance and deliver two more screenplays.

The first screenplay was a direct result of Edwin's earlier effort and Hugh Lynn's continuing interest. Conducted in January 1924 in five readings over a span of nine days, it was intended as both a commercial venture and a means to acquaint movie audiences with the power of the unconscious mind. Edgar—in trance—was told: "You will give an original story that might be used as a scenario and one that would outline the Psychic Work as done by Edgar Cayce."

The result was the screenplay provocatively titled *Why?* It was a scenario which depicted the psychic activities of a young handyman named Abe who worked for a wealthy New York family. While delivering a load of firewood for a dinner party, he becomes engaged in a conversation with a guest who has some experience with hypnosis. Deemed to be a suitable candidate for a psychic experiment, Abe agrees to be hypnotized. Much to the surprise and delight of the wealthy New Yorkers, Abe—in trance—is revealed to have psychic abilities, including the power to compose and play mesmerizing music. He begins to play the piano and the scene suddenly shifts to ancient times—Medieval Europe, Rome, and Greece—where the same dinner guests are acting out a drama similar to the one taking place in present day. Only in these scenes, the true natures of the participants are more obviously revealed. The images that Abe conjures at the dinner party are disconcerting at first, leading the guests to become confused and resentful, but as Abe plays a haunting melody, the guests find insight and truth. "Each sees in this . . . a portion of their individual selves . . . as though it were in answer to many of their secret thoughts," the Source tells us.

The word "reincarnation" doesn't appear anywhere in the Cayce screenplay, but this is the theme that is presented. In the context of when it was given, just days before the Cayce family would be grappling with what became known as the Life Readings, it would seem that the psychic-scenario of *Why?* was as equally for the benefit of the Cayce family as it was for movie audiences. Edgar, like Gertrude and Hugh Lynn, would need help coming to terms with a concept that would forever change the scope and larger message of their work. This may have been a filmic preview of their own journey ahead.

A few months after giving readings for *Why?*, Edgar was back in trance working on another screenplay. Only this script, titled *Bride of the Incal*, was far grander in scope and took seven sessions to complete, ultimately comprising what amounted to a fully developed silent-film screenplay. Alf Butler, whose idea it was to conduct the reading, was a Cayce student in the same Bible Study class as Edwin Williamson. He had since left his position at a Selma bank and was working as a Paramount film distributor in Birmingham, Alabama. Gloria Swanson, then a leading silent-film star, was looking for the right script, and Butler was sure Cayce could deliver it.

As Butler would write in a letter to Edgar:

> You know it has always been my idea that your scenarios ought to get over swimmingly. Once you break the ice . . . all our worries . . . will be over. Perhaps you may recall how Jack London wrote his heart out without selling a thing till way late; then [he] could scarcely write fast enough to supply the demand. It's the same with what you will be able to turn out. And you will have the additional advantage of producing the greatest diversification of plots and themes that have ever come down the pike. Your stories would never get in a rut [because you] have more . . . ideas than any dozen authors combined.

Bride of the Incal lived up to Butler's expectations. In what can truly be termed a precursor to the Indiana Jones adventures, the story focuses on an intrepid team of American tourists in search of legendary Inca gold hidden high in the Andes Mountains. Unlike *Why?* which was more similar to a stage play, this one has all the elements of a classic action thriller: ancient treasure dropped into a lake to keep it out of the hands of greedy Conquistadors, remote jungle caves and temple ruins, and a hidden passage leading to a sacrificial stone altar for would-be Incan brides wishing to be united with the supreme deity, the wondrous Incal.

Into this setting comes the protagonist, Rene Lowe, and her fiancé, Tom Stone, who travel to Peru to visit Rene's brother, an American diplomat. As the men in the story increasingly fall prey to an all-consuming greed for Inca gold, Rene falls under the spell of the mysterious

Deio, who purports to be the direct descendant of the high priest of the now vanished Inca Empire. What Rene and Tom don't know is that the cunning and duplicitous Deio, of mixed Spanish heritage, is hatching a plan to use Tom to uncover the hidden resting place of Inca treasure, while at the same time luring Rene into a temple under the pretext that she is to be initiated as a high priestess. Deio intends to sacrifice Rene to appease modern-day Incan warriors who have been safeguarding the treasure for centuries and plans to keep the lion's share of gold for himself. It is only when Tom comes to his senses, realizing that earthly riches cannot compare to the love he feels for Rene, that he courageously tunnels under the temple and saves the day. Rene becomes a bride, not to the Inca deity, but to Tom, her betrothed.

Like the previous two screenplays, *Bride of the Incal* didn't find much traction in Hollywood. On a positive note, however, correspondence with the studio heads raised considerable interest in other Cayce's psychic talents, eventually leading Paramount Studio founder Jesse Lasky and film producer William (Bill) Goetz to request business and health readings.

Other industry players and entertainers would join them. Gloria Swanson, best known today for her starring role in the classic *Sunset Boulevard*, would embrace a holistic health regiment based on her study

Paramount Studio founder Jesse Lasky, c. 1915.

Movie Mogul Bill Goetz and wife, Edith Mayer Goetz.

of Cayce readings. Noel Langley, who would achieve fame as one of the screenwriters of *The Wonderful Wizard of Oz*, would write a book on Cayce's Life Readings, and "Boy Wonder" Irving Thalberg, who was instrumental in producing such films as *Grand Hotel*, *Mutiny on the Bounty*, and *The Good Earth*, would briefly entertain turning Cayce's life story into a film.

Considering how many influential film producers were interested in Cayce's work, it is ironic that while Edgar's trance-induced film career never became a reality, the budding child actress Hugh Lynn directed in Selma, Ethlyne Williamson, was a success.

While Cayce was dictating his own screenplays, Edwin was seeking

Ethlyne Claire, Cowgirl, c. 1929.

to take advantage of his performance-at-a-distance début at Churchill's by moving his family to New York. Unable to sustain himself by writing screenplays, he and wife Loula focused on getting their children into the movies. After winning a teenage beauty pageant, whose prize was a screen test, Ethlyne signed on with an agent and was cast in the 1924 film short *Sandra*. She next landed a recurring role in a Universal Studios film series shooting in New York called the *Newlyweds and Their Baby*. The success of the series brought her and her family to Hollywood.

Using the stage name Ethlyne Clair, she would go on to appear in forty-seven films with such stars as Monte Blue, John Barrymore, Joan Blondell, Louise Brooks, and Boris Karloff. Most notable were *Riding for Fame*, *Painted Ponies*, and *Hero on Horseback*, in which she co-starred with rodeo champion Hoot Gibson. They made for a winning combination; he was always the happy-go-lucky cowboy, she was the cowgirl looking to rope him in.

After the Cayces left Selma, Edgar would continue to help the family by giving them medical readings. Most significant was one for Ethlyne, who was cured of a potentially fatal case of pneumonia, thus permitting her breakthrough with Hoot Gibson. Malcolm, who went on to become a popular Chicago children's radio show host, also received trance medical advice, and his children—Edwin's grandchildren—would receive readings as well.

Malcolm Williamson at WLS Chicago, a radio station founded in 1924.

Edgar and Hugh Lynn, with whom Ethlyne corresponded, were pleased to have helped launch her career, however modest their contribution actually was. The truth of the matter, as eventually became clear, was that the Cayces were likely better off as a result of their failed Hollywood efforts.

Ethlyne indeed became a celebrity, but the journey was not a happy or fulfilling one. In a candid interview she gave before her death in 1996, at age 91, she described having been drummed out of the industry for having rejected the repeated sexual advances of the powerful Darryl Zanuck. Ethlyne's only regret, however, was having been typecast as a cowgirl instead of a beautiful screen vamp. When asked to name her favorite movie, she said simply, "I hated them all."

A "gusher" in West Texas, c. 1921.

EDGAR DAVIS:

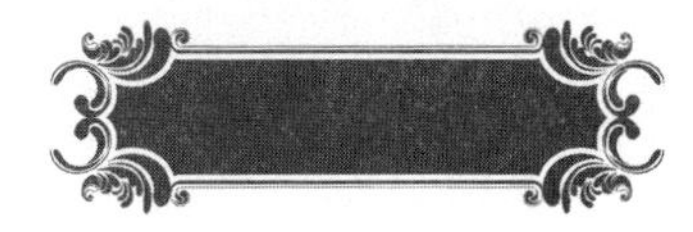

TEXAS WILDCATTER

Over half of the young men in Cayce's Bible Study class would not return from World War I. In dreams and visions, Edgar would see their bodies dead on the battlefield, their souls reaching out to him to communicate with loved ones. David Kahn, too, would reach out to Edgar, but by letter. Upon his return from France, Kahn wrote to Cayce asking to meet with him to discuss forming a "psychic partnership." Although Edgar was still fearful of entering into another partnership and making a "business" out of the trance readings as he had done back in Hopkinsville, he liked Kahn enough to consider a number of potential joint ventures. Among them was the idea of using psychic advice to drill for oil.

Edgar initially rejected the idea on principal: it was contrary to how he believed the readings ought to be used. Further, experience had taught him that using the advice in this way rarely turned out well for him or the recipients of the readings. In one notable case, Joe Dickey, the young man using trance information to gamble at the race track, had resulted in migraine headaches for Edgar and a nervous breakdown for Dickey.

Kahn believed that using trance information to search for oil wasn't the same as exploiting it to help one person gain unfair advantage over another, as would be the case in using it to gamble at the racetrack. Underground oil reserves belonged to the people who owned the mineral rights to the land where it was found. He couldn't see any harm in helping people, for a percentage of profits, to locate it.

The Cayce Petroleum Company

OF TEXAS

EDGAR CAYCE, PRESIDENT
SELMA, ALABAMA
VICE-PRESIDENTS
Jos. B. Long, Cleburne, Texas
W. E. Barrow, San Saba, Texas

Capitalization 2,000,000 Units

J. T. McConnell, Secretary-Treasurer, Meridian, Texas

TRUSTEES
Edgar Cayce, Selma, Alabama
M. C. Sanders, San Saba, Texas
Dr. H. B. DePew, St. Louis, Mo.

SAN SABA, TEXAS, Oct. 29, 1921.

Yours very truly,

The Cayce Petroleum Company
of Texas,
Edgar Cayce
President.

A– Declaration of Trust, of which all parties dealing with it must take notice. Declaration of Trust entered into by the Trustees of Said Company, dated 20th day of September, 1920, and recorded on 20th day of September, 1920, in Office of County Clerk, Johnson County, Texas.

Cayce Petroleum Company stationery signed by Edgar Cayce.

This is what Cayce, partnered with David Kahn, proceeded to do. Their journey would take them throughout Oklahoma and Texas and to the formation of the Edgar Cayce Petroleum Company, whose anticipated proceeds would fund a hospital with a dedicated staff of physicians and nurses willing and able to treat patients using his trance information. While Cayce and Kahn were prospecting, it would be Gertrude, Leslie, and a staff of three others who kept the photography business operating in Selma. Edgar was gone on one trip to Texas for so many months in the early 1920s that Gertrude dispatched Dr. House from Hopkinsville to bring him home.

"The oil was there," Edgar later admitted to a friend. His company just couldn't turn what they discovered into dollars and cents. Such was the case of a venture that brought Cayce and Kahn to Luling, Texas, in 1920 where they would cross paths with "wildcatter" Edgar B. Davis, whose personal life story and adventures are perhaps as extraordinary as Edgar Cayce's.

Edgar Cayce in Texas, prospecting for oil.

Luling, with a population of 15,000, was widely considered "the toughest town in Texas," a reference to both the hardscrabble cotton farmers and cattlemen who lived there and to the harsh and unforgiving environment. An impoverished town of false front stores surrounded by endless cotton fields, Luling was the westernmost stop of the Sunset Branch of the Southern Pacific Railroad and the northern terminus of a freight road to Chihuahua, Mexico—the end of the line so far as most Texans were concerned.

Unlike the previous oil-well readings which Cayce had given, the first Luling reading, conducted in Cleburne, Texas, did not identify an exact geographic location to drill for oil. Kahn was instructed only to go to Lockhart, in Caldwell County, where they would meet an unidentified man on the steps of the county court house. He would tell them where to put their drilling rig.

Strange as this advice was to Kahn and Cayce, the Texas oilman whom they most trusted, Joe Rush, wasn't surprised at the mention of Luling. He related how his previous employers, Michigan "wildcatter" Morris Rayor and Fort Worth attorney Carl Wade, had been called to Luling in a similar way, back in 1914. An "otherworldly" voice had spoken to Rayor through a Detroit medium, directing him to Luling. Rayor had brought his psychic there, and on her direction, they had spent nearly half a decade punching one dry well after another before going bankrupt.

Another oilman who had given Luling a try was Oscar Davis, from Brocton, Massachusetts, whose various family members had visions of vast oil reserves. He had prospected in Luling until his death in 1918 and found nothing but underground pools of saltwater. Henceforth the area had developed a reputation as a "faith location," the place where "spirits of the dead" guided—or perhaps misguided—oilmen to drill.

Despite Rush's admonition not to follow in the footsteps of the previous prospectors and reputable geologists who declared that there was no oil to find in Luling, Cayce and Kahn drove to Lockhart where, as predicted, they met a man on the courthouse steps.

Kahn introduced himself to a gentleman who walked with a cane and was old enough to be his grandfather. "I'm here investigating any possible oil leases," Kahn told him.

The old man turned out to be a county judge intimately familiar with local geography as well as its archives and records. He directed them to drill in Rag Town in Luling, where the town's black population lived. He then sent them across the street to talk to the state geologist who would show them the land records, as indeed he did. The geologist advised them to talk to Minnie Phillips, a white landowner who pulled much weight with Rag Town's primarily black population. Along with the advice came a warning: Phillips was the "toughest of the toughest" in a town where Wild-West style shootouts were still commonplace. She didn't take kindly to strangers, oilmen in particular.

The Phillips Ranch, their next stop, was no more than a ramshackle dirt-floor farm house amidst miles of dusty and windswept cotton fields. She greeted the Cayce team with the barrel of a shotgun, which she poked through a crack in the door.

Kahn didn't initially introduce himself as an oilman. He explained that he was from Kentucky and had served in the U.S. Army. As he was still wearing his lieutenant's uniform and spoke with an accent, his claims were convincing. He didn't view what he said as dishonest as he technically was still allowed to wear the uniform by virtue of the fact that he hadn't yet received his decommission. The fact that it was waiting for him back in Lexington was beside the point.

His words were enough for her to open the door wider, but not enough for her to lower the weapon. The conversation continued with Kahn explaining where he was from. She opened the door even wider. An aging barefoot woman, dressed in rags, stood before them.

Minnie Phillips queried Kahn. Did he know a man named Phillips in Lexington? In fact, Kahn did. Phillips was his pharmacist, the same man who had filled his family's prescriptions, including those recommended for his sisters and brothers in the Cayce readings. The pharmacist turned out to be Minnie's brother. This new synchronicity convinced Cayce and Kahn that they were indeed on the right track, but where it would lead them remained to be seen.

After further discussion, it was agreed that Joe Rush would drive Phillips into town where she could wire her brother to obtain a character reference for Kahn. On the way to the telegraph office, they could stop for provisions, paid for by Kahn, and if she was able to reach her brother, they would then share a meal and they would tell her why they had come. All turned out as hoped for. Minnie's brother confirmed Kahn's identity and moral character, and they sat down to a meal. But before Kahn raised the subject of why they had come, he inquired about her health.

As Kahn later related the story, she hadn't been in good health for years, and her son had developed tuberculosis. This was why they had left Lexington and come to Texas. The dry air was thought to be curative. "But now he is in Kansas City and I am here protecting these poor colored people from the oil swindlers," she told Kahn.

This was when Kahn told her that they were oilmen. The same power that permitted his partner Edgar Cayce to diagnose illness had brought them to her doorstep.

"There's a lot of oil around here," Phillips confided. "And they don't have to drill more than a hundred feet to get it."

Phillips knew about the oil because on rainy days, the cattle wouldn't drink the water. The surface was covered by a thin layer of petroleum. Natural gas bubbled out of the nearby San Marcos River in such quantities that children enjoyed igniting it with kitchen matches.

Before continuing the discussion further, Kahn volunteered Cayce's services. He laid newspapers over the dirt floor and Edgar lay on his back. Kahn then conducted a health reading for Phillips. Cayce described, among other conditions, a circulation problem that interfered with the nerve endings in her neck. Phillips was in tears when the session ended. Cayce seemed to know every ache and pain she had. "I never saw anything like this in my whole life," she swore.

The second reading Cayce gave was to determine how much oil was in Luling and how to drill for it. Cayce told of a fabulous "sea of oil" trapped in a giant salt dome directly under her ranch house. He also identified a nearby dead tree, with two prongs of the trunk jutting skyward. Thirty feet from this tree, and three hundred feet down, was said to be the richest oil deposit in south central Texas.

That night, or soon after, Cayce Petroleum made a fourteen-month lease arrangement with Phillips and the farmers she wished to protect. Their company would pay a dollar per acre per year for a year for the right to drill plus a $1,000 non-refundable bond should they fail to break ground within the first six months, and it would cover all the costs of drilling the wells and bringing what they pumped to market. A portion of the profits would belong to Cayce Petroleum; the lion's share would go to Phillips and the black community of Luling.

Cayce and Kahn left Luling in 1920 with the intention of mounting a drilling expedition. But after six months on the road trying to raise the funds—encountering one problem after another—all they accomplished was delivering a load of lumber to Phillips to build the rig. To Kahn, it seemed as if the otherworldly forces that had led them to Rag Town had suddenly turned against them. Most investors wouldn't take their story seriously, and those who claimed they did, weren't forthcoming with cash. This was when Edgar B. Davis, brother of oilman Oscar Davis, arrived on the scene.

Edgar Davis and Edgar Cayce had much in common. Davis stood over six feet tall, was respectful and well-mannered to everyone he met, was an ardent Christian believing in the power of prayer, and heard spirit voices calling him to drill for oil in Luling. The important difference was that Davis was a dedicated businessman and was made of sterner stuff than Cayce when it came to drilling for oil.

Four years older than Cayce, Davis had grown up and attended

Edgar B. Davis, c. 1917.

high school in Brockton, Massachusetts, forgone college, and followed his older brother's lead working for the Walkers Shoe Company, where he eventually became a partner. Under Davis' management, the company was the first to nationally advertise and might well have been the first in the world to put a logo identifier on the shoes themselves—what Nike would so successfully do a century later. Davis might have made his career in the shoe business had he not suffered a nervous breakdown. At age thirty-four he was hospitalized in a sanitarium, where he had a mystical experience. A voice he believed belonging to God gave him a mission to promote the brotherhood of mankind.

Davis sold his interests in the shoe company and boarded a steamship for a round-the-world tour. In Asia and India he studied Buddhism and Hinduism, and while still a dedicated Christian, became a firm believer in reincarnation. At this point, and for decades to come, he wouldn't join a particular church or denomination, believing that organized religion, no matter where in the world he encountered it, was more about man's laws than God's laws. The splendor of God's creation, he said, was his chosen temple of worship.

In Singapore, Davis met a Dutch rubber plantation manager who showed him around his fields and gave him a job. Davis subsequently had another mystical experience. Using what little money he had left from selling his shares of the shoe company, he opened the first American owned rubber plantation in Sumatra, then a second plantation in Ceylon. Strangely—according to what associates later claimed—Davis had advantages over other foreigners in the rubber business. He never got sick from tropical diseases or suffered from sun stroke in the heat, nor was he ever bitten by the cobras and other extremely venomous and potentially deadly snakes that infested the rubber tree groves.

His success in the rubber business put Davis on the board of what would later become known as U.S. Rubber. Among other accomplishments, he began marketing Keds, the first national sneaker brand to use soft rubber soles. Before he sold his interest in the business in 1918, his net worth was estimated to be in excess of $3.5 million. This was also the year he made what he called his first substantial "thanks offering." He gave over $1 million to his former employees. Recipients of his largess not only included his company's top executives, but the lowliest plantation worker.

After a brief and unsuccessful career on Wall Street, during which he attempted to coordinate rubber production with Detroit auto interests, Davis turned his attention to Luling where his brother Oscar had been drilling. His motivation was yet another mystical experience: God had sent him to deliver Luling and Caldwell County from the oppressive cotton-based economy that enslaved both the poor black and white population. "We ought to recognize that rich and poor have a common interest," he would later write. "If one suffers, all suffer. Greed on the part of the rich or envy on the part of the poor are the boomerangs which come back to plague us all."

In 1921, after his brother's death and when Davis inherited Oscar's leases, he set about drilling on property adjacent to the site that Edgar Cayce had selected. No details are now known of what transpired when Davis met Cayce. All Kahn reported was giving Davis the Cayce readings and other files on the Edgar Cayce Petroleum interests in Caldwell County, and claimed that Davis—acting on the Cayce readings—began drilling on land formerly leased by Cayce Petroleum.

The truth is difficult to ferret out from the existing lease agreements, but there is no question that Davis prospected in the same Rag Town area as Cayce. In all likelihood there was more to the meeting than handing over the Cayce readings. As future events would reveal, Davis and Cayce got on well and their shared passion for the scriptures and belief that God spoke in dreams and visions would have given them much to discuss. It would also not be unreasonable to believe that they held prayer sessions, as was customary for both men when prospecting for oil. They parted ways amicably and would meet again five years later.

When asked by the press why he had selected Luling to drill for oil, Davis simply said that that the "voice of God" told him to go there and to invest his entire life savings into prospecting. Further, he claimed that the wildflowers growing on the edges of the cotton fields told him precisely where to drill. Farfetched as the reporters believed this to be, the explanation was consistent with what would subsequently come through in three readings conducted for Davis after Cayce left Texas. The Source said that Davis indeed heard God's voice, as well as the voices of "elementals"—spirit entities which lived among plants that Cayce saw as a youth.

Davis lost a substantial fortune in six dry wells. Nearly bankrupt, he turned for financing to Frank Seiberling of Akron, Ohio, with whom Davis had once served on the board of U.S. Rubber Company and whose family would receive numerous Cayce readings. Seiberling himself would receive three readings, and his daughter, who would later be instrumental in the founding of Alcoholics Anonymous, was given thirty-eight readings.

Like Davis, Seiberling was also said to be a businessman who was guided by God. Most important to later events, Davis and Seiberling had worked together in a previous incarnation, as had Little Anna and her father, and had developed skills that would be extremely beneficial to them in the present. Together they had the ability to tap into the "spiritual source" of supply that could manifest into "material riches."

The Davis and Seiberling team, however, didn't initially prove any more successful than Davis' earlier endeavors. At one point in their venture together, when Seiberling's funds had run out and Davis had given up his New York townhouse to move permanently to Luling—doing as his vision said, to invest everything he had in prospecting—Davis didn't have the money for a shave and haircut, let alone meet his payroll obligations.

"You just can't imagine how broke Mr. Davis was," Luling newspa-

Frank A. Sieberling, co-founder of Goodyear Tire & Rubber Company.

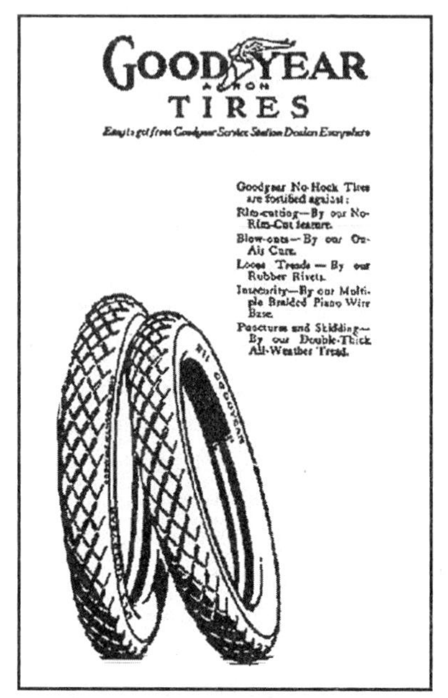

Goodyear Tire ad, c. 1916.

per editor Hal Bridges later recalled. "He often didn't have a quarter for a shave. Yet he was always optimistic. He owed us $285 for some printing. I told him to forget it, but he didn't. One day he came in, all smiles, to say he had just remembered $300 worth of municipal bonds he had tucked away at his family's summer home. Davis' secretary located these bonds along with an additional $80,000 worth of English war bonds that he had also forgotten."

On August 9, 1922, the year after Cayce Petroleum had forfeited their Luling holdings, Davis' first well came in. Reporters would later claim that the well was a "gusher," but this was not the case. The well, however, did have "legs," as oilmen used the term, and would consistently produce more than a hundred barrels a day for more than a decade.

The well that proved his unwavering faith in Luling was drilled nearby. The geology and production were just as described in the readings for the Cayce Petroleum Company. Davis punched a hole in a massive salt dome, releasing a veritable jet stream of hot oil—enough in the first few days to turn a cotton field into a lake of steaming "black gold." Davis received $500,000 in advance for a million barrels of oil and used the money to "punch out" sixteen more wells in Luling, earning him upwards of $12 million.

Stories told about Davis in Luling are now legendary. In one instance, he was said to have been driving into town, had a sudden vision of a new "faith location," asked his driver to pull the car over, stepped into a field, and pulled a ragweed out of the ground. "We'll drill here," he said, pointing to the hole where the weed's roots had been. Just as he would do yet again several weeks later with a dowsing rod—he struck oil. So convinced that he was being divinely guided that he once insisted his team drill over 7,000 feet into the ground—deeper than any hole that had ever been drilled in central Texas. The resulting well shot oil hundreds of feet into the air and, before it could be pumped into holding tanks, left a shoulder-deep pool that filled a nearby valley.

After reading about the discovery of the Luling oil fields, Kahn approached Davis for help building the Cayce hospital. Davis didn't return his letters. He had other plans for his wealth.

Davis' first order of business was to invite the entire town of Luling, both blacks and whites, to a celebrate God's gifts at two giant barbecues on forty acres of meadow land he had purchased for the event along the shady San Marcos River, south of town. "Come one, come all," advertised Davis.

Come they did. Fifteen thousand or more people were met by massive electric "welcome" signs posted on the road. Japanese lanterns hung from the trees over two massive outdoor dance floors, bandstands, and long rows of barbeque pits. Thousands of pounds of beef, lamb, frying chickens, crates of soda, and gallons of ice cream were consumed. Cigars were made available by the case. Entertainment featured two bands brought from San Antonio and opera stars from New York.

In the weeks to come, after paying off the money he owed Frank Seiberling and others, Davis gave everyone in his organization, from top to bottom, bonus checks ranging from a low of $5,000 to as high as $200,000. His secretary's tuition to chiropractic school was paid in full with the only provision that she would return to Luling to provide health treatment, which he himself would underwrite, to any townspeople who desired it. A black janitor, working in the building where Davis had first set up his business, was given a fully furnished new home. Even this wasn't the end of his largess. Davis had thirty-two brand-new automobiles delivered to townspeople who had sustained him during his difficult first year in Luling.

Davis would eventually build a country club and golf course for whites, and a country club and athletic field for blacks, endowing both clubs with enough funds for residents to use them for free. Eventually there came an Edgar B. Davis scout camp, community center, and schools. Today there is a hospital, considered the finest in central Texas, named in his honor and built on the donated land upon which his office once stood.

In short, Davis transformed Luling as he believed God had directed him. A city that was once considered "the toughest town in Texas" is now one of the most friendly and prosperous. Kahn and Cayce would, no doubt, have also used oil-well proceeds for charitable purposes, but their funds would more likely have gone to building a hospital on the East Coast, not in Luling, Texas.

Though the subsequent readings given to Davis do not directly pertain to Luling, they suggest a phenomenon that appears in other readings: that the spirits guides or entities who directed the prospectors to Luling wouldn't let the oil be found unless they were convinced that the proceeds were to be used for the benefit of its residents. For example, readings Cayce gave for prospectors seeking treasure from the legendary Lost Dutchman Gold Mine in the Superstition Mountains outside of Apache Junction, Arizona, were told that the treasure wouldn't be found without the cooperation of the Apache spirits charged with protecting it. Perhaps the same was true on this occasion.

The Lulling adventure was just the beginning of the contact that Cayce would have with Davis. Five years later, the oilman now turned Broadway theater producer, invited Edgar to New York to attend a show he had commissioned called *The Ladder*. Its topic was about reincarnation. Similar to the screen drama *Why?* that Cayce had produced in trance, Davis' play centered around the actress Antoinette Perry (after whom the Tony Awards are named), playing the part of a young woman who has visions of previous lives in 1300, 1670, and 1844. At

"Does Edgar Davis regret that the play has failed?"

"Has it failed?" Frank Davis replied. "What is failure? The most useful and successfal man I have ever known is a schoolteacher who never has had so much as twenty thousand dollars in his life, yet has influenced -- always for good -- the lives of more than five thousand pupils who have passed through his shhool in forty years, with his influence widening to all the families of those pupils. If the sole test of success is money-making, 'The Ladder' has not succeeded. But Edgar Davis' main purpose was not to make money out of the play. As an incident of the production he would have liked to make money to spend in other good works -- but primarily his purpose was to bring to the attention of a great number of people his philosophy of life. If half a million people have seen the play, and most of them have liked it and, presumably, spread the thought that underlies it, can it be called a failure? Edgar Davis has lost no sleep whatever over the fact that the money invested in his play has not resulted in financial profit."

Letter written by Edgar B. Davis' brother about the failure of *The Ladder.*

the play's climax, she returns to the present to marry a man she had previously rejected.

The play opened in New York in 1926 and would become one of the most spectacular long-running flops in all of theatrical history. Plays that received such universally bad reviews invariably shut their doors in a matter of days. Davis, however, kept his show running for a full two years by giving away free tickets by the thousands, frequently held charity performances, and feted critics and opinion makers to sumptuous dinners. As the *New York Times* critic begrudgingly reported, the production was "being kept alive, to our knowledge, for propaganda purposes."

Edgar and Gertrude Cayce weren't impressed with the show, despite the screenplay that had previously come through and the fact that reincarnation, by this point in the Cayce work, was much on their minds. The Source, too, was unimpressed. In a reading in which Davis asked whether he should keep the show running for the benefit of mankind, the answer was a decided "no." The play might be reconfigured to become a Broadway success, the Source suggested, but as currently presented, failed as both entertainment and education.

When Davis finally gave up on Broadway, he thought to turn to politics, entertaining the notion that he might run for President. The Source was again consulted and steered him back to the private sector where he could use talents he had developed in previous lifetimes, most particularly in the Roman era, during which he had held a high-ranking position as the land and human resources manager under Caesar.

Davis once more entered the Cayce story in 1936 and 1937 when Davis and his partner Frank Seiberling decided to work together again—this time to bring about a merger of the world's two largest rubber companies. Both men individually consulted Cayce for advice. The Source repeatedly said that the merger was a good idea and could be beneficial to man, but that "cooperation" was essential before the undertaking could succeed. Davis and Seiberling would have to have the other's best interest at heart "for the increase" to come about.

The proposed merger soon became bogged down in a complicated web of divided interests. Cayce was brought in again, this time by Seiberling's son-in-law, Milton Harrison, who was attempting to bring about an accord before their disputes were turned over to the attorneys. "There has developed, unfortunately, what could eventuate into a very serious division between the two men and we are doing everything we can to avoid such a split," Harrison wrote to Cayce. "The information, which is gained by us and which we hope to gain additionally through you, will be unquestionably very beneficial in avoiding ill will and in promoting a renewal of faith and thus good will. With Edgar Davis, especially, the approach through a psychic source, in my opinion, is the only approach."

Cayce—in trance—repeated what had been said earlier, calling for the two men to learn to cooperate by putting the other's interest ahead of his own. In Luling, by previous agreement, Davis had been in charge. Seiberling had only lent him money, which had been paid back. The men were in a different situation this time around. They would have to relate as true partners, something that required they set their egos aside, otherwise suffer the consequences. The advice Cayce gave was most insightful and relevant to us today because it outlines exactly what is required when entering into such a partnership.

> [They must] do that which is spiritually just and right, without the material or financial considerations . . . For when there are injustices of any nature perpetrated by any organization or group to any force or power, or any portion of such an organization, it

> produces the . . . rust that doth corrupt, and sooner or later it brings dissension, discussion, disease in the minds of all . . . Would that all corporations, all organizations, know and realize, the law of the Lord is as the two-edged sword . . . Unless good is done to all, good cannot grow out of same. For what ye sow, ye reap!

Milton Harrison pled with Davis and Seiberling to reach an accord. Together, they could accomplish much good. Apart, they would fail.

The case landed in civil court. A settlement was eventually reached, but in dollars only. The two men never resolved their differences. Both men lost their vast fortunes. Edgar Davis died at age 78 in 1951, the result of a fractured skull he sustained stepping off his front porch in Luling. Frank Seiberling passed away in 1955 at age 95.

Gladys Davis, c. 1922.

Gladys Davis:

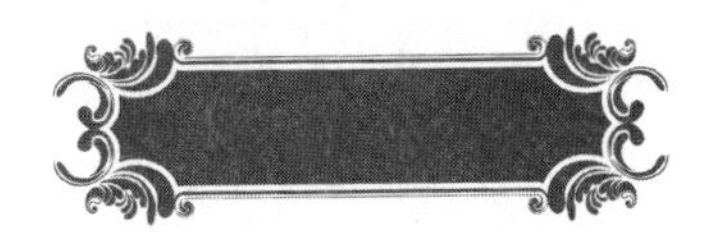

The Young Woman With a Notepad

The readings became such an important part of Edgar and Gertrude's lives in Selma that they dedicated a room in their Broad Street photography studio to conducting them. The location they chose for their "spook room," as Edgar called it, was a former storeroom on the second floor. He wanted to decorate it with furniture that his friends gave him, along with photographs and personal possessions. He realized, perhaps only intuitively, that having mementos from friends was important to the quality of the readings themselves. Somehow or other the readings were a collective effort, which was why Edgar speculated that the Source used the pronoun "we" at the beginning of trance sessions, as in "Yes, *we* have the body of Amanda Fay DeLaney . . . "

Along with the room, the Cayces had "Cayce Art Co." stationery printed up, and Edgar sent out a mailing to friends and family encouraging them to spread the word that readings would be given twice a

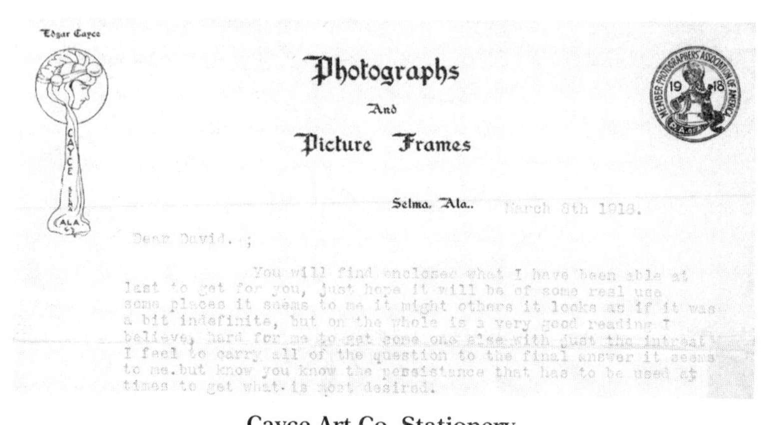

Edgar Cayce

Photographs

And

Picture Frames

Selma, Ala.. March 8th 1918.

Dear David.-;

You will find enclosed what I have been able at last to get for you, just hope it will be of some real use some places it seems to me it might others it looks as if it was a bit indefinite, but on the whole is a very good reading I believe, hard for me to get some one else with just the intrest I feel to carry all of the question to the final answer it seems to me.but know you know the persistance that has to be used at times to get what is most desired.

Cayce Art Co. Stationery.

day. He also advertised for a dedicated stenographer whom they could train to transcribe the readings.

Transcribing the readings was more difficult than one might suppose because while in trance, Cayce sometimes spoke rapidly, often using conjunctions, prepositions, and relative pronouns so profusely that normal rules of punctuation could no longer be applied. Without a stenographer suited to the task, the Cayce readings were less valuable and at times completely useless. Edgar interviewed and tested more than twelve secretaries before he found one both capable and willing to do the job.

Her name was Gladys Davis. Other than Edgar himself or Gertrude, who conducted the readings, she would become the single most important part of the work—the person who, more than anyone else, elevated it to a professional level. The "work" as it is known today wouldn't exist had it not been for Davis making duplicate copies of the readings for the files and on a deeper level, making it possible for Edgar to consistently do what he did best. Davis infused into the work what has frequently been described as an "aura of loving protection," the likes of which the Cayces had never before experienced. She and Edgar had such a connection and bond that for many years after his passing, visitors stepping into the A.R.E.'s Cayce vault, where she worked as archivist, would overhear one-sided conversations between her and what is presumed to have been Edgar's spirit.

In 1923, the year she came to know Edgar, Gladys had turned eighteen years old, just two years older than Hugh Lynn. Tall and blond with broad shoulders, delicate features, and blue eyes, she was the eldest daughter of an Alabama tenant farmer (peanuts, cotton and corn) whose joy and passion in life was having foot-stomping family get-togethers where he entertained on his fiddle and the others joined in with tin whistles, accordions, or whatever instruments were available. The eldest of five children, Gladys had two brothers and two sisters, Lucille, and Mary Frances (nicknamed Tiny) who married at the age of fourteen.

Gladys was far more capable and independent than her other siblings, so much so that after her father's passing in 1924, and for years to come, she was her family's sole source of financial support. As she was the most studious and described by friends as "sharp as a tack," it had been a foregone conclusion that Gladys would became a schoolteacher. But after attending Selma High School for one year, she saw her first typewriter, a new invention just then appearing in Selma, and enrolled at Central City Business College to learn how to use one.

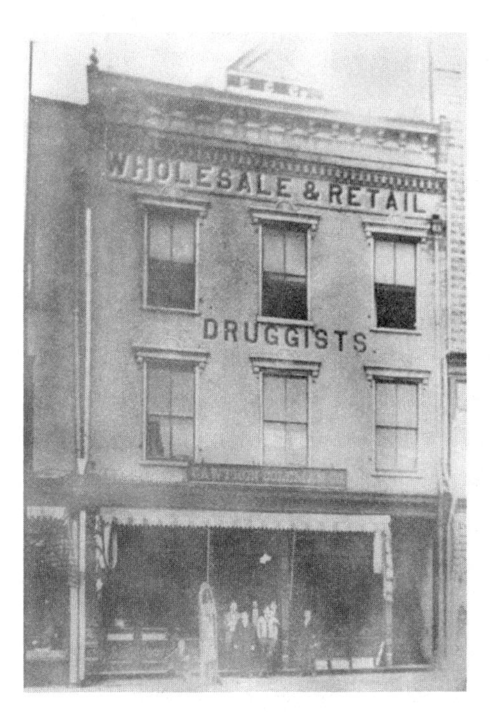

Cawthon-Coleman Drug Store, c. 1920. (Courtesy of Old Depot Museum, Selma, Alabama.)

Upon graduation at age fifteen, she took a job at the Cawthon-Coleman Drug Store where she substituted for the regular stenographer while she was on vacation. As the drug store was located on the first floor of the same building which housed the Cayce photography studio, she gradually came to know the family. The pharmacists did much business with customers who had obtained medical readings upstairs, and although it would be another two years before she would get to know the Cayce family personally, she remembered seeing family members going up and down the stairs to their home and studio.

Just as Davis knew something about the Cayces, Edgar's family was familiar with hers. Gladys had gone to the same high school as Hugh Lynn and he was friends with her sister Tiny when he was in seventh grade. He often walked Tiny home after school, exchanging books and comparing homework assignments with her, and sometimes took her to the drugstore for sodas.

In addition to Hugh Lynn, Tiny had come to know Edgar through her membership in Christian Endeavor, the church outreach program in which Edgar was deeply involved. Though their mother was a Seventh-day Adventist and the others Methodists (they would nevertheless benefit from the readings and welcome Glady's income from

Edgar Cayce's Selma, Alabama Christian Endeavor Fellowship. Edgar is at the top far right; Hugh Lynn is kneeling second from left.

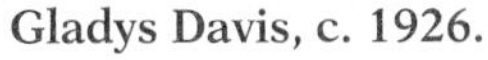
Gladys Davis, c. 1926.

Edgar's father, Leslie Cayce (The Squire), c. 1922.

her work with the Cayces), her family's enthusiasm for the non-denominational Christian Endeavor brought the families together even though they were not members of the same church. Tiny and the rest of the Selma branch of Christian Endeavor had gone with Edgar to Birmingham when he was honored for his outstanding work with the young people.

Despite the acquaintance between the two families, Gladys was still confused about which member of the Cayce clan did the psychic readings and what exactly they were about. She assumed that the one giving the readings was Leslie, the distinguished older gentleman she described as "dapper," who frequently came into the pharmacy. She herself had ventured upstairs, not to have a reading, but to have her photo taken. As Edgar was likely in Texas at the time, the responsibility had fallen to Leslie. This further confused her about who the "psychic diagnostician" was.

When Gladys worked at the Cawthon-Coleman drugstore, she remembered seeing Edgar when he had come into the drugstore and said "Good morning, Miss Gladys," as if he knew her personally. She remembered the incident because the manager jokingly told Edgar to stop

Tissier's where Gladys counted nuts and bolts. (Courtesy of Old Depot Museum, Selma, Alabama.)

flirting with his secretary by calling her "Miss Gladys." Edgar ignored him. From that moment on, and for two decades to come, he would invariably call her "Miss Gladys," and she would call him "Mr. Cayce."

Gladys' friend Ruth de Bardeleben soon set her straight about which of the Cayces was the one who gave the readings. The psychic was the son Edgar, the tall man who had taught Sunday school at the First Christian Church and the man who called her "Miss Gladys." Ruth excitedly told Gladys she had heard that people who followed what Mr. Cayce said in trance were cured of whatever ailed them. Gladys knew this to be true from others as well, just as she knew that the information coming through in the readings was not always medical. Her employer had obtained information that had led him down an Alabama river where he had located some gold doubloons, presumed to have been pirate treasure.

After the drug store's regular stenographer returned from vacation, Davis then applied to Tissier's Retail and Wholesale Hardware Store where she obtained more permanent employment as a stenographer, earning seventy-five dollars a month. As she would later reminisce of the experience, she gradually became depressed, thinking there had to be more to life than inventory lists of coal buckets, hammers, nails, nuts, bolts, plows, and cultivators.

One day her friend Willie Graham, the manager of the china department at Tissier's, paid her a visit. Graham, who at times recruited Gladys to record the history of chinaware from salesmen for store customers, asked if she would take down a Cayce reading for her three-year-old nephew. As it turned out, every stenographer in town was there, including many who were not the least bit interested in auditioning for a job, even if one was offered to them. They wanted to see for themselves what went on in the Cayce "spook room." The scheduled trance session that afternoon was to be conducted for Virgil Graham, who was suffering from a nervous disorder. Prospective stenographers were being invited to sit in on the reading and test their skills.

As it was nearing lunch time and Davis herself was more than curious about the mysterious Cayce's business, she joined Graham in the photo studio's converted second-floor storeroom. In the center of the room was an armless sofa with chairs arranged around it. When Gladys and Graham arrived, there were three other stenographic candidates already in the room, and she felt lucky to find an empty seat. Among the candidates was her friend Maud Doughty. Gladys glanced around the room and spotted both Edgar and Leslie seated in chairs. Edgar quietly got up and moved a small table over to where she was seated and smiled at her. He then went to a long couch and sat down. Next to him sat the elder Cayce, Leslie.

Edgar explained what was about to happen and told the women it was better to be accurate than to try to make sense out of what was said. Then the trance session began. To Gladys, it looked as if Edgar was about to take a nap. He took off his shoes, loosened his tie, lay back on the couch, and closed his eyes. Leslie, seated in the chair beside the couch, leaned forward and looked into his closed eyes. After a few minutes of silence, Edgar's eyelids fluttered, and Leslie spoke, beginning with instructions to find the body of Miss Graham's nephew.

Edgar began, " . . . Now we find throughout the system . . . "

He then proceeded to describe the boy's body in detail. What followed was nearly incomprehensible to those auditioning for the job. Gladys, too, had trouble following his words, but rather than try and understand what was being said, she took the words down as they were spoken. The language was quite unfamiliar, and she became more baffled with every passing moment.

In the midst of his diagnosis, Edgar used several highly unusual phrases, such as "perineurial gland" and "pneumagoastric center." Treatment recommendations included a "wet-cell" and another electrical device known as the "Abrams Oscilloclast," which was to be attached to the patient's "wrist and seventh dorsal."

Gladys kept writing, despite how little sense the words made to her. "I was determined to get it all down, no matter what," she said.

At some level she realized just how extraordinary what was taking place was. The "sleeping" Cayce was diagnosing Virgil's nervous condition as if he were a physician peering into his brain and, in addition, was prescribing the use of a device manufactured by a person whom most of the medical profession thought should be arrested.

Davis, who would become a thorough investigator of the readings, looked into the matter of the Abrams Oscilloclast as she did the anatomical references presented in the readings. As she would discover, Dr. Albert Abrams had once been a highly respected physician who had studied in London, Paris, Berlin, and Vienna before becoming professor of pathology at a clinic in San Francisco, which would one day become part of the Stanford University Medical School. All this, however, was before he shocked medical profession by announcing in 1912 that the proper manipulation of certain nerve centers in the body could relieve an assortment of ailments, including epilepsy and what would today be diagnosed as Parkinson's—conditions that were generally considered curable only by use of the knife.

The supposition underlying his device and much of his other work was actually similar to Cayce's in several notable cases. This supposition was the concept that in order to remove disease in a living cell, it was necessary to go beyond the cellular tissue and reach the electrical structure of the human body. If the electrical system was not "vibrating" normally, the entire body would be out of balance. Based on this approach, Abrams would cause another furor when he contended that

The Abrams Oscilloclast recommended by Cayce.

he could manipulate the sex of an unborn child through the use of electrical vibrations on a pregnant woman. Though a wealthy man thanks to the various electronic devices that he had patented and sold, Abrams was completely rejected by his professional colleagues and died five months after Cayce gave the Virgil Graham reading, dismissed by the medical profession.

What Gladys took away from her research was not only a greater appreciation for what came through in the reading for the three-year-old boy but also a far more expansive understanding of the root principles in the medical readings than virtually any nonphysician who would be associated with the Cayce work. Sadly, the Grahams did not likely study the reading the way Gladys one day would. The recommended treatments were apparently not followed, and child was believed to have died.

Davis, of course, didn't know these things on the day that she auditioned for Cayce. She barely understood what he had said, let alone what was being recommended. However, she was the only stenographer present that afternoon who had the requisite amount of words on the page. Her friend Maud Doughty admitted to Gladys that she was certain she wouldn't get the job because she was "too shocked" by what went on to take down a single word.

Gladys typed up two copies of the reading and was asked to give them to Miss Graham. She hoped that Mr. Cayce would also get to see her transcription and maybe even offer her the job. "Somehow I knew he would," Gladys later wrote. Still, she was relieved when Miss Graham came into the hardware store and told her that Mr. Cayce wanted to speak to her.

When Gladys arrived at the photo studio, Edgar came out of his darkroom, drying his brown-stained hands on a towel. She later described the feeling she experienced in his presence as "a lovely sense of renewing an old friendship." She also appreciated how respectfully he treated her. "I felt comfortable with him. I had never really had any adult, a man especially, talk to me . . . like I was an equal . . . He seemed actually interested in me as a person. I found out he was that way with everybody."

Edgar told her that she had transcribed the reading "perfectly," and they would need her full-time. Beyond transcribing the readings, he didn't know what her duties would be. She might have to travel back and forth to Texas as he was doing. There might also be trips to New York.

Gladys accepted the job and in that instant glimpsed what was in store for her. As if reading her mind, Edgar looked at her steadily with a sparkle in his blue-gray eyes and said softly, "No more nuts and bolts."

Gladys began what would become her life's work a few days later. She would not only bond with Edgar but also with Gertrude, who worked with her for the first month helping her practice doing the transcriptions. Gertrude would read aloud previous trance sessions, and Gladys would sit in the chair next to her taking her words down. They got to know each other quickly, sharing the stories of their lives, their trials, and their triumphs. Gertrude took a motherly interest in Gladys, and Gladys acted as the daughter Gertrude and Edgar had never had.

Later when she and Edgar actually began working together, Gladys proved her worth immediately. Young and beautiful though she was, she was much more business minded than the Cayces and established procedures that became the system by which all future readings would be conducted. She would take down in shorthand what was said in the readings and later type two copies—one for the client and one for

A sample of Gladys's shorthand readings.

Steno notebook cover.

Gladys would take down a reading on one page, then turn the page and continue on, one reading after another. When she reached the end of the notebook, she turned the pad over and started in reverse until it was filled up.

This notebook holds 63 documented readings in shorthand!

In 22 years she used approximately 300 of these notebooks for the readings and an additional 200 for Edgar Cayce's correspondence.

Page 1, upper left corner, shows this is one of 11,457 readings recorded. (This page ultimately was assigned reading #2805.)

When Gladys took the reading down in shorthand, she would proceed to type a copy of the reading then for her own reference, cross out the section she had typed.

the files. Her penchant for saving "one for the record," conducting follow-up research, and compiling background material was what ultimately resulted in the collection of not only over fourteen thousand readings but also thousands of letters and other documents—all of which she indexed and cross-referenced, making them that much more useful and valuable to the many doctors and others who subsequently studied them. The fact that she would include in these records personal details from her own intimate medical history is but one example of the many ways she put the Cayce work above her natural desire for privacy. From the moment she transcribed her first reading, the work always came first

Looking back on that first transcription, Gladys would chide Edgar by asking him how he knew she had gotten it down perfectly right when, by his own admission, he didn't remember a thing he said or did when in trance. "I just knew . . . " was always his response.

Edgar, at this point, likely didn't give much thought to his offhand remark, nor did Gladys. It was simply a matter of intuition. They wouldn't know differently until Gladys obtained her own readings, but these wouldn't be conducted until the following year. And by this time, life would dramatically change for her as well as for the Cayces.

Evangeline Adams (1868-1932).

EVANGELINE ADAMS:

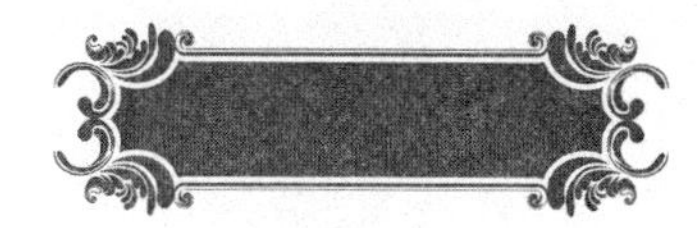

RULED BY STARS AND PLANETS

Edgar's quest for funds to build a hospital took him to Dayton, Ohio, where business tycoon Arthur Lammers, impressed by readings conducted on behalf of an adolescent cancer patient, pledged $500,000 to further the Cayce work. In addition to a hospital, he wanted a library and study center, which he intended to call the Cayce Psychical Research Center.

At Lammers' request, Cayce gave the first in a series of readings on oil development investment opportunities, the potential for a Cayce hospital and research center, and how best to use Edgar's ability. Although Cayce never developed a deep personal relationship with Lammers, and less than twenty readings were conducted on Lammers' behalf in Dayton, their brief partnership forever altered the scope and substance of the work. A new kind of information began coming through in the readings: the influence that the stars and planets have on human behavior and how information could be obtained through the readings that could be used to guide a person to better understand himself and his place in the universe.

Arthur Lammers, 1920s.

Astrology was not a new subject for Lammers as it was for Edgar. Thirty-five-year-old Lammers and his wife, Zelda, were friends of Evangeline Adams, the most respected and famous astrologer of the 1920s. They also had a passion for Eastern philosophy, metaphysics, and theosophy. They would hold séances in their sprawling Dayton home, a Victorian mansion with stained-glass windows, oriental carpets, a giant pipe organ, and an extensive library of esoteric books and manuscripts on such subjects as medieval alchemy, yoga, and spiritualism. "Supernatural Sundays" at the Lammers house, with the alluring Zelda entertaining on the pipe organ, was the place to be for well-heeled Dayton intellectuals on a quest for enlightenment.

Cayce may have visited the Lammers' home on only three occasions during his initial month-long visit to Dayton. He wasn't known to have examined the books in the Lammers library or attended a séance. It was not until the series of readings were underway that he was introduced to Evangeline Adams or the larger circle of Lammers' spiritually-minded friends. Lammers arranged for Edgar to stay in a small efficiency apartment on Fifth Street. Readings were given in downtown Dayton at the Phillips Hotel close to the Tribune Building, home of Dayton Photo Products and Lammers Printing—the companies from which Lammers derived his fortune. The Phillips Hotel was where Edgar spent much of his time, took his meals, and conducted the first Lammers' readings in June 1923. The last reading in the series was conducted at the same hotel in February 1924 after Edgar had visited Selma to see his family and to conduct what had become a long backlog of medical readings.

Linden Shroyer, Lammers' personal assistant and accountant, conducted many of the readings in this series, and Bertha Rosenberg, Lammers' secretary, was the primary stenographer. The readings would touch these people as they would Lammers. Rosenberg and her family would subsequently receive health readings as would Shroyer and his family. Further, Shroyer would eventually leave the Lammers Company and come to work for the Cayces.

All manner of questions were put to Edgar in the Lammers readings: where a hospital was to be built (near a large body of water in Virginia or South Carolina was the response), dietary advice for Edgar's psychic development (he wasn't to eat red meat), who was best suited to conduct and transcribe the readings (women, as they were said to have a greater capacity than men to understand psychic phenomenon), who on the planet could obtain the most accurate trance information from Cayce (a man identified as Russian Edwin Roth, at that moment living in or visiting Bavaria), and how to bring about world peace. Unfortunately, Edgar continued to eat red meat, no effort appears to have been made to locate Roth, and whatever answer Cayce gave about world peace was either not recorded or subsequently lost.

More important in the greater body of the Cayce work were answers to life's most important questions: the purpose of man's existence on earth and what to expect after death. The responses were so remarkable that they became the basis for "Psychic Phenomena through the Subliminal," a privately published booklet which contained the first lengthy verbatim transcriptions of Cayce readings. Lammers would write the introduction, and Gladys Davis would coordinate its eventual publication and distribution.

Lammers' first question was a request for an explanation of what physiologically happened to Edgar when he entered trance and provided information. Similar to Cayce's answer to this same question for Ketchum, the Source described a process of "subjugation" in which Edgar's "subconscious" or "soul forces" took control over his conscious or physical self. In other words, he went to "to sleep" in order to "wake up."

Lammers continued by asking what kind of questions should be asked of Cayce. "Only those that are in accord with spiritual and soul forces and laws," the Source came back.

Here and elsewhere in the series, the Source specifically said that proper questions should consist of those that lead to relief from pain or suffering so long as they are not at the expense or detriment of another individual. The same was true of spiritual and business related questions. If the desire of the seeker was for good, this brought harmony, accuracy, and a more direct communication with God, the ultimate source of all knowledge and understanding. This was described as one of God's laws.

Discussion of God's laws was expanded upon in subsequent readings in this series. "Divine Laws," as the Source made clear, could neither be ignored nor put aside. A person breaking man's laws suffers the consequence if she or he gets caught, but when breaking God's laws, he or she always gets caught. In other words, the right question for the right reason had to be asked for the good to manifest.

The most important of God's laws cited was the "law of love"—a commandment which appeared in many subsequent readings. Put most simply by the Source: "Love is Law, Law is Love. God is Love. Love is God." This amounted to the same thing as "the gift of giving" without "hope of reward or pay," or serving others.

Like Ketchum before him, Lammers wanted to know if it was possible for anyone other than Edgar Cayce to accomplish the kind of psychic work he was doing. The answer shocked and surprised Lammers, as it did Cayce. "All can do it," the response came.

If there was any doubt about what had been said, the Source repeated itself. "All can already do it. As to the degree of the development, only the law of concentration through subjugation [is] brought out into play and only need[s] the opportunity of self-expression."

The revelation here was that psychic ability was a gift everyone was born with. It needed only to be developed. That development, the

Source further explained, was what constituted "evolution" on the earth plane. This concept shed much new light on the phrase that had and would consistently appear in the readings: "mind is the builder."

Here, and in nearly two hundred readings to come, the concept was clear: the physical is the result of what first exists in the mind. Darwinian evolution, though understood as physical, was the result of a mental evolution that preceded it. And mental evolution, as clearly stated in the Lammers' readings, was spiritual or psychic in nature.

Lammers was pointedly told that as humanity came to more fully recognize the innate psychic abilities possessed by everyone, such psychic talents as "thought transference" would become commonplace, and this was a direct result of humanity returning to God, the creator. Development would "evolve" in such a way that direct communication with the Divine would take place on a conscious level.

The novel concept here was a greater understanding of what Cayce was doing in trance and what the Source claimed everyone would eventually be doing. Psychic experience, according to the readings, could not be reduced to mere physiology or science without spirituality. Man's quest to understand himself was presented as a journey to find God. This was a subject that would be expanded upon in a second series of published readings when Cayce and his family eventually settled in Virginia Beach and a group of housewives had asked Cayce how they could develop their psychic abilities. This was why these readings, compiled into book form, were not titled *How to Become More Psychic*, but *A Search For God*.

Cayce could take comfort in this and so many others things that came through in the Lammers' readings because the information squared perfectly with his fundamentalist Christian beliefs. However, there was far more to the story of a soul's journey back to God that came through in the Lammers' readings.

Asked what constituted man's soul and whether the soul ever dies, the Source replied that the soul was "that which the Maker gave to every entity or individual in the beginning, and which is seeking the home again or place of the Maker. [The soul] may be banished from the Maker, [but] not [by] death."

This response fit comfortably into Cayce's deeply held beliefs. The Bible had clearly stated there was a heaven and a hell. However, as a natural extension to this question, Lammers wanted to know more. In the first known reading to make clear reference to what happens when a person dies, the Source said: "The spirit of all that have passed from the physical plane remain about the plane until their development carries them onward or are returned for their development here."

Lammers must have picked up on this reference to reincarnation or a soul's return to Earth for development. Edgar may have missed it. But what followed when Lammers asked the next logical question would tax Cayce's imagination more than anything that had yet come through in the readings.

"What is meant by the banishment of a soul from its maker?" Lammers asked.

"All insufficient matter is cast onto Saturn" came the response.

Here was the first clear and undeniable reference to a planet playing a role in the movement of souls. Lammers suspected that this was verification for astrology, and he would dedicate the last reading in the series to what would become the most controversial aspect of Cayce's work: astrology and soul development in this life and the next.

If there was still any doubt that astrology figured into the equation, Lammers directly put the question to him: "Do the planets have an effect on the life of every individual born?"

"They have," the Source came back. "Just as this earth's forces were set in motion . . . each [soul] comes under the influence of those conditions . . . in which such is expressed through the breath of the Creator."

In subsequent readings on this subject, the Source challenged skeptics who would dismiss the notion of astrology by posing a question: "Astronomy is considered a science and astrology foolishness. Who is correct? One holds that because of the position of the earth, the sun, the planets—they are balanced one with another in some manner, some form—yet that they have nothing to do with man's life or . . . the emotions of the 'physical being' in the earth. Then why and how do the effects of the sun . . . influence [life on earth] and not affect [man and] man's emotions?"

"I said all that?" Edgar was quoted as asking when he was given the Lammers' transcription to read. "I couldn't have said all that!"

Lammers assured him that he had. That Edgar was in Dayton, six-hundred miles away from the many friends who would have dismissed astrology as a serious topic of discussion, and perhaps even heretical, was perhaps why the Source had waited until now to introduce this concept. Here in Dayton, Edgar was among ardent believers.

Ultimately, however, the person who convinced him of the potential truth of what was coming through, and encouraged the readings to come, was the charming, gracious, and erudite Evangeline Adams. To her, the readings Lammers received not only made perfect sense, but they also explained aspects of astrology beyond what even she imagined. Without Adams' counsel and encouragement, Edgar would have had considerable more difficulty taking what became a giant leap into uncharted territory. This was likely the reason why Lammers arranged for him to meet her. Edgar needed to be convinced of the truth of astrology by someone who made it her life's work, just as Lammers was encouraging Cayce to give up photography and dedicate his life to giving the readings. By bringing Cayce to her offices, Lammers seemed to be saying that her success could be Edgar's should he follow on her path.

His meeting with Adams took place on a weekend trip that he and Lammers made in 1923 to New York City. By previous arrangement, they were met by Adams' secretary, Emma Brush, and shown into the

Evangeline Adams, c. 1925.

astrologer's tenth floor suite of rooms at the Carnegie Hall Tower on 7th Avenue and West 56th Street. There were no shaded lights or exotic furnishings; the reception room was light and airy with Currier & Ives prints, signed photos of famous clients, and a wall of file cabinets containing records and birthdates of some five thousand or more people she and her team corresponded with. Near the entrance was the receptionist's desk where clients made appointments in person or by phone and where visitors could find brochures. Many of these brochures were written by Adams herself, along with stock mimeographed copies of interviews and biographical materials. Down a narrow hallway were anterooms filled with teams of female secretaries, stenographers, and mathematicians at work stations.

The stout fifty-five-year-old Adams, who wore wire-rim glasses, a long string of pearls, and a conservative black dress, was not what Edgar had expected from someone commonly associated with "fortune-telling." Born into a Boston family who had given the world two signers of the Declaration of Independence and two presidents of the United States, she had studied science and medicine at Boston University, and though she preferred being simply addressed as "Miss Adams," she could justifiably have called herself "Dr. Adams."

In the three decades since she had begun practicing astrology, her clients included financier J.P. Morgan, opera singer Enrico Caruso, King Edward VII of Great Britain, boxer Jack Dempsey, screen stars Gloria Swanson and Charlie Chaplin, and Seymour Cromwell, the president of the New York Stock Exchange. Eventually there would be many more, including educator and mythologist Joseph Campbell and playwright Eugene O'Neill, who would both later testify to the truth of her astrological assessments of them. Before her death in 1932, she would host a top-rated radio show, write four best-selling books, successfully defend her astrology practices in New York courts, and eventually become an icon in women's studies programs throughout the world.

Edgar was as entranced by her as nearly everyone who met her. "Regal" was how many visitors described her, yet "scholarly, almost professorial." As her biographer would write, "something in her person was already reminiscent of a formal but kindly maiden aunt, who wisely counsels without condemning." There was more to her appeal for Edgar. She collected miniature elephants, just as he liked to do, and kept a Bible at hand's reach. More significantly, Adams was a gifted intuitive—something that was clear to Cayce as it would later be to Tom Sugrue, Cayce's future biographer, who would visit Adams in preparation for a lecture he later delivered at the Cayce hospital. Adams' many accurate prophesies were based on her astrological cal-

"Never have I cast a horoscope that put me on my mettle the way yours has."

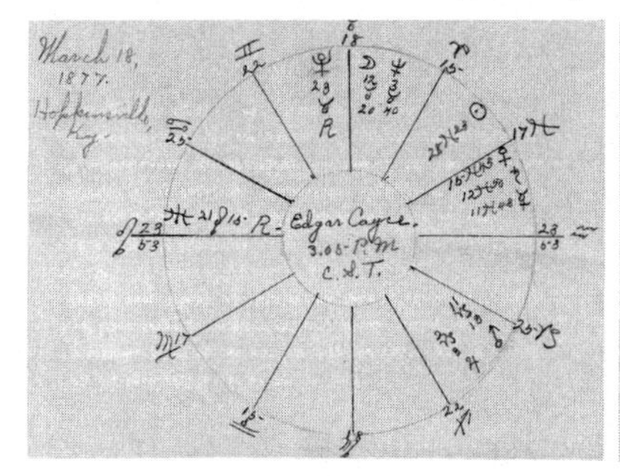

Edgar Cayce's Natal Astrology Chart, 1943.

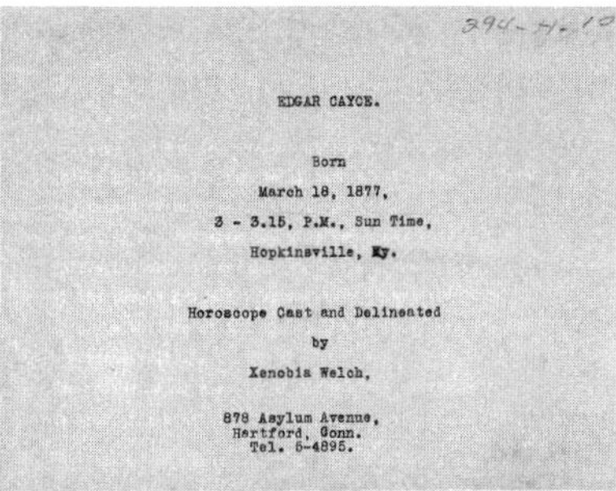

394-H-10

EDGAR CAYCE.

Born
March 18, 1877,
3 - 3.15, P.M., Sun Time,
Hopkinsville, Ky.

Horoscope Cast and Delineated
by
Xenobia Welch,

878 Asylum Avenue,
Hartford, Conn.
Tel. 5-4895.

Cast by Xenobia Welch, a student of Evangeline Adams.

Although your greatest desire has always been to serve humanity, you prefer doing it royally - with no recompense. The day you con-cented to accept remuneration for your work in the occult, that day marks the hardest won battle you will ever have with yourself.

Evangeline's student Xenobia Welch's final remarks in her report on Edgar's chart.

culations, but she possessed a "presence" not unlike Edgar himself, though Cayce lacked her education and sophisticated manner. Perhaps Edgar read her aura and liked what he saw. Based on what transpired it was clear to him that she had a true gift and there was more at work than simply reading his chart.

After showing Edgar into her book-lined study, she told him some of the illustrious history of astrology, naming King Solomon, Plato, and Napoleon as practitioners, and showing Edgar the circular charts on which horoscope calculations were made. She then obtained the date, time, and place of Edgar's birth. For the next forty minutes she consulted a globe on which to pinpoint the latitude and longitude of Christian County, Kentucky, and a thick, leather-bound volume called an ephemeris, which she used to calculate the position of stars and other celestial bodies at the time of his birth.

Using this information, Adams drew a circular chart showing the position of the planets when Edgar was born at 3 p.m. on March 18, 1877. Everything she told him of his past and future, Cayce later said proved to be true, including something he found most disturbing. He was told that he would never be materially happy or achieve the kind of success he presumed would eventually be his. Cayce thought she was mistaken because his long-held dream of building the Cayce hospital looked soon to become a reality. Lammers had promised $500,000. Edgar was making plans to sell his photo studio and bring Gladys with his family to Dayton to help get the project underway.

Author Tom Sugrue and others close to Edgar would have further contact with Adams as more readings were conducted. The information coming through in these readings compared favorably with how Adams taught astrology, although a great deal more complex. Most important to the Cayce readings was that a person's free will plays a greater role than the planets in determining how one's life unfolds. Everyone shapes his own future; the stars and planets merely "impel" rather than "compel." Further, given the kind of detailed information revealed in the later readings, it would be next to impossible for anyone without psychic gifts to accurately describe an individual's personality traits, tendencies, talents, weaknesses, and future challenges based solely upon his or her birth date.

In most horoscope readings to come, Cayce would emphasize the specific influence that various planets exerted on the individual. The role of the constellations, however, such as Cancer, Leo, or Virgo, was considered relatively insignificant in sharp contrast to the Adams' approach which holds the "sign" a person is born under as the chief determining factor in shaping an individual's personality and interactions with others.

Cayce also asserted that the influence of the planets was not necessarily what it was for Adams. As in standard astrology, Mars was associated by Cayce with high energy and anger, but the Source consistently emphasized the planet's "internal" influence rather than the "external" behavior. The emphasis was on constructive growth through control of the human will—that which reigned supreme. Nor were all individuals affected equally by the planets. As many future readings would show, some individuals were more influenced than others and in several notable instances, were not affected at all.

Important differences were also noted in the influence particular planets had on behavior. Saturn, the ringed planet, was historically represented as a love of tradition and an opposition to change. In contrast, the key words that Cayce related to Saturn were "sudden" or "violent" change bringing a shock to the system. Similar to Adams' approach, however, Mercury governs the mind, reason, and intellect, while Neptune brings greater spiritual insight and development.

The most significant revelation, which is what caught Adams undivided attention and in turn other astrologers, was not the influence that planets have on human beings, but why. In the fourth Cayce reading on astrology, the Source stated that the "influence as is given by many . . . is defective [in that] many of the forces of each [planet] are felt more through the experience by the entity's 'sojourn' upon those planets."

Cayce would most pointedly reference sojourns again in an astrological reading for a thirty-year-old secretary: "It is not so much that an entity is influenced because the Moon is in Aquarius . . . but rather because those positions in the heavens are from the entity having been in that sojourn as a soul . . . not as a physical body as known in the Earth, but as a body adaptable to the environs of Jupiter: for there's life there—not as known in Earth!"

By these and other Life Readings, the Source came outright and said that the soul of an individual could actually "reside" on another planet and in other dimensions, as Cayce had referenced earlier about banishment to Saturn. This was a place, or dimension, not unlike the Roman Catholic vision of purgatory. But here, the purpose was a means to prepare an individual, through "soul development," to meet the Creator. Earth served this function as well, for here souls had opportunity, by working with others, to test what they had learned.

The cosmic plan, as presented, called for the individual soul to experience creation in its full diversity and complexity. The ultimate goal was for the individual to use his or her free will to meet the challenges that would facilitate the return to God and hence evolve closer to the Maker. "[Man must pass] through all the stages of development until the will is lost in Him and he becomes one with the Father." As Edgar well knew, this was similar to the message put forth in the Lord's Prayer of "Thy will be done."

The hardship for Edgar was digesting the vast new information which, thanks to Lammers and now Adams, suddenly began to pour out of him in trance.

In the first dedicated "horoscope" reading he gave for Lammers on October 11, 1923, Cayce described Lammers' soul as "ruled by Jupiter" with "Venus in the eleventh House," and hence that he was well "balanced" to deal with individuals whose birthday comes in March—as did Edgar Cayce's. Clearly, this was positive news and bode well for the building of a hospital. Also presumed to be good news, Lammers was said to be destined for ever greater wealth, which would be a legacy passed on to his children. The only caveat was that Lammers' upwardly mobile trajectory could turn "destructive" unless he kept his "appetites" in check.

This reading apparently was similar to a horoscope provided to Lammers by Adams and supported the concepts that had come through in the early Dayton readings. It was the last line of the reading that was the shocker. After a description of Lammers as "strong-willed" and "self-reliant," the reading said that this was his "third appearance on this plane" and that "he was once a monk."

Arthur Lammers and family in Dayton, 1920s.

Arthur Lammers:

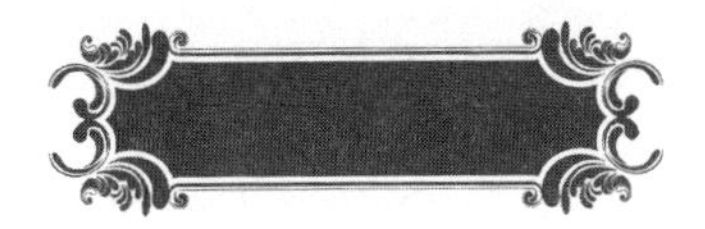

Once a Monk

Lammers had never been a monk. Nor was there the remote possibility he would ever be one. A theosophist, he was a student of many spiritual traditions. Moreover, he and his wife Zelda took much pleasure in their three—soon to be four—children and in the luxurious lifestyle their printing and photo-engraving businesses afforded them.

A week passed before Lammers asked the Source for an explanation. This was not because he and Cayce weren't interested. Edgar was nervous about what might come through. Reincarnation was even further removed from accepted Christian theology than astrology.

When they finally asked, the Source confirmed that Lammers had been a monk in the incarnation previous to his appearance as a printer in Dayton. "In this we see glimpses in the life itself of the entity as was shown in the monk . . . and [his soul] wafts itself through all times and ever remains . . . "

Further, the Source said that Lammers had been "upon this earthly plane" three times. His life as a monk, where he had lived in a cloister in Spain, was most relevant as the Source suggested he had worked in the scriptorium and hence his interest in typography and texts. He was a scribe then, a printer now.

The same was true for Edgar, as became clear in the next reading they conducted. While Lammers had reincarnated three times, Edgar had seven important or most notable physical appearances on the earth plane and further, that his "soul forces" were better developed, presumably leading him closer to God or in more direct communication with the Divine forces.

The door had been thrown open. In one new reading after another, the Source, without being prompted, added this type of new information. A reading for an oil business partner George Klingensmith, who had pledged financial support for a Cayce hospital and research institute, outlined several past lives and added a curious sidenote: he and Lammers, Linden Shroyer, and Cayce had been together in a previous incarnation. Klingensmith was further told that he and the others were working together in Dayton now because they were trying to accomplish in this lifetime what they had previously failed.

Still reluctant to go down this road, two weeks passed before Edgar permitted Linden Shroyer to ask specific questions about his incarna-

Mansion of Zelda and Arthur Lammers in Dayton, Ohio.

tions. "Give the name and profession of each of the appearances on this plane," the Source was instructed.

The information came through so quickly that it seemed the Source had been waiting for this question and to be asked in this particular way. What hence forth became the model for all future Life Readings. Shroyer was said to have been a Norsemen and before that a Persian soldier. And similar to what had been said about Klingensmith, he had been present during the Grecian wars.

Attention was then turned back to Edgar in a second Life Reading. Edgar was said to have been a soldier in the vicinity of Dayton, which was why, the Source suggested, he had once again been drawn "to this spot" in his present incarnation. He resonated with it because of his past association with it. Earlier, Edgar had been a settler in Jamestown, Virginia, which also, by no apparent coincidence, was near Virginia Beach where the readings were now indicating was the most suitable location to build the Cayce Hospital.

Were people drawn in the present to locations where they had lived or worked earlier? This seemed to be the implication. But it was difficult to say for sure as the farther back in time the Source chronicled Cayce's previous incarnations, the more removed they seemed to be from Edgar's experience. Before Jamestown, Cayce had lived in France at the time of Richelieu and prior to that was a chemist studying under Aristotle. He, too, as it would be revealed, was a participant in the Grecian wars, most specifically the siege of Troy.

The Source, perhaps knowing the difficulty Edgar was having with this information, noted something special about his incarnation before Greece, when he lived in the "plains country" of Arabia. The Source said that his human remains from this lifetime still existed and could be found in a cave 714 miles from a city called Shushtar.

The Source further identified what it suggested was Edgar's most important incarnation. He had lived in Egypt and was reported to be a high priest named Ra Ta, who was cast out of the Pharaoh's court. Stranger still was his first incarnation, which the Source referred to as the creation of man, "when the morning stars sang together and the 'sons of God' came together and spread the news of the glory of the coming of man."

Edgar didn't leak the news of the Life Readings to Gertrude and

Gladys, back in Selma, who were soon to join him in Dayton. The subject seemed too outlandish to be presented in a letter, and even so, as he would later freely admit, Edgar didn't understand the substance or purpose of the information coming through. Gertrude and Gladys would have to experience it for themselves, which they soon did.

The two women and toddler Edgar Evans arrived by train in November 1923, soon after Edgar had received his second Life Reading. He met them at the station and accompanied them to the Phillips Hotel, which would be their temporary residence until they could move into the apartment on East Fifth Street. The plan was for Leslie to remain in Selma to finalize the paperwork on the sale of the photo studio. Hugh Lynn was also to stay behind in Selma to complete his junior year in high school. By the time he graduated, the funds were expected to be in place to begin building the hospital. However, where it was to be located still remained uncertain. Despite the repeated advice coming through in the readings that it would be best that the hospital be built in Virginia, near or adjacent to the Atlantic Ocean, Lammers—the principal funder—was adamant that it be in Dayton, close to his base of operations.

Just days after Gladys and Gertrude were settled, Edgar introduced them to the new type of information coming through. They chose to make five-year-old Edgar Evans the test subject of the next Life Reading for the simple reason that he was too young to complain and what came through would be meaningless to a child who hadn't yet learned to read or understand the information put forth. In essence, they were taking one small step after another. Thinking that if they chose, the team could retreat back to doing the health readings which they were more accustomed to conducting.

Edgar Evans was said to have had four notable previous incarnations, including ones in Germany and India. However, specifics were not given as they had been for Lammers. The Source instead provided parental advice to Edgar and Gertrude, along with warnings as to various illnesses or injuries to watch out for based on astrological influences and specific dates during which the child would be prone to have a *fire*-related accident.

Gladys, who seemed to take the information coming through in stride, was the next person to have a Life Reading. In her case, she was not only present to witness the reading, but she also took the notes and later transcribed it. She described the experience as frightening, "but in a good way."

Gladys' past lives numbered four and included a stint in the court of Louis the Fifteenth around the same time as Edgar had been there. In this incarnation she was a member of the royal family and had been seduced by the Duke of York with whom she had a child. Before that she had incarnations in Persia and Egypt. Previous to that, she had lived in the house of a ruler in a place called "Alta," which, according to the Source, existed "ten thousand years before the Prince of Peace came."

This was the first of the Life Readings in which the recipient went on record to share both her emotional response to the reading as well as truths she discovered in them. Her Persian incarnation was a case in point. The Source said that in this lifetime she "was taken by the invading forces," and because of this "she now has the aversion to those cutting instruments, for in that manner the bodily destruction came." The information took her breath way. Since early youth she had had a fear of being cut and stayed away from knives. If compelled to use one in the kitchen, she was so nervous that she invariably cut herself. Her incarnation in which she had been seduced and apparently betrayed by the Duke of York also rang true. As she admitted to Gertrude, she had an intense fear of men.

Gertrude stepped forward for a Life Reading the following month. Her most recent incarnation was in the French courts during the same period when Edgar and Gladys had been there. A follow-up Life Reading revealed that she had been a royal courtesan named Lurline. That she, a Kentucky-born housewife, had been up to no good in the French courts seemed to be preposterous. But there was one curious aspect that gave it a modicum of credibility. Unbeknown to either Edgar or Gladys, Lurline was the same name she had given to a beloved childhood doll.

Hugh Lynn was given the next reading for much the same reason that his brother had received his. He couldn't complain. Beyond the astrological information that was part of all the Life Readings, which the Source said resulted in a deep love of nature and the outdoors as well as an inclination to defend "personal principles at any cost," the reading indicated six incarnations. Among them was an incarnation in Egypt where he had been a Pharaoh. Similar to Edgar's own Life Readings, the Source indicated his physical remains could still be found, in his case in the north corner of one of the pyramids, presumably in mummy form. This appeared so unbelievable that no further questions about Hugh Lynn's past lives were asked, especially the most obvious: why a soul who had been a Pharaoh had been reborn two thousand years later in Kentucky as the son of a struggling photographer and a twenty-seven-year-old housewife.

This was when Lammers figured back into the story of the Life Readings, or more precisely failed to make an appearance. In December, little more than a month after the family had made their move to Dayton, the funds Lammers had promised were not forthcoming. Bills weren't being paid. Foremost among them was what Edgar owed at the Philips Hotel. The family had actually put off the move to their rented apartment for the sole reason that they had no money to check out.

Lammers was also increasingly more difficult to reach. He had arrived late to what became their last business meeting in November when they were to discuss arrangements for printing the brochure of Cayce's early Dayton readings. The meeting turned into a heated argument with Shroyer and Klingensmith. When the tempers settled, Lammers explained why he had been difficult to reach and had put off paying the bills. He was having legal problems related to the Lammers Photo Products Corporation. These matters, he swore, would soon be settled, and the Cayce hospital project would be back on schedule. However, the situation didn't improve.

By January 1924 the bills were still not being paid, and Linden Shroyer, Edgar's primary contact for Lammers, was also left without funds. Unfortunately for him, the news reached him in Florida where he had traveled on Lammers' behalf to close a business deal. Shroyer found himself having to cover his own hotel bills and the train ride home. When he arrived back in Dayton, Lammers' office doors were locked, never to be reopened.

The situation for the Cayces was more dire than might otherwise have been because money due the family for the sale of the Cayce photo studio didn't arrive as they had anticipated. Rather, the Cayces received hundreds of dollars in bills for back taxes that his father had failed to pay when Edgar was in Texas. The savings that the family had set aside in Selma had gone to moving Gertrude, Gladys, Edgar Evans, and their belongings to Dayton. The only remaining cash the family had—a single gold coin Gertrude had left from her dowry—had gone to buying food and train fare to bring Hugh Lynn home for the Christmas holidays.

How could Lammers have left them in the lurch without so much as a warning? Except for the Source, there didn't seem to be anyone to turn to for answers. And this was when the greater significance of what was coming through in the Life Readings came into focus. The information pertaining to astrological influences and previous incarnations was not for entertainment or pleasant diversion from their immediate challenges. Rather, it was as important as the medical advice being given to patients in desperate need of help. Being forewarned of possible sources of interference and challenges was being forearmed. The details coming through in the readings were like markers on a road map that indicated where a person was headed because of where that person had been. Learning to 'read the readings,' so to speak, was a way of avoiding potholes, or in a worst case scenario, outright collisions.

The Source had stated this best in Hugh Lynn's reading: "Man's consciousness is gained through what he does about the knowledge of what he is, in relation to that from which he came, and toward which he is going." The Source also made it clear that the knowledge gained through the Life Readings was not the same as specific memories from previous incarnations. Forgetfulness of previous lives was by design, not only for the purpose of maintaining "free will," but also for protection, as conscious memories from earlier incarnations could potentially become a burden.

The "memory" that a person takes with him into a subsequent incarnation was presented more in the form of a lesson that has been learned or remains to be learned. Unless that "lesson" makes for a better person, it has no lasting value. This is what the Source referred to as "karma" or the impact that one incarnation has on another. "To find that ye only lived, died, and were buried under the cherry tree in Grandmother's garden does not make thee one whit better neighbor, citizen, mother, or father!" the Source spelled out. "But to know that ye spoke unkindly and suffered for it, and in the present may correct it by being righteous . . . that is worthwhile!"

Although the focus in many of the future readings was on what might be termed "bad karma," the Source devoted a greater number of readings to what might be called "good karma" or talents, abilities, and attitudes that were earned as a result of successfully meeting previous challenges. Having met those challenges, a soul would be given "greater responsibilities," which could come in the form of wealth, station in life, good health, or highly developed abilities and talents. These were described as "responsibilities" because they, too, were karmic and had to be used in a manner that was in keeping with the Divine purpose. As Edgar's own Life Reading would later reveal to him, his ability to communicate on a psychic level was a direct result of his "soul development" in Persia, most specifically a painful out-of-body experience in a cave outside of Shushtar, what is modern-day Iran, where the readings had said his physical remains from that incarnation could still be found.

The writing had been on the wall in Lammers' own readings, only the team had failed to notice. The first red flag was a reference that Lammers, because of astrological influences from Neptune, would find the greater opportunity for development so long as he was not near the water or with people associated with water. This was in striking contrast to Edgar, who was specifically told he should be near the water. Perhaps it was Lammers' inclination not to be near water which explains his adamance that the hospital be built inland. Why hadn't they probed the Source for an explanation for this anomaly? And why hadn't they asked the larger question regarding whether or not Lammers was the best choice to fund and manage the building of a Cayce hospital?

Another red flag was raised in regards to Lammers' relationship with Klingensmith, Shroyer, and Cayce. According to the readings, they had all fought together in ancient Troy, and their effort had resulted in failure. When this information had been given, Edgar had thought of ancient Troy and the siege of that city as myth—the product of legendary Greek poet Homer's vivid imagination. The Source presented the story in *The Iliad* as fact and identified the Dayton participants as having engaged in "destructive purposes" which had resulted in failure.

What had happened back in Troy that was relevant to their experience in Dayton? The Source had virtually come right out and told them to ask this question, but the team had failed to follow up. Now, when it was too late, they went ahead and probed for information. In the days ahead, the Cayces pieced together what they soon realized was a band of brothers' story of betrayal and tragedy.

Lammers had been no less than Hector, the leader of the Trojans, who courageously defended their city for nine years. Though the readings provided more information than what had been presented by Homer—Hector does die in a violent duel to the death with Achilles, but his ultimate demise as described in the readings has his head cracked open against the city's wall—there were enough similarities that there could be no mistake that the Source truly was referring to the same event. Most notable, a Trojan horse containing soldiers hidden inside, is rolled into the city, which is subsequently pillaged and burned.

The key to understanding how Lammers' incarnation as Hector figured into the Dayton drama seemed to rest in the team who had assembled around him and the nature of his betrayal in Troy. As the readings would reveal, Cayce had once been a guard at the gates of Troy, and Lammers' accountant, Shroyer, had been Cayce's attendant. Klingensmith, who lived in Hector's household, had also been implicated in the conspiracy. The result of their actions was Hector's death and the ultimate destruction of the city with its inhabitants. As became clear, most but not all of the principal players in this lifetime were reunited, and due to Hector's violent death, Lammers was on the lookout for treachery. There was "no mutual trust" the readings indicated.

The readings suggested that Lammers in the present, suspected or believed that Cayce, Klingensmith, and Shroyer were trying to maneuver around him by pushing to establish the Cayce hospital in Virginia and not in Dayton, as Lammers was demanding. This may also have been the reason, it was later understood, why Lammers had sent Shroyer to Florida. He was trying to put distance between him and the others.

A more careful study of the readings also highlighted Lammers' weakness and what was described as Hector's downfall. The Source

Trojan Horse by A. Yakovlev, 1911.

had specifically said that Lammers' future financial success depended upon his ability to control his "appetites." The reference here wasn't only to his diet, but to pride and arrogance which had gradually come to dominate his decision-making, as it had back in Troy. In an effort to expand his printing business by taking over a competitor, he had become overextended. He had also failed to anticipate a change in leadership at the National Cash Register Company, his single largest client.

As Shroyer and the Cayces later discovered, Lammers had always maintained a cordial relationship with John Patterson, NCR's founder and chief. But Patterson's death in 1922 and the ascendency of his son, Frederick Beck Patterson, changed the dynamics. Frederick wanted to overhaul the company, and when Lammers wasn't willing to accommodate new demands—he wanted to conduct business as usual—NCR began buying from Lammers' chief competitor. Rather than capitulate to demands—as had been Hector's choice in Troy—Lammers metaphorically fell on his sword. He would fight to the death, only his arena was the state civil courts.

After a short and intense 1923 standoff in civil court, which Lammers' attorneys advised against, Dayton Photo Products and Lammers Printing went into bankruptcy. When Lammers was late for

Linden Shroyer, Gladys Davis, and Edgar Cayce in Datyon, c. 1923.

the meetings regarding the publication of the Cayce brochure, he was fighting off the creditors in the process of foreclosing on his mansion and repossessing his automobiles. Shroyer eventually shared with the Cayces the blow-by-blow story of what happened. The trouble was that there was no way to move forward with the hospital plans without Lammers.

After he shut off all communications with the Cayces, Lammers moved his family to Cincinnati, where he had been born and where his in-laws could provide housing and a modest livelihood. It was here in 1954 at age of sixty-four that he died. Several decades would pass before Lammers' children would reach out and make contact with what had become the A.R.E. By this time, however, the principal players on the team which had once been together in Troy had passed away as well and based on their readings, presumably are on a path or sojourn that once again would bring them together to lessen their karmic burdens.

The Cayces, bankrupt themselves, were left stranded in Dayton.

Christmas 1923 turned out to be the leanest holiday the family had ever had. Hugh Lynn, who arrived in Dayton from Selma by train, found his father at the station shivering in the cold. He, like Gertrude and Gladys, didn't have the funds for overcoats. Christmas dinner consisted of the smallest "bird" on the dining table that Hugh Lynn had ever seen. "I could fit it in the palm of my hand," he later said. Gladys would note that there was so little money that she had started using butcher paper to transcribe the readings.

But even their lack of income wasn't the greatest challenge facing the team in the New Year. Just as Lammers, Klingensmith, Shroyer, and Cayce had been together in past lives, so had Edgar, Gertrude, and Gladys.

Edgar and Gladys, 1943.

Edgar and Gladys:

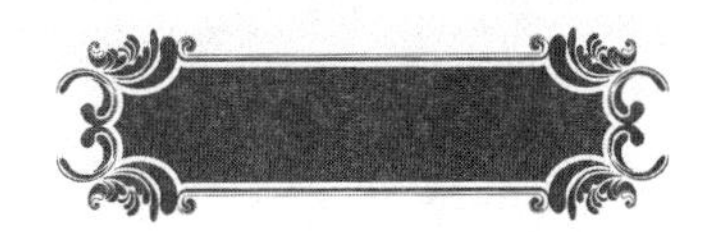

Eros or Agape?

The readings chronicling the fall of Troy linked a relatively unknown figure–a Dayton printer, albeit a wealthy one–to an important and heroic figure from antiquity. In the years to come, other famous personages would also be identified. Tacitus, the preeminent Roman historian, came back as radical statesman Patrick Henry, whose stirring words, "Give me liberty or give me death," helped to incite the American Revolution. Thomas Jefferson was identified as a person who reincarnated as a young child periodically abandoned by his alcoholic parents. John James Audubon, the great naturalist and artist, incarnated as a widowed Alabama housewife who earned a modest income hand-coloring picture postcards. Late in life, Cayce himself was identified in a previous incarnation as Lucius of Cyrene, said to have been the author of the Gospel of Luke.

Critics of the Cayce work would hone in on the identification of these and other world figures in the Life Readings as evidence that what came through couldn't possibly be true. However, in defense of what might reasonably be deemed to be the "famous person syndrome," only a very small percentage of the people who would receive Life Readings were identified as famous, and that list didn't include Cleopatra, Napoleon, or Abraham Lincoln, with whom legions of people then, as today, immodestly claim psychic kinship.

Cayce well understood such criticism because he himself was similarly skeptical. The way he was ultimately able to fathom the mystery rested in the soul tasks that the once famous frequently had to bear, and how they drew to themselves people and situations by which they would be sorely tested. A former coal miner identified as Nero, the Roman emperor who launched the first great persecution of the Christians, was paralyzed from the neck down in an automobile crash and totally dependent upon Christian charities for every detail of his personal care. An historically famous French artist, who had used his talents in a previous lifetime to parody homosexuals, was reborn as a homosexual in a homophobic household.

Cayce also came to understand that these souls were never alone in their struggles. They came back in soul groups to try and complete some long-term "good" that had been started in previous incarnations and were drawn to others of similar past-life experience that responded to particular patterns or cycles of human history. This appeared to be the case not only for relatively small soul groups, such as Lammers, Klingensmith, Shroyer, and Cayce, but in far larger waves of incarnates, such as American revolutionaries who come back to help guide the nation during particularly troubling times. This, however, was a revelation yet to be explored. The focus in Dayton was on the more intimate and personal connections, which is what prompted Gladys on May 31, 1924, to request a second Life Reading. This time she wanted to know her possible connections with Edgar and Gertrude. How was it that an eighteen-year-old Alabama girl, fresh from secretarial school, had in a matter of months become such a large part of the Cayce work?

As previously noted in the readings, Gladys had had an incarnation in the French courts. Now she was told how she, as a young woman named Gracia, had been one of the daughters of Louis XIV, described by the Source as "of beautiful figure and loving in every manner." After years of being raised in a nunnery, she rejoined the royal family and was seduced at the age of seventeen by the philan-

The Duke of York.
(King James II of England)

King Louis XIV of France.

dering James, the exiled Duke of York, whom history notes later became King James II of England. According to the new information, she had entered the relationship based on the premise that she and James would be married, presumably after a church-ordained annulment of his existing Catholic marriage. The relationship resulted in her giving birth to the Duke's child out of wedlock, who was none other than Edgar Cayce in his fifth incarnation.

Toward the soul that was Cayce in this incarnation, the Source said, "the love does not cease in the heart but all is centered in the offspring of that love [Edgar]." This message would be repeated in another of her Life Readings: "In the courts . . . when they were mother and son, the greater portions of the body beautiful became the system of one and the life of the other." In other words, theirs had been an extremely powerful mother and son connection.

The story then becomes tragic. When the Duke does not marry Gracia, there is a court scandal. Gladys' mother, the queen, reportedly lost favor with King Louis who banished her and her daughter to a convent. The child Edgar, now without a mother, is then killed by the capricious king as he is a potential threat to the thrones of both England and France. Gladys, who is forced to become a nun, is devastated. "There is brought the great dread and the inability of any [other] to satisfy that desire of the heart and life, to fill the longing for one who has become dearer than life itself to [Gladys Davis.]" At age thirty, unable to cope with the loss, Gracia dies of a broken heart.

The Source succinctly summed up the greater message being conveyed. Gladys "should find [her] rest in [the] heart, soul, and mind in the life of that individual . . . Edgar Cayce . . . The affection which was lost in that plane should be manifest in this present [incarnation], for Gladys Davis [will] only find its rest in this earth's plane with that entity Edgar Cayce."

Gladys had been given what amounted to a single piece from which grew an elaborate mosaic. However, one thing was clear. She had good reason, according to the readings, to give up a comfortable home and secure employment in Selma and come to Dayton to work with Edgar. That she hadn't received a paycheck since her arrival and was sharing a bed with Edgar Evans, still in diapers, was made all the more heartrending. She was a mother seeking reunion with a child who had been taken from her. Perhaps, too, as was noted by Gertrude and others, Gladys seemed to be the only stenographer in Edgar's life who could record his trance discourses with the seeming familiarity of a mother listening to her son.

The same day this reading was given, Edgar went back into trance to ask the Source about his French incarnation and his relationship to Gladys. Would the information be consistent?

The Source came back:

> The entity [Edgar Cayce] was of tender years . . . born of [Gladys Davis] the beloved of the court, and of the ruler's son of the territory just across the waters [England]. And the change necessary in court proceedings prevented the culmination of this ruler's recognizing the earthly fatherhood of [Edgar Cayce]. The great trials came to the entity . . . when the separation was effected between mother and son, [and] the young life was gradually taken out on account of the jealousy arising in the court. For the king became fully aware of the lad's appearance, and the possibility of [him] becoming the ruler forced others to play the traitor to the mother, who loved the entity so well.

And just as Gladys was said to have deep love for the child that was taken from her, Edgar's feelings for her were deep and abiding. "The lives of each have ever been bound in the other's life, and the conditions as exist are only the outgrowth of endeavor in [the] earth plane . . . The outward manifestations of the inward desires of the heart and soul . . . find in each the answering chord in the other's affection that will never, never, never be found in any other."

In this passage the Source was not only saying that they had shared love in the French incarnation but suggested that that they had been together many other times as well. The Source advised: "Be faithful one to the other, irrespective of earthly conditions, [for] these two have ever been together," and "Be thou faithful unto the end and receive that crown that is ever for the faithful in heart, soul, and body. Be kind, affectionate, loving, ever giving, ever preferring the other."

Here and in the readings to come, the Source was describing a love that transcended a single incarnation. The recommendation was clear: they must always put the other first, ahead of themselves, in order to do the greater good for themselves and others in their work together. Two days later, in another reading, this was expanded upon. And what came through was more powerful than any single reference to reincarnation or astrological influences:

> [Edgar Cayce and Gladys Davis] have had many experiences together, and their soul and spirit are well knit and must of necessity present each that they may be one. For we find in the beginning that . . . these two–which we shall speak of as 'they' until separated–were as one in mind, soul, spirit, body . . . in the first earth's plane as the voice over many waters, when the glory of the Father's giving of the earth's indwelling of man was both male and female in one. In flesh form in earth's plane we find . . . both were confined in the body of the female [in their first incarnation], for this being the stronger . . . form. Yet with the experiences as have been brought in that plane and period, we find then the separation of the body. For the desire of the flesh being to give of self in bodily form to the other, it brought the separating of the spirit and soul from the carnal forces when next brought to earth's plane . . . Hence . . . the separation . . . yet bound together in physical affections one for the other.

Exactly what was being said or described was not easily understood. In some distant time, right back to man's first incarnations on Earth, the souls of Edgar and Gladys had been one–both male and female in the same body or spirit entity. Out of desire to experience sex, they had separated and for reasons not yet made clear, had been unable to reunite as a single soul.

This theme was expanded upon in the information to come. In their Egyptian incarnations, Gladys was said to be the offspring of the controversial union of Edgar, the high priest known as Ra Ta, and Gertrude, who was said to be the favorite dancer of Pharaoh Hugh Lynn. In a strange corollary to the French incarnation, Gladys was the child who died young when she was taken away from her parents by the jealous Pharaoh. They were together again when Edgar, and then Gladys, as lovers in Persia, died together in the cave in Shushtar. Not only could Edgar's body still be found there, but the love that he had experienced with Gladys in that incarnation was, according to the Source, evident in marks that they would find on their bodies, which were indicative of how they lost their lives.

"Both suffered physically, and they each bear in the body at present a mark designating these conditions," the Source said. "On the female body [Gladys Davis], just below the left breast, to the side and on the edge of the breast itself, the mark, and an answering one on the body of the male [Edgar Cayce], in the opposite proximity of the breast."

Again came the message that they were meant always to be together: "At present we find they are again together . . . united in soul and in spirit . . . and through the joy and the pleasure of selfless service they may again know the meaning of . . . those joys . . . that bring . . . peace, and again [the] uniting of body, soul, and spirit in the next [incarnation]. Remain faithful, therefore, unto the end: gaining those joys through daily acts of selflessness for and with others, remembering that . . . they–and all souls–become knit one with the other."

As both Edgar and Gladys would later admit (confirming the "designating" marks referenced by the Source) they felt a strong and at times overwhelming desire to be in one another's company. The Source stated the challenge plainly: Each of them felt "the crying of the soul's desire, both in the carnal and the answering of the oneness in each."

Gladys Davis and Gertrude Cayce,
c. 1924.

Like the proverbial good news accompanied by the bad news, nineteen-year-old Gladys Davis was being told something that seemed to exist only in romance novels. She had found her soul mate, described in the readings as her "twin soul." She and Edgar had once been a single entity, which was why they had such immediate affinity with one another. The bad news was that her mate was a happily married man twenty-seven years her senior and that his wife was her new best friend. And if this wasn't enough, her mate's wife, according to the readings, had to remain married because of the bad karma that had been created back in Egypt, when Gertrude abandoned Hugh Lynn, the pharaoh, for Edgar. In other words, Edgar and Gertrude were meant to be together as husband and wife in their present incarnation.

If there was any doubt of this, the Source had spelled it out in Edgar's first Life Reading, only he and the others who had read it hadn't understood its greater import. "In the plane before this . . . in the court and rule of the second Pharaoh, Hugh Lynn Cayce, or Rameses . . . the high priest [Edgar Cayce] gave the religious element and force in the age . . . yet was cut short [by giving into temptation] and taking [Gertrude] and leaving the shores of this country [which resulted in baby Gladys' death]. That same entity that was taken is at present in this earth's plane, the companion and mate as should be in the present sphere, Gertrude Cayce."

Gladys didn't openly discuss what she had learned in these readings. The truth of how she felt, however, is both evident in the questions that were later put to the Source and also in her medical records which she, as the first Cayce archivist, entered into the files as they related to uterine cancer treatments that were recommended in her readings. Her cancer, the readings made clear, was a result of stress from sexual repression. In one physical reading after another, the Source recommended that Gladys undertake exercises, meditation, and therapy to combat depression and physical problems stemming from that stress.

Edgar, too, felt the stress. He experienced deep kinship and love for Gladys and was inclined to express that love as he would if she were his wife. Yet, for the sake of his marriage, he could treat her only as a daughter, and even this, only in the role of a beloved secretary.

One can only imagine how Gertrude, who conducted several of these readings, must have felt. Although she was Edgar's wife "in the flesh," there was another bound to him "in spirit" and according to the readings, attached into eternity. Back in Hopkinsville, she had long fretted over the "third other," the Source, which had inserted itself into their relationship. Now there was a love triangle that trumped anything that had ever come before. Gertrude, age forty-three, was still recovering from three pregnancies and a life-threatening case of tuberculosis. She had aged twenty years in the past five. Gladys, a mere teenager, was fresh-faced and beautiful.

Like Gladys, Gertrude never went on record to say how or what she was feeling. All that is clear is that a discussion between her and Gladys must have taken place-given the kinds of questions they would ask the Source in their readings. From these questions it is clear she understood that the circumstances in Dayton in which they found themselves were karmic and, more important in the larger picture, that how each of them chose to handle the challenge would determine their future challenges or blessings to come.

"For the best development each must give of the other self in no uncertain terms if the best would come [from the Cayce work]," the Source said. "For they [Gladys and Edgar] are knit in one and their completeness will only be found in the other." As this intimacy might prove to create a challenge for their respective family members, the Source was requested to counsel them. The reply came: "Ever in that same loving relation as one holds for the other, for in fact they are one and their relation to each other's family ties should be the same . . . Patience endureth all things, yet if we have not the love that is found between these in their relations, we become as a sound or as a tinkling of the vibration without the answering chord."

The concept of an answering or resonating "chord" was similar to references Cayce made to what he experienced in prayer, only here was something more fundamental and transcendent: a true union of souls, both physical and mental. In this regard, the Source specifically said that sexual relations between Edgar and Gladys, if handled discreetly, would not be inappropriate if they so desired and would enhance their "unity." Physical relations between them could be very special indeed and different from those between other consenting adults, because Edgar's body was truly hers, and her body his. However, the Source again qualified its response. Their work would be judged, now and into the future, by how they comported themselves in this incarnation.

The decision was made to abstain from any carnal experience, if not for the sake of Gertrude, but for the greater work. If they were to turn themselves over to giving readings full time, as they had now wholeheartedly agreed to do, they had to put their trust in one another and in the Source, else there was no point in doing what all three of them now understood to be their life's work.

In the years to come, many people involved with Edgar and Gladys believed that there was something special between them. Townspeople in Virginia Beach would always question why it was that a beautiful young woman remained unmarried, not go out on dates, and conversely give herself–heart and soul–to a married middle-aged man. They had no idea of the real struggle and challenges that were put before Gladys, Edgar, and Gertrude.

Gladys, however, had a profound reason for holding to her commitment, as did her "twin soul." Her work was his work and Gertrude's too. They would ultimately be together. Just not in this lifetime.

Later readings would reveal that Gertrude had also found her twin soul in her son Hugh Lynn.

Morton Blumenthal, c. 1922.

Morton Blumenthal:

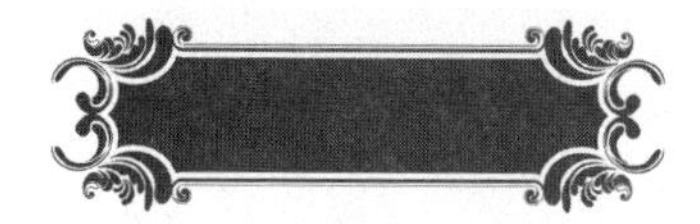

The Mythic Achilles

Lammers had introduced the team to a dream that had seemed to be well within their grasp. Under the right leadership, a Cayce hospital and psychic research center could potentially touch the lives of thousands. What Evangeline Adams had accomplished by bringing astrology into the main stream, Edgar Cayce could do for holistic medicine and perhaps much more, given the new insights that were being gleaned from the Life Readings. Still, the team needed a business manager—someone who could not only help the family climb out of debt and raise funds to be build a hospital, but could also streamline the process of how readings were given and received. On August 13, 1924, the Source named several suitable candidates, including one of David Kahn's new friends, Morton Blumenthal, a twenty-nine-year-old Jewish stockbroker from New York.

Kahn had met Morton through a mutual friend in Altoona, Pennsylvania, where Morton had been born and where Kahn was in the midst of negotiating a business deal to expand what had become a modestly successful furniture manufacturing plant. They got along

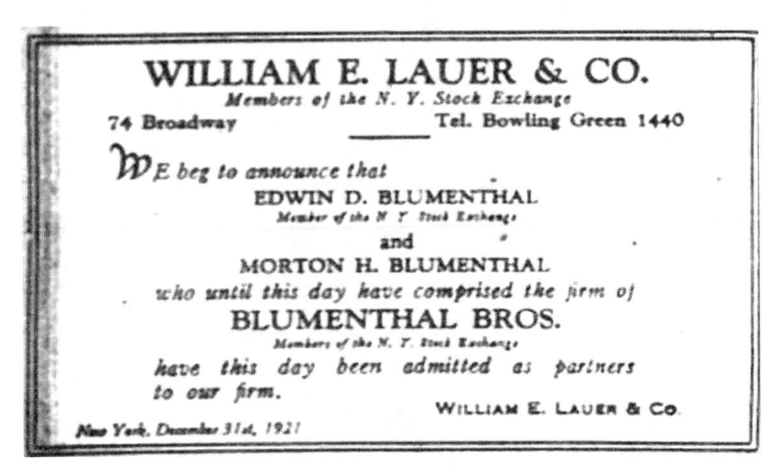

WILLIAM E. LAUER & CO.
Members of the N. Y. Stock Exchange
74 Broadway Tel. Bowling Green 1440

WE beg to announce that
EDWIN D. BLUMENTHAL
Member of the N. Y. Stock Exchange
and
MORTON H. BLUMENTHAL
who until this day have comprised the firm of
BLUMENTHAL BROS.
Members of the N. Y. Stock Exchange
have this day been admitted as partners to our firm.
WILLIAM E. LAUER & CO.
New York, December 31st, 1921

The William E. Lauer & Co. announcement, 1921.

instantly. Morton was the son of a shopkeeper, who had died when Morton was a child. He and his brother, Edwin had supported their mother while working their way through school and eventually landing positions at the prestigious William Lauer brokerage house on Lower Broadway.

Beyond Morton's business acumen, he was a prolific reader and had studied philosophy at the University of Pittsburgh and Columbia, where the core programs included classes in metaphysics as well as social philosophy and jurisprudence. Though Jewish, he could quote long passages from the New Testament and was as familiar with the work of Helena Blavatsky as he was with Aristotle, Plato, and Henry James. As Kahn would enthusiastically write, Morton "had a burning desire to understand the secrets of the universe." The enterprising Kahn, always the salesman, also noted that Morton had an ear infection and suggested that his friend, Edgar Cayce, could help.

The first reading Blumenthal received was not the success that either he or Kahn hoped it would be. No overt mention was made of an ear infection. Rather, the Source provided a general diagnosis of his health with an emphasis on improvements that could be made to his circulation and nervous systems. Overall, he was in good health. A second reading was conducted to clarify the first. The problem he was having with his left ear wasn't an infection the Source said, but the result of the circulation problem detailed in the first reading. This satisfied Blumenthal that Cayce had, in fact, been correct in his diagnosis. It was the business and marital advice that was tacked onto the second reading that made him enthusiastic about the potential of the readings. Intrigued, he agreed to share with Kahn the expense of bringing Edgar to New York, where they could meet in person. Funds to take him there, along with a modest stipend to cover the household expenses while he was gone, were promptly sent to Dayton.

Edgar was impressed when he met Blumenthal at the Hotel Cambridge in early October. Slightly built and short in stature with fine aquiline features, Morton was handsome and sophisticated with a keen intelligence and a businessman's practical approach to life. Unlike his brother Edwin, with whom he partnered at the brokerage company, Morton was introverted and much preferred an intimate conversation over a leisurely home-cooked meal at his apartment where he lived with his mother, than a night out on the town.

Edgar Cayce in his Sunday best, 1922.

Morton was not as impressed with Edgar as he with him. As Morton later admitted to Kahn and would later write of the experience, he was put off by Cayce's lack of education, poor attire, and slow Kentucky drawl. What he found inspiring was what came through in their first New York trance session, which was conducted by Kahn on October 10th. In what was likely the first Cayce reading given on the stock market—what would eventually comprise over five hundred such readings—Morton asked which holdings in his portfolio would be the most profitable. With the same uncanny accuracy Cayce had described oil deposits in Texas, he counseled Blumenthal to steer clear of commodities and utilities and go with "rolling stocks and oil" which the Source indicated followed easily identified and repeated trading patterns.

Four days later, Dave Kahn conducted the first of what would be four Life Readings on Morton. The astrological information that came through was not unique in the greater body of Cayce's Life Readings, but notable in that Blumenthal was said to be positively influenced by Neptune. Unlike Lammers, he would find strength and success near the water. Also hopeful for a partnership were references to Morton's accomplishments in past lives where he had assumed positions of leadership. As a reward or a responsibility for past-lives well spent, he had been granted much in the way of worldly goods and further, according to the readings, could expect at age thirty-five in 1930 to be given greater blessings, at which time he would assume a position in which many others would rely upon him. How he chose to use what he was given, whether in the "correct manner" to bring "satisfaction to self and others" or conversely "distress," would determine whether or not the riches would remain under his stewardship. Should he succeed in remaining true to the spirit in which these blessings were granted to him, he would be able to rise above the karmic cycles of sojourns that repeatedly had tested him. His present incarnation, in other words, could be his last.

If this were not enough to raise Blumenthal to the top position on the list of potential business managers for a Cayce hospital, what came next confirmed his suitability. Among several of his important previous incarnations, he was identified as the mythic figure of Achilles, who had overcome Hector and led the Greek army's assault on the city of Troy. Just as the Source had identified Lammers as having been the real life Hector, Blumenthal was identified as his nemesis, anointed by the Gods, the readings said, to be invincible in battle.

Had Edgar, Klingensmith, and Shroyer conspired with him, at

Achilles in Battle,
artist unknown, c. 1877.

Lammers' expense, to facilitate the taking of Troy? This was the implication. Further, it seemed synchronistic that Achilles should appear in the readings after Hector had been given his chance and was found wanting. The Source did not reveal the details—only that it was abundantly clear that Blumenthal figured prominently in the same soul group as Edgar.

The question that wasn't asked, but perhaps should have been, was the metaphoric significance of how Achilles, said to have been invincible, had died after nine years, just before his army succeeded in capturing Troy. The Source merely supported what had been said in the Homeric legend. Achilles died from a wound to his heel inflicted by Hector's brother, Paris. While Hector's death would be described in detail in the readings and later in dream interpretations, Achilles' demise was not. Had he somehow lost favor with the universal forces that had made him invincible?

Readings were also conducted for Morton's brother, Edwin. He, too, it was revealed, was part of a team who had formed eons earlier, long before Troy. Together with Morton, Edwin had seen to the rebuilding of Jerusalem. Together they could build and alternately destroy cities, the Source indicated. Of particular interest were references to Edwin's capacity for psychic development.

Edwin Blumenthal

In Edwin's readings, more than for any other individual who had or would receive trance advice, the Source outlined a detailed plan on how to best develop psychic abilities. The recommendations included a daily regime of rising at an early hour to pray and meditate, a list of what foods to eat, and suggested twenty-to-thirty-day periods of complete solitude. Edwin, who would receive stock market advice as did his brother, was told that if he followed this advice, he wouldn't need Cayce to successfully trade on the market. He would be able to do it himself.

Cayce left New York more excited than he had been since meeting Lammers. He was thus delighted when two weeks later, on November 2nd, Morton and his mother visited Dayton to obtain more readings and to explore how a potential partnership might work. As Morton would later write of the experience, he was stunned by the sheer poverty in which he found Edgar and his family living. "The two boys, Hugh Lynn and Edgar [Evans], looked undernourished," and "Gertrude was thin and wan, her fingers almost skeletal in appearance."

Morton found the conditions so bleak and squalid that before sitting down and getting to know the family, he dispatched his mother to the grocery store. She returned with several bushel baskets of dry goods, meat, and vegetables. Gertrude immediately proceeded to make a meal, which Morton said the Cayces promptly scarfed down. How the family was living in such abject poverty when giving health readings for some of the Dayton's wealthiest families was beyond him. They obviously needed a business manager.

Morton took control of the situation immediately. In addition to sending the Cayces a weekly stipend, in return for which he and his brother would receive daily business and spiritual readings, he brought Gladys and the entire family to New York on what was the first true vacation they had ever had. Gladys, who had never been in a city larger than Dayton, described the trip as her dream come true. Accompanied by Morton and staying in a suite of rooms at the Hotel Cambridge adjacent to his own, they attended a Broadway show, ate dinner at the Plaza Hotel, and went dancing at a New York nightclub. On their second day in the city, while Edgar and the boys took in the sights, Morton's mother took the women shopping and treated them to lunch in a fancy restaurant.

The Plaza Hotel, c. 1920s.

Edgar was only too pleased to give readings for Morton, his family, and their friends. Among them was one for newspaper columnist and financial wizard Merryle Rukeyser, with whom Morton had taken courses at Columbia University. Freda Blumenthal received the first of what would be many readings, as did Edwin's wife, a wealthy socialite. The most important reading, from Morton's point of view, was for twenty-year-old Adeline Levy, the future Mrs. Blumenthal, who was visiting from her home in New Orleans.

Morton was not what would be termed a lady's man, though he had dated widely. Miriam Miller, a show-girl, had been a favorite and was also the first of the women in his life to receive a trance reading. Now it was Adeline's turn, and he held out great hope that the Source would endorse what he himself believed to be true: that she would make an ideal companion. Jewish as he and intellectually inclined, she came from a wealthy and prominent family, traveled widely, but was not flashy or ostentatious. Morton's instincts were correct, according to what came through in trance. The petite dark-haired beauty was ideally suited to be his wife. She had been no less than Helen of Troy, for whom Morton, as Achilles, had waged war on that city. Just as Gladys had found her way back to Edgar, Morton had found his soul mate in Adeline.

Thus, two partnerships were established on the same trip to New York. Morton would marry Adeline, and he would become the Cayces' business manager. How this would play out was anyone guess, but based on the information coming through in the readings, the partnership with the Cayces could bring results well beyond what even they could imagine. A Cayce hospital was just a beginning, the Source suggested, of what they could accomplish together.

To get them started, Edgar was put on a retainer of $50 a week, and Gladys would be paid $25 a week as his stenographer. Kahn's assumption and Cayce's, too, was that readings were to be given on the stock market, which indeed were conducted. What came as a surprise was Morton's deeper interest in the more fundamental foundation of the work—how God and the Divine forces worked to bring about the greater good. A practicing Jew, Morton wanted readings on the life of Jesus Christ. Did Jesus the man actually exist, and were the accepted details of his life as put forth in the Bible accurate?

In many respects—given how often Biblical admonitions and allusions had appeared in the readings—it is curious that questions such as this hadn't been asked before. Perhaps Edgar was reluctant to find out the truth, as had been the case with astrology. Likely it was this and more. Cayce, a dedicated and fundamentalist Christian, had been hard pressed to accept the concept of reincarnation and was still wrestling with how the cycling of a soul through time reconciled with the Scriptures. But at Morton's behest, the readings were conducted. To Edgar's relief, "the Jesus readings," as they were henceforth called, didn't contradict what was said in the Bible. Rather, they greatly expanded what was believed to be true of the life and times of Jesus Christ.

The most exciting revelations concerned what happened prior to the Messiah's birth, a topic not covered in the Bible. According to the readings, preparations were made to welcome the soul that was Jesus several hundred years before his birth in Bethlehem. These preparations were made by a group known as the Essenes or the "Brotherhood." They were described in the readings as "a noncelibate religious order within Jewry," whose primary purpose was to be the channel through which Jesus would incarnate. At the time Cayce provided this information, the discovery of the Dead Sea Scrolls was still more than a decade away and next to nothing was known about them. The Cayce readings not only confirmed what was proven true by the Qumran discoveries, but they also explained the archaeological evidence of Essene settlements and religious practices that were discovered a half century after Cayce's passing.

The Jesus readings would detail how Essene priests selected two maidens who were to be dedicated as potential channels for the Messiah. Among them was Mary, who had been raised in the Essene community since the age of four, and between the age of twelve and thirteen was the "one chosen" by the Angel Gabriel. Indeed, according to the readings, Immaculate Conception took place. This was explained by the soul relationship between Mary and Jesus as well as their relationship with God. Like Edgar and Gladys, Mary and Jesus were "twin souls," thus making it possible, with God's help, for Mary to conceive and still remain a virgin. There was far more detailed information to come, such as the so-called missing years of Jesus after his birth and prior to meeting John the Baptist and beginning His ministry. The

Jesus writing in the sand.
Each read something different.

Source revealed that Jesus had undergone training in India, Egypt, and elsewhere; that he had a brother and a sister, and that Mary Magdalene was a sister of Martha and Lazarus.

Eventually an entire book was compiled out of the details shared in the Jesus readings, along with references to when early Christian and Gnostic accounts of His life were edited out of what became the Bible, and how some stories were misinterpreted or incomplete. Such was the account of Jesus writing words in the sand when a woman, accused of adultery, was about to be stoned. The Bible reveals only that Jesus wrote in the sand. Cayce—in trance—reveals that the words he wrote miraculously appeared differently to each person who was present. They read only of their own sins.

Morton, more than anyone else, steeped himself in the Jesus readings and was so moved by them that he eventually converted to Catholicism. He was also the only person in the circle of confidants who urged Edgar to not only pay close attention to the advice coming through in the readings, but to also do exactly as the Source recommended. "If the readings say Virginia Beach, then that's where you should go," he told Edgar.

Morton further made the move possible. He increased Edgar and Gladys' salary, rented them a house in Virginia Beach, and provided $1,000 to get them there. The family didn't know what to expect—the city was merely an isolated summer community on the windswept Atlantic shores, hundreds of miles from anyone they knew—but it was where the readings had said they ought to go. The prospect of living in a home of their own after two years spent in hotels and efficiency apartments would be a welcome treat.

In September 1925, the Cayces and Gladys arrived by train in Norfolk and then continued by trolley to Virginia Beach. It would be several months before Morton, or anyone else, joined them there for a visit. The family was surprised, even shocked, by how desolate a location the Source had selected. Off-season the place looked like a ghost town comprised of two and three-story cottages, rooming houses, boarded-up souvenir shops, and a restaurant. The single hardware store was also the pharmacy. As Edgar soon found out, it was owned and operated by Virginia Beach's mayor who doubled as its postmaster.

The readings given for the Blumenthals, conducted twice a day and nearly every day but Sunday, were sent by mail or wired to New York. Now, in addition to the stock market readings and the ongoing Jesus readings, Morton began asking the Source to interpret his family's dreams, which would one day also comprise enough material to fill a book. Although Morton and Edgar had experimented with doing dream readings earlier in the year and the Source had specifically told the team to "pay more attention to dreams, for this is where truths are given," it wasn't until the family reached Virginia Beach that their true worth was revealed.

The most important of the early dream readings was given for Adeline, who was now pregnant with her and Morton's first child. In the first of what became a series of readings on behalf of the child, Adeline reported a "weak-minded" boy or child appearing to her. In trance, Cayce cautioned her to be extremely careful about controlling her thoughts, as mind was the builder. If she dwelt or obsessed over the dream, she might indeed give birth to a "weak-minded" child.

Adeline and Morton would work hard to maintain a positive attitude and put such thoughts out of their mind. However, a perfect storm of events threatened to throw Adeline into a depression. Over a period of less than nine months she suffered the unexpected death of her best friend, the passing of her mother, and finally the suicide of her father.

Morton and Adeline's baby, Morton Jr., was born on April 4th, 1927. By all appearances he was handsome and healthy, with blue eyes and blond hair, and grew up to be lively and rambunctious. He would also become "weak-minded" and ultimately be confined to a mental asylum.

Similar to the warnings given to Morton and Adeline was a dream interpretation warning given to Edwin and his wife. "[I dreamed of a] leak of what seemed to be liquor on our foyer rug, out of bottle . . . or keg," Edwin reported. Cayce—in trance—interpreted the message: "As is seen, this is as the warning to the entity as respecting liquors in and about the place, and in the use of same . . . Let not these conditions become the stumbling block either to health, position, or influential surroundings." The truth turned out to be as accurate as it had been for Morton Jr., only this time the family was able to act on the advice more effectively. Edwin's wife had a drinking problem, which she had assiduously kept secret. When confronted, she revealed the truth and, with intervention, was helped.

In the midst of the on-going readings, Morton began to devise a financial plan to make the Cayce hospital a reality. His first initiative was to send letters out to the hundreds of people who had received help from the readings. To his profound disappointment, they received so few responses that this plan was abandoned. The new plan was to use the Source to build a portfolio of stocks to buy a Virginia Beach property suitable for the hospital, and if all went well, go ahead and begin construction. The concept had much merit, as the stock market readings given to the Blumenthals over the past several years had been so successful that the two brothers had tripled their net worth and were about to buy their own seat on the exchange.

Though it was indeed true that nearly everyone in the market at this time was making money in what was a boom market, the information that was coming through Cayce was unique in important ways. Cayce—in trance—at times would quote daily figures as if he were a ticker tape machine. And in addition to market indicators, there came insights into decisions being made by CEOs and major shareholders, which could be used to sell short and buy long.

Also unique, and unlike the oil well and medical readings, the stock market advice coming through wasn't necessarily from the Source, or at least the same well of information as was assumed to generate most, if not all the advice being given. On several notable occasions, who or what came through during the stock market readings stopped and introduced themselves.

In addition to Morton's deceased father, there was millionaire motion-picture distributor Marcus Loew, Bamberger Department Store

Investment advice from the grave:
L. to R. Felix Fuld, Marcus Loew, and Elbert Gary.

chain founder Felix Fuld, and Elbert Gary, who helped to organize the U.S. Steel Corporation. All, with the exception of Morton's father, had died relatively recently in respect to their appearance in the readings. The best that Edgar and Morton could surmise was that they were acting as some kind of a team, working together on the other side to bring riches to the Blumenthal brothers, and by extension, the Cayces. From whom or what they were taking their marching orders was not clear. Strangely, the matter was not addressed until years later and then only in connection with a comprehensive series of questions put to Cayce to try and determine who or what was the source of his information.

For the time being, Morton and his brother were content that a consortium of spirits, if indeed this is who or what was coming through, continued to provide them the edge they needed to finance the building of a hospital.

Edgar Cayce standing in front of the soon to be completed Cayce Hospital, 1927.

Beyond readings on the stock market, dreams , and those health readings that were being given, yet another new type of reading was now becoming commonplace: those dedicated to "the work." These readings not only sought recommendations from the Source on the business plan to be adopted in the creation of the hospital, but also who should be hired and how they were to be paid. Readings were conducted to fine-tune the blueprints, prepare budgets, obtain the work permits, and to learn from whom they should purchase medical equipment.

Friends and neighbors in the sleepy Virginia Beach community, where cows sometimes strayed into the streets and nearly all full-time residents had chicken coops, couldn't have guessed how the occupants of the Cayce's modest three-bedroom bungalow spent their time or what was about to be built on a grassy knoll overlooking a remote stretch of the windswept beach. As envisioned in the blueprints and what soon began taking shape on what has become the corner of 67th Street and Atlantic Avenue, the Cayce Hospital for Research and Enlightenment was to be four stories with thirty bedrooms, a lobby, a dining room, a lecture hall, a library, and doctor's quarters.

In the days ahead, Dr. Thomas and Carrie House with their son, Tom Jr. moved from Hopkinsville to join the team. Edgar's father, Leslie, would begin doing chores at the hospital as would Annie Cayce, Edgar's only unmarried sister. Gladys' cousin, Mildred Davis, would come to help in the business office, joining Linden Shroyer who would help run business affairs. With varying degrees of success, all would be vetted by the Source.

In the summer and fall of 1928, the first months of hospital construction were marked by an attitude of cooperation and harmony. Edgar, Morton, and many others felt a "presence" watching over them and were gratified by a dramatic visitation in July of that year. In the course of a reading that was already in progress, an unexpected announcement interrupted the session.

"Hark!" came Source's booming voice. "There comes the voice of one who would speak to those gathered here."

Morton, Gertrude, Gladys, Dr. Thomas House, and others sat in stunned silence as the Archangel Michael introduced himself. Gladys would later remark that with his appearance came a "vibrational change" in the "energy forces" around them. The windows began to rattle in their frames, and a wind blew through the room with such force that she felt as if her stenographic pad was being pulled from her hands. Tears began to well in their eyes—Edgar's included—as the angelic presence spoke:

> ***I am Michael, Lord of the Way! Bend thy head, oh ye children of men. Give heed unto the way as is set before you in that Sermon on the Mount. For even as the voice of the One who stood beside the sea and called all men unto the way, that those that would harken might know there was again a staff in David . . . for in Zion thy names were written, and in service will come truth!***

An entirely different kind of work reading was being given. The participants gathered in the room, and those involved in creating the hospital were told that they being given a great opportunity and also a frightening responsibility to serve God. The hospital, though still far from opening its doors, would become a reality. But what they had yet to accomplish was more difficult than the construction still to come. They would have to learn to cooperate with one another. As Archangel Michael made clear, among the participants in the venture were those who had been pitted against one another in previous incarnations. Their success was dependent upon them acting as one entity under God.

Though shocked, surprised, honored, and altogether humbled by the appearance of what they presumed to be their guiding spirit, Edgar and Morton knew all too well what was being asked them, for a tug of war for control over the hospital had already began.

The most notable incident occurred when Morton, wiring them from New York, called a sudden halt to construction. He had received billing statements for twice what he had expected. Edgar had then informed him that significant alterations had been made to the plans, including adding a bath between each of the ten second-floor bedrooms, and another bathroom in the hall on the third floor. Edgar had, by his own admission, given permission to the contractor to go ahead with the changes.

Up until this point, Edgar had believed that he was in charge of the building operation. After all, how could Morton oversee construction from the floor of the New York City stock exchange, and if not Morton, then who? And further, hadn't the readings specifically said that Morton ought to be manager of the partnership? The Source hadn't said he was to be the lawgiver on all that was to take place. Morton agreed, in principle, that Edgar was right and called the construction crew back to work. He also admitted that he couldn't supervise the daily operations. He felt he was needed in New York where he was buying and selling stocks to make the hospital a reality. However, the truth of the matter was that he wanted to control what was taking place and as the chief and albeit only significant benefactor, believed that his word was final. This would, in retrospect, be his Achilles' heel.

Edgar Evans Cayce in Virginia Beach, c. 1930.

Edgar Evans:

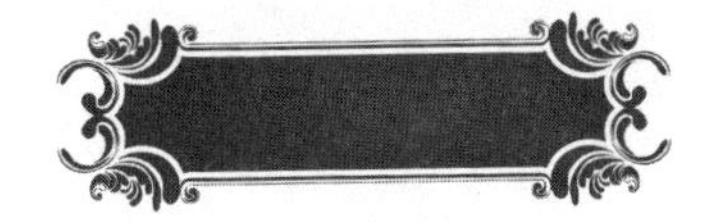

In Atlantis

While Morton was raising money for the hospital using the stock market readings, Edgar launched his own initiatives designed to generate income to support its operation. These efforts were to locate new oil fields, to find buried treasure, and to patent innovative engineering technology coming through in medical and scientific readings.

One treasure-hunting endeavor brought Edgar's Source to the Bahamian island of Bimini where, according to the readings, a storeroom of pirate gold could be found buried close to a distinctive combination of landmarks. Edgar gave four readings dedicated to finding it. But mere days before a search party could land on Bimini to begin the search, a devastating hurricane erased the landmarks identified in the readings and destroyed the hotel where they had booked rooms. Although the treasure was not found, from the readings came riches of another kind: a geographical location for the mythical continent of Atlantis.

References to Atlantis had appeared in several early Life Readings,

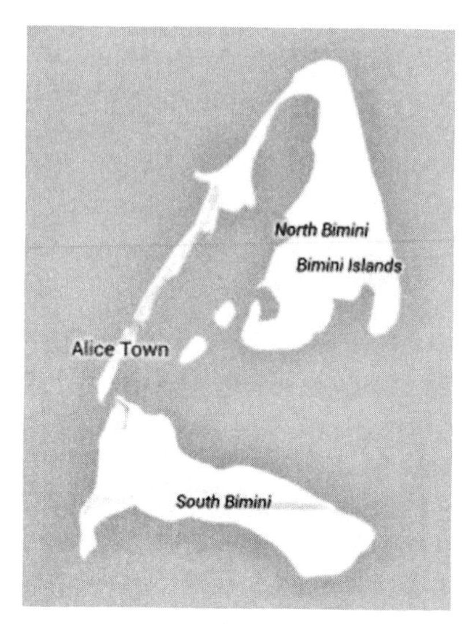

Bimini Island in the Bahamas directly east of Miami, Florida.

but until the hunt for treasure on Bimini, the Cayces and their friends hadn't thought of the vanished or submerged continent as a place that had actually existed. Just as they had previously opened their minds to the possibility that ancient Troy had existed, they now did so with Atlantis. Their understanding began to change in a reading conducted on March 2, 1927, when the Source said that a temple of the "Poseidians" was once located near Bimini. This triggered further inquiry and would result in an intensive investigation that would one day lead to a study of six hundred Life Readings that mentioned Atlantis, Poseidia, or Alta—the various names the Source associated with the lost continent. The story that emerged, whether poetic invention or actual events, was a saga covering some 200,000 years before recorded history.

Throughout his life Edgar Evans Cayce, whose Virginia Beach bedroom looked out on the Atlantic, would embrace the Atlantis readings more than anyone else. His Life Readings were the first to detail events in the mythic kingdom and suggested both the magnificence and tragedy of Atlantis. Just as Hugh Lynn's passion became the Life Readings and he would eventually write books and articles on reincarnation,

Edgar Evans would become an Atlantis expert which allowed him to lecture and author his own book based on his study of the readings. To him, the study of Atlantis wasn't a fanciful exercise in historical plausibility, but a stirring and convincing means to probe frightening parallels between Atlantean culture and modern times.

The first mention of Edgar Evans' connection to the "land of the Poseidians" was in his second Life Reading, which had been conducted back in Dayton in 1925. Edgar Evans was said to have been born with considerable mechanical and engineering skills which he had developed in his Atlantean incarnation, and he had carried these skills though all of his subsequent lifetimes. Among other incarnations, he had been a mechanical engineer in Germany who had helped to develop the first steam engines and before that in Egypt, where the readings suggested he had played an important role in developing technology that had helped to build the pyramids.

The Source went on to describe how his innate and well-earned engineering talents would be much in demand in his present life. How he chose to use them, the readings further suggested, wouldn't only impact his future career but would also potentially play an important role in future world events. Here was a good reason for the inquisitive and scientific-minded Edgar Evans to feel compelled to know more. Answers were provided in the series of readings dedicated to Atlantis begun in 1932, and in subsequent years additional information was drawn from the Life Readings of those identified as having lived there.

In the third reading in this Atlantis series the Source came right out and said that Atlantis had existed and was once a large continent whose borders stretched between the Gulf of Mexico and the Mediterranean. "That the continent existed is being proven as a fact," the Source said and went on to describe archaeological excavations then being conducted in Mexico.

The Source claimed in a second reading that evidence of Atlantis had actually been found in the Yucatan in the form of a stone marker or tablet, which was at that moment being shipped to a museum to Pennsylvania, though archaeologists didn't recognize what they had found as being from the ancient kingdom. Evidence of Atlantean culture was also said to exist in the Pyrenees Mountains, Morocco, British Honduras, Peru, and Central America. Further, the Source identified

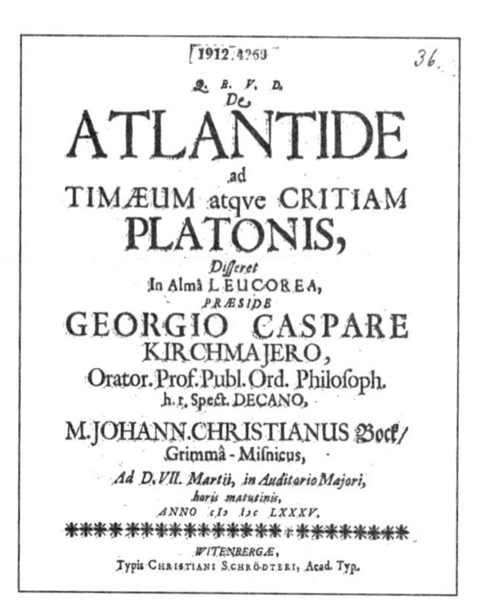

[1912.4?69 36.

Q. B. V. D.

De

ATLANTIDE

ad

TIMÆUM atqve CRITIAM

PLATONIS,

Differet

In Almâ LEUCOREA,

PRÆSIDE

GEORGIO CASPARE

KIRCHMAJERO,

Orator. Prof. Publ. Ord. Philosoph.

h. t. Spect. DECANO,

M. JOHANN. CHRISTIANUS Bock/

Grimmâ - Misnicus,

Ad D. VII. Martii, in Auditorio Majori,

horis matutinis,

ANNO cIↄ Iↄc LXXXV.

****

WITENBERGÆ,

Typis CHRISTIANI SCHRÖDTERI, Acad. Typ.

Plato's *On Atlantis,* copy c. 1685.

portions of the British West Indies and Bahamas as parts of the once great continent that were still above water, most particularly Bimini.

The initial mystery was why descriptions in the readings were not of an "island," as had been specifically referenced in Plato's dialogues, dating to the fifth century B.C., in which Atlantis is described in a conversation among Egyptian priests. This was explained quite simply: Plato had only heard stories of what remained of the huge continent after successive waves of cataclysmic destruction caused massive portions of the continent to be submerged under the ocean. Students of the Cayce readings had to look much further back in history, several thousand years before Plato to the dawn of man's first incarnations on Earth, to understand the greater story. This was when Atlantis was a kind of cosmic Petri dish for souls incarnating on Earth.

The Atlantis readings describe a being named Amilius as the first soul or entity that God created. Along with the other souls that God would create, he didn't manifest in flesh and blood, but was an entity the readings described as "pure light." This is what, according to the readings, was symbolically referred to in Genesis when God said, "Let there be light." God was not saying let there be physical light or light from the sun, but rather, "light" of spirit or Divine light. Further, when

God said, "Let us make man in our image," He was saying, according to the readings, that He and Amilius co-created man in their spiritual image.

The Atlantis readings further describe how the first wave of light beings entered the earth realm and began experimenting with matter. According to the Source, these beings built bodies for themselves "much in the way and manner as the amoebae would [appear] in the waters of a stagnant bay, or lake." Their purpose was to experience physical reality through "sound, taste, and touch," something that couldn't otherwise be experienced in the dimension in which they existed. As symbolically described in the Bible, this led to the desire for carnal relations, as had been detailed in the information Edgar and Gladys had received in their Life Readings.

The unforeseen consequences of carnal relations drew mankind farther from God. Souls became trapped or "hardened" in what were described as a wide variety of "inferior" physical forms. The readings suggest that there were beasts with humanoid-like appendages, reminiscent of creatures such as the half-man and half-beast Minotaur discussed in ancient Roman and Greek mythology. These monstrosities or sub-humans were burdened by cumbersome bodies and low intelligence, though in subsequent years would lose some of their animal attributes. A more superior life form was needed to become "the temple of the soul."

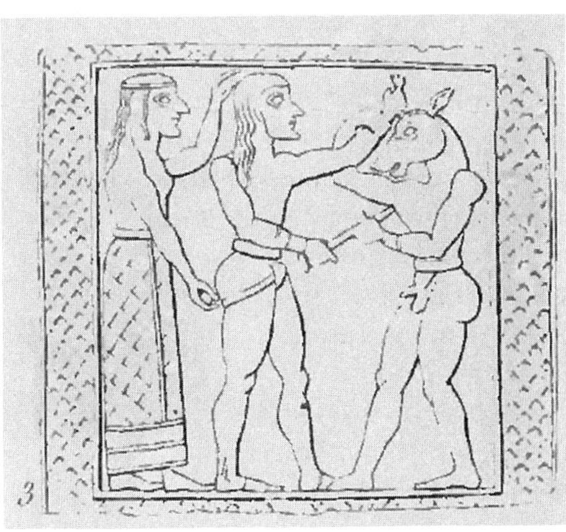

A depiction of the Greek Myth Theseus and the Minotaur.

The Source would again draw a connection back to the Bible. Amilius was said to have incarnated as Adam, the "first son of God." He did so by his free will to try and liberate the lost souls who had become trapped in the physical plane. Adam created a companion in Eve, the first "twin soul," and together they sought to help the trapped souls return to God through the power of free will.

Atlantean culture developed first because this was where Amilius, as Adam, and many of his fellow "sons of God" first began working together to subdue the beasts of the earth and bring souls back to God in the superior human body. Together the sons of God established a temple dedicated to the "Law of One," which was to serve as an example or model of morality to point the way. As Adam's "work" had begun in Atlantis first, that continent had a head start over other cultures that co-existed on the planet.

Though the population of Atlantis would pass through the same stages of human development that Cayce described as five other "root" races on the planet, they progressed much more rapidly because, thanks to Amilius, they had found a means to keep peace and work together for the common good. Psychic power among the Atlanteans was highly developed and described in the readings as "gifts of the spirit." Among the Atlanteans these powers permitted foreknowledge of events to come and a more intimate or direct knowledge of plant and animal life.

The technology described as being developed in Atlantis was said to be far beyond anything that existed elsewhere on earth. At a time when nomadic tribes in what is now Europe and Asia were presumably still living in caves, Atlanteans had learned to farm, replenish the soil with fertilizer, build canals for irrigation and bathing, and develop specialized metallurgical techniques. Poseidia, the Atlantean capital, was built such that river water was channeled through aqueducts and canals to be used as thoroughfares and then into pools where residents bathed and played sports.

Over time Amilius or Adam confronted unforeseen challenges. "Divisions [arose] between those of the Law of One–the sons of God who had retained their purity–and the sons of Belial," the readings said. The sons of the Law of One differed from the sons of Belial who sought "the gratifying, the satisfying, the use of the material things for self, without thought or consideration as to the sources of such, nor the hardships in the experience of others." Further, Cayce said, "They were those without a standard of morality. The sons of Belial had no standard, save of self." Bloodshed and territorial wars resulted from the disregard for the rights and freedom of others. The few took control over the many for their self-gratification. In response, Amilius established temples or shrines in an effort to remind the population of their divinity.

According to the Source, "[The] first upheavals [in Atlantis] were brought about when the activities of the sons of Belial brought to the daughters of the children of the Law of One the abilities for enjoying the pleasures of excesses of every nature in human relationship as well as those related to same." Much the same was stated in another reading: "[They gradually began] polluting themselves with those mixtures that brought contempt, hatred, bloodshed, and those that build for desires of self without respect of other's freedom, other's wishes."

While this was taking place, the Atlanteans continued to make remarkable technological progress. Among their accomplishments were inflatable flying devices made of animal skin, in which they traveled to developing cultures, such as in Egypt and Sumeria, with whom they shared some of their culture and technological advancements. Foremost among their technological advancements was a type of crystal device called the "Tuaoi" that Atlanteans could use to directly contact God. The readings suggest that the general populace gradually lost the ability to use the Tuaoi as it was intended, and a class of high priests then acted as intermediaries.

A problem that both the Atlanteans and the other cultures continued to have was the menace of huge carnivorous beasts or "prehistoric animals" that trampled the forests, destroyed the fields, and consumed vast quantities of food. Birdlike raptors hovered in the skies, feeding upon whatever could be scavenged. These creatures were a danger to mankind everywhere. Herein lay the root of what would cause yet another upheaval which would contribute to the ultimate destruction of the continent. Atlanteans decided to use their advanced crystal technology to hunt and slaughter the beasts. Technology which was intended to help man communicate with God became a weapon, resulting in earthquakes which divided the continent into five different land masses.

A hypothetical Tetrapteryx as imagined by William Beebe (1915).

Similar in some respects to the Tuaoi—perhaps a derivative of the same crystal technology—Atlanteans had now developed a "power station" fueled by what was described as a "firestone." Around 28,000 B.C., according to the Source, the firestone was "unintentionally tuned too high" and resulted in an earth-shattering explosion which heated the ground and caused volcanic activity, leaving only three of the five islands—those named Poseidia, Aryan, and Og. The volcanic eruptions, or explosions, were of such magnitude that a tsunami flooded across parts of the world. According to the Source, this was the great flood depicted in the Bible for which Noah and his family built their ark. Large segments of the Atlantean population had to be evacuated; many of whom were associated with the Law of One who made their journey to other parts of the earth, most notably Egypt, the Yucatan, and Peru. As they were far more advanced than those of the cultures in which they settled, they would become high priests and spiritual guides among the developing cultures.

Here, as in so many instances to come, the readings provided missing links in the great cosmic puzzle presented in the Life Readings: Ra Ta, or the soul of Edgar Cayce in his latest incarnation, had been one of the Atlanteans who escaped to Egypt to become a high priest. Even more revelatory was what came through about Amilius, or Adam, the first soul to incarnate in human form. Where Ra Ta was said to have incarnated to help "prepare the way," Amilius was "the way." He was said in the readings to have incarnated as Enoch, the Biblical patriarch to whom God would reveal the mysteries of the universe and who was also known in Egypt as Hermes, the architect of the great pyramid. There were other incarnations as well: Melchizedek, a priest and king of ancient Jerusalem; Joseph, the faithful and righteous leader in Egypt; Joshua, the Israelite leader; and Zend, the father of Zoroaster. In his last appearance he would incarnate as Jesus.

A greater picture of the world history—fanciful critics said—came as a result of the Atlantean readings. However, unlike the medical readings, they didn't know what to do with them. To corroborate the Source's depiction of Atlantis would be as difficult as trying to prove the Jesus incarnations. What little substantive progress Edgar Evans made in later years to try and corroborate what had come through on Atlantis, such as tracking down the archaeological discovery that was said in the readings to be on its way to Pennsylvania, met with failure or were dismissed by critics as pseudoscience. Moreover, what came through the readings in 1933, covering the third and final phase of Atlantean destruction, was beyond rational belief and was hence deemed unworthy of serious consideration. However, given scientific developments soon to come, the information was not as implausible as originally thought.

According to the Source, the Atlanteans—now warring with one another—developed technology that was powered by a limitless source of electrical energy. This was described as a concentrated beam of light, much like a laser beam, emanating from what Cayce called "the mighty, the terrible crystal." The Source used the word "atomic" to describe the type of "electrical energy" or "electricity" being harnessed by the Atlanteans to power the device and to rebuild in the wake of the devastation at the end of the second destruction of Atlantis. They were also said to have used "rediscovered gases, and those of the electrical and 'aeratic' formations [those being charged with gas] in the breaking up of the atomic forces to produce impelling force . . . or of changing the faces or forces of nature itself." The principle innovation as described in the readings which fueled the "eternal flame" was "such as we may find in those that make for the active forces in that of uranium." Today, descriptions of atomic energy and laser technology aren't science fiction as they were eighty years ago when Cayce gave these readings.

There were other interesting revelations given. For instance, according to the Source, persons who had incarnations in Atlantis "are all exceptional . . . They either wield woe or great development. And their influences are felt, whether the individual recognizes it in himself or not [in the new generation of incarnates on Earth]."

Edgar Evans Cayce (1918 to 2013).

The personal reason Edgar Evans became obsessed with the subject was that he was one of those souls said to have witnessed the Atlantean cataclysm. Not only this, he had been one of the Atlantean scientists responsible for the destruction that ultimately led to the end of the first phase of life on the continent. This was presumably why, in his first Life Reading, the Source suggested that there would be many who would "dread" his soul's return to the earth plane. The Source counseled Edgar Evans that he must always "keep close to the spiritual guidance [of Christ Consciousness]," and "depart not from same." The suggestion here was that Edgar Evans had the potential to do great harm in his present incarnation should he indulge that selfish part of himself which created such misery in Atlantis.

Edgar Evans took this warning to heart, as did his parents. A precocious child with intense mathematical and scientific interests along with a passion, as Tommy House and Dave Kahn observed, "to blow things up," his family channeled his tendencies to civil and electrical engineering. Upon his later graduation from Duke University and despite temptations in the form of job offers to work for military contractors, he steered clear of using his talents to participate in building weapons systems.

Few people outside of the immediate Cayce family felt such relief when during World War II he removed himself from combat or any weapons operation duty and instead joined the Army Signal Corps. While older brother Hugh Lynn joined General Patton in Europe, Edgar Evans was building a radar tracking station in Trinidad. As he said in his high school valedictory speech, successfully finding one's place in life meant meeting one's "responsibilities to God, to others, and to self" in that order and with devotion. This was how he chose to live his life, and before his death at age ninety-five in 2013 what is most remembered.

Marion Stansell at age 20.

Marion Stansell:

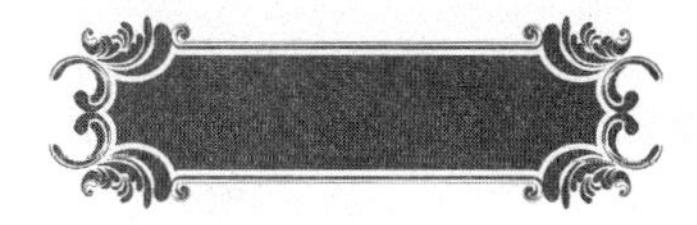

The Perpetual Motion Motor

Edgar Cayce had identified sixty people as having lived in Atlantis when he was asked in February 1928 to give readings for an invention that seemed as improbable as anything said to have been created in the antediluvian world: a perpetual motion motor.

The readings came at the request of Lucy Cooney, a woman from Birmingham who had received life-saving medical advice on a brief trip that Edgar and Gertrude made to Alabama to generate interest and support for the association which would operate the hospital. While visiting with Lucy and her husband, Robert, she shared the remarkable story of a neighbor, thirty-five-year-old Marion Stansell, an amateur inventor and engine mechanic who operated a Birmingham gas station and auto repair shop. Like oilman Edgar B. Davis, Stansell had visions in which he allegedly received direct communications from God. The Cooneys wanted to know if the visions were authentic and whether the Source could help him achieve his life's dream: a perpetual motion motor.

The story that the Cooneys told the Cayces was altogether fantastic.

Stansell had had a near-death experience while recovering from a gunshot wound and mustard gas poisoning in France during World War I. While recuperating in a hospital ward, he had contracted a virus infection and in his already weakened condition suffered heart failure which led to him being declared dead. Similar to others who reported near-death experiences, he claimed to have risen above his body and to have watched hospital staff hovering over him. He then became aware of his family back in Birmingham, who were praying desperately for his safe return home. In his vision, a "spirit guide" appeared who then escorted Stansell to what he described as a dimension inhabited by the recently dead. Not wishing to continue his astral journey, he asked to meet Jesus with whom he pleaded to be permitted to return to earth so that he could care for his family. Christ told him he could return if he committed himself to doing God's will. He would be given a formula for a mechanical device that could save the planet from certain environmental destruction. Twenty minutes after being declared dead, Stansell reawakened. Physicians were not only shocked to find him living, but that his infection was gone and the mustard-gas burns were fully healed.

Thanks to the Cooneys, a meeting was arranged with Stansell at Birmingham's Tutwiler Hotel where a medical reading was conducted on February 1. In trance, Cayce confirmed that Stansell's body had undergone a healing. He wasn't fully recovered and treatments were recommended to improve his overall health, but these were similar to recommendations given to many other relatively healthy people over the years. Most noteworthy, the reading indicated that Stansell had considerable "psychic talents" and that through "dreams and visions" he would be able to view blueprints for a revolutionary type of motor. According to the readings, this motor was designed in the spirit realm by De Witt Clinton, the deceased former governor of New York, who in his last incarnation on earth had been the creative force behind the development of the Erie Canal and other large-scale engineering projects. Having by now conducted upwards of a hundred or more stock market readings in which other entities had made appearances or stepped in to provide information, Cayce wasn't put off. He accepted the information as given.

This reading, and others to come, also suggested that with the trance

De Witt Clinton, the deceased former governor of New York. More guidance from beyond the grave.

assistance of Edgar Cayce, Clinton could provide precise technical information to Stansell. Further, the Source made clear that Stansell would require a dedicated team of like-minded Atlantean entrepreneurs—among them Morton Blumenthal and Tim Brown, Dayton auto parts inventor and manufacturer—to see the invention through to completion. Not only would motor-related readings eventually be given for Brown, whose creative efforts helped to establish Delco Electronics ignition systems, but readings would also be given to Charles Kettering, who would become chief of research and development for General Motors under William Sloan. Mr. Sloan's family members were also recipients of Cayce readings. Stansell, it seemed, was in very distinguished company, both in the flesh and blood and on the other side.

Blumenthal was as excited by the information as was Tim Brown and requested the first of twenty-one readings dedicated to the Stansell motor. The first, conducted at the La Salle Hotel in Chicago on March 8, 1928, set the tone for the many others to come. The device, as outlined, was to be constructed and operated in a large water-filled metal tank. Inside the tank would be suspended a drum containing compressed air or vapor which would rotate when the device was activated. Around the sides and inside the drum were metal sprockets, like pins sticking out of a pin cushion. These were described as functioning along the lines of spark plugs on an engine block. A "camshaft" running through the center of the drum would be connected to a caterpillar-type drive shaft to harness the motive force created by the rotating drum.

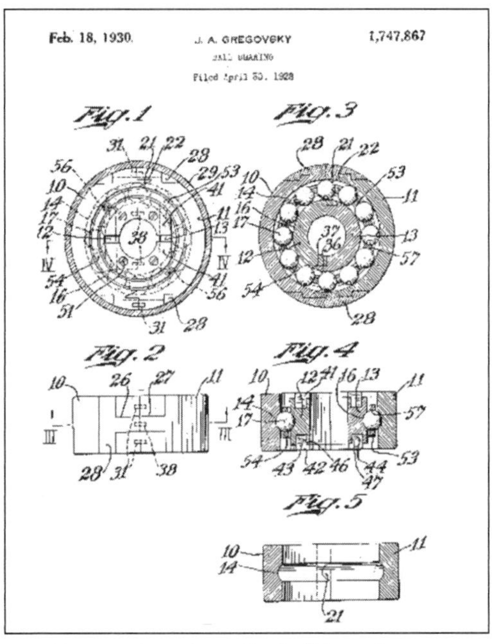

Patent drawings for ball bearings used in the Stansell motor.

In the theory presented by the Source, positively charged particles in the bottom of the vapor-filled drum would contract as they rose to meet negatively charged particles at the top. The result would be a rotational force causing the drum to spin and drive the camshaft. The action taking place in the metal drum was compared to the rotation of the earth: once put in motion, the drum would spin indefinitely until it was physically stopped. There would be no exhaust fumes or dangerous emissions, and it would require no fuel beyond that necessary to initially put the drum into motion.

Robert Cooney, acting as Stansell's business agent, tried unsuccessfully to explain to Cayce the basic science underpinning the invention. "The phrase 'getting something from nothing' is incorrect," he would write. "We know there is no such a thing as nothing. We do know that everything is a force or some form of energy. We do not know the relation of these forces of energy to each other—or, in other words, the Relativity of Force—but we can assume that this relationship exists. Therefore, in the case of our motor, when we look at the two substances, [essentially] water and air, we look at them as forces, and by using a mechanical contrivance to accentuate and retard these forces at the right time it is possible to utilize the resultant force or component force. This is what has been done in the Stansell Motor."

Edgar didn't himself enter into discussion of the science of what came through, but he did appreciate a warning referenced in the first reading to all participants who sought to work together to build the motor: "There must be perfect cooperation of the self and the will with those who would assist in perfecting this from the material side. Also there must be perfect cooperation with inner self to obtain that information."

With Edgar on board to give readings, Brown and Blumenthal jumped at the opportunity to help Stansell realize his dream. In the process, they naturally hoped for income to operate and expand the hospital and to enrich themselves as well, for the technical revolution that a perpetual motion motor would create in industry would be monumental. Imagine a world with an unlimited supply of clean energy freely available to everyone. No pollutants or emissions. No transmission lines. And enough power to fly a plane or drive a ship around the world.

Excited by the prospects, a contract was drawn up between Brown and Blumenthal to pool their resources and install Stansell at the Brinkman Engineering Company, a state-of-the-art motor technology incubator in Dayton, Ohio. It was also an expensive place to develop their invention as the partners would discover. In the first few months of experimenting at Brinkman, Brown and Blumenthal spent tens of thousands of dollars assembling what turned out to be two nonfunctioning motor prototypes.

Stansell's son, and others who saw the prototypes, described them as looking similar to a box-shaped evaporative cooler with a barrel-shaped drum suspended in the middle. This configuration remained the standard, though devices of varying sizes were created and subsequently scrapped as engineers began using more precise tools and materials as specified in the readings. When each new model was built, Brown requested and received numerous additional readings to explain why a particular model failed to operate as expected and to delve deeper into the underlying physics. Unlike previous engineering advice provided by the Source to various inventors who had approached Cayce in previous years, most notably Thomas Edison and Nikola Tesla, the Stansell motor partners were simultaneously compiling new theoretical concepts as they were actually building their invention. Most remarkable of all, and unprecedented in the history of science, highly qualified and credentialed engineers were working with a psychic.

To these engineers and others to come, Cayce used terminology and concepts which were consistent with accepted physics of his day, yet framing them in terms of a more comprehensive vision of what he termed God's laws. "Life in its manifestations is vibration," one such discourse began. The type or "wave length" of vibration, he said, determined how it acted in a given environment or dimension. "Vibration that is creative is one thing, vibration that is destructive is another . . . yet they may be from the same source, as in the electrical forces . . . in the [human] body . . . Remember, life is vibration, so is mind, so is matter." Accordingly, Cayce would state, "electricity . . . is the same energy . . . [that is called] God. Not that God is an electric light or an electric machine, but vibration that is creative [building rather than destructive] is of the same energy as life itself."

Most relevant to understanding how the Stansell motor operated, the Source drew a distinction between that energy which was of the "spirit" and that which was of "earthly manifestation." This was described as the Divine law of "polarity" acting upon the "First Cause," or God's energy force. In the Divine or spiritual realm, energy was described as positively charged or expanding. Earthly or material manifestation was both positively and negatively charged. Negatively charged vibrational energy, Cayce said, contracts rather than expands and creates, in essence, energy in motion.

Also according to Cayce, the action taking place between the positive and negatively charged particles was gravity or that in which "everything . . . is drawn to a common center . . . [Gravity is but] the centralization of the vibratory force [on the material plane]." Cayce further suggested that what was commonly understood as the magnetic attraction that a compass needle had toward earth's positive pole was one and the same thing as gravity. An apple falls to the ground for the same reason that a piece of metal clings to a magnet. The Earth's rotation or "radial force" was a result of gravity too or the displacement of "compelling forces." By altering the combinations of vibrations, one could change gravitational pull on the various elements to create, as the Source confirmed possible, an anti-gravity device.

The team members, however, were less interested in building an anti-gravity device than they were in the particulars of the Stansell motor. Simply put, it was said to operate on the principle of alternately changing the gravitational pull of vapor in the drum housing the motor. The sprockets or "sprankles" as they are referenced in the readings were tuning forks that transmitted the vibrational level of the vapor in the drum and acted on the gasses trapped inside, causing them to alternately rise to the top of the drum and then sink to the bottom. This action was described as being the same kind of centrifugal force as found in nature. By first setting the drum in motion, man was doing what God had done in the First Cause when his "directive force" or the release of vibrational energy created the universe and set the Earth and other planetary objects spinning in space.

Tim Brown, who with Stansell took the lead in development of the engine, apparently had the clearest understanding of the purported scientific principles being put forth, for much of the correspondence from Brown in Dayton to Edgar in Virginia Beach and Morton in New York was merely an attempt to explain what he thought the readings were saying. The problem was putting theory into practice.

Over the course of what became a three-year struggle to create an operational device, the Source provided a wide variety of technical reasons why each prototype failed to work. The greatest challenge, as Brown described it, was assembling the motor parts in proper order while submerged in water and simultaneously maintaining the right pressure inside the drum. Not only this, the various parts had to be assembled in the correct sequence or negatively charged gases in the drum would mix with the positively charged vapor. A lesser challenge, but still troublesome, was putting the assembly into motion when the device was precisely set along an east and west axis line. The Source said that this was necessary, Brown surmised, because the Earth's positively and negatively charged poles would otherwise interfere with the action taking place inside the drum.

One new prototype after another was built and then discarded. Among several enhancements, grooves were cut into the sprockets or tuning forks, a modification which was believed would speed the transfer of the vibration of the water in the tank to the vibration of the vapor in the drum. When the metal drum was judged to be too fragile for proper experimentation, a thicker metal skin was used, and its surface contours polished smooth. As Brown would note, with each new prototype variation all the other elements in the assembly had to be adjusted and new readings conducted to determine if they had gotten the configuration right.

Cooney appears to have been the first of the Stansell partners to bail on the ongoing experimentation. Brown simply dug in his heels. He was convinced that the principles behind the Stansell motor would not only make the partners rich but would also result in a technological revolution as important as the industrial revolution.

Certain that the team was on the right track and that only a minor reconfiguration of their most recent prototype would make the device operational, Brown and Blumenthal moved forward to have the device patented. In a reading on March 7, 1929, the Source was asked to estimate how much income their invention could generate. The response was "$10,000,000." This was surely reason to celebrate, along with the remark in a reading for Edwin Blumenthal that their latest configuration was correct. However, along with exciting news that they were nearing the completion of their invention, came a reminder similar to the one referenced in the first readings: the partners were to remember that "mind is the builder," and that proper thought must be given to their intent and purposes. As in the previous oil-well readings and again discussed in the Life Readings and now revisited in the science readings, endeavors of this kind required an accord before the good would manifest.

Oklahoma rancher and oilman Curtis Wilmot had said this best in a letter to Cayce back in 1923: "All hands have to be pulling together with a common purpose," and that common purpose couldn't be for the desire for riches but for "God's purpose," or the "First Purpose."

As optimistic as Blumenthal was at the time, the problem was not putting the machine in motion, but keeping it in motion. Regardless of how it was configured, it didn't rotate for more than a few revolutions before stalling. With the collapse of the stock market in the winter of 1929 and after the entry of a second psychic as chief consultant on the Stansell motor project, their business venture was over. Later still, after a fire destroyed the Brinkman Engineering Company in 1942, the prototype Stansell motors were sold for scrap metal. Twenty years later Stansell would pass on. All that had come out of the motor readings was an innovative design for ball bearings which Stansell, Cooney, and another partner patented but were unsuccessful in bringing to market.

However, throughout the years of prototype construction, Morton never lost faith in the device but let it go anyway. The ostensible reason was because his other grand project—the Cayce Hospital for Research and Enlightenment—had by this time become a reality.

Marion Stansell (and his wife). He worked on the motor right up until his death in 1963.

Thomas Joseph Sugrue (1907-1953).

Tom Sugrue:

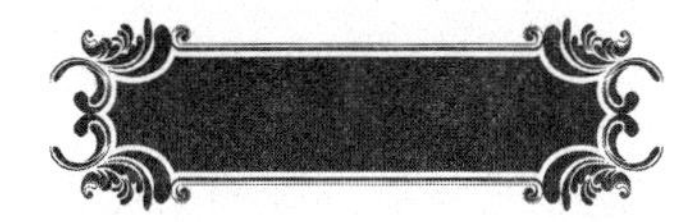

In the Shadow of the Pyramids

Edgar and Hugh Lynn worked alongside the construction crew putting the finishing touches on the main hospital building. Joining them on the scaffolding was Hugh Lynn's best friend, Tom Sugrue, on summer recess from college. Twenty-three-year-old Sugrue had more enthusiasm than talent as a carpenter, but he took to the concepts put forth in the Cayce readings as did few others. No one in Cayce's lifetime would write so extensively about Edgar or do more to popularize his work. But despite the tens of thousands of words that would pass through his typewriter, Sugrue kept secret the compelling personal reason he had such faith in Cayce. Nor would he reveal how he was a member of the same soul group being given an opportunity to accomplish in this lifetime what it had failed to do in ancient Egypt.

Sugrue's introduction to the Cayce work came in 1926 when he met Hugh Lynn at Washington and Lee University where they were both sophomores. Tom was wearing a beanie, strumming a ukulele, and singing an Irish ditty. The slight, redheaded young man from Naugatuck, Connecticut, asked Hugh Lynn where he was from. Hugh

Lynn told him Virginia Beach, and Tom responded with a disparaging remark that would set the tone for the next twenty-five years of their relationship.

Sugrue wanted to be a writer more than anything else. He had been out of high school for two years and was working as a teller at a Connecticut bank when the bank president asked him to write a story for the local newspaper about the company picnic. The article was well received and inspired him to enroll at Washington and Lee University. From the moment he and Hugh Lynn met, they argued over practically everything, sometimes settling their disagreements with a fistfight. They fought about the most mundane things—from how to decorate their dorm room to who was getting better grades. They argued about where they would live when they graduated, what was the best fraternity, and most of all, about religion.

Tom, a devout Catholic, had once considered studying for the priesthood. He not only rejected what Hugh Lynn had to tell him about reincarnation and the Jesus stories that Hugh Lynn claimed hadn't made it into the Bible, but he thought them absurd. Hugh Lynn finally challenged him to come to Virginia Beach and meet his father. Tom only agreed to do so, he said, with the intention of proving that "Cayce was a fake."

In private, Hugh Lynn revealed the great hopes he had for Tom in a letter to his father: "I have met one fellow . . . who will someday be well known as a writer . . . He is very interested and I am anxious to get him placed [on the list of those to receive Life Readings]. We get along miserably together, both too sarcastic and disagree on many big ideas, yet must have had some attraction [in a previous incarnation]."

A reading was arranged in June 1927 when Tom and Hugh Lynn came to Virginia Beach on their summer break to help with the hospital's construction. No sooner had Tom arrived than he began pontificating about the "ruse" of psychic phenomenon. Hugh Lynn and Gladys were happy to give him enough rope, as they said, "to hang himself."

Tom was not initially impressed with what came through in his Life Reading, as there were things that Hugh Lynn could have previously shared with his father. The Source discussed the influence various stars and planets had on Tom's behavior and described him as being "high minded" and a lover of the beautiful—whether in music, poetry, literature, or the outdoors. The Source said he was "one that is attracted to few, yet attracts many," that he was "eccentric in a manner . . . well seeing, well meaning . . . yet not well grounded."

Sugrue couldn't argue otherwise. He wrote poetry in addition to an unpublished novel, was an accomplished musician, and liked nothing better than being outdoors. A compelling argument could also be made that he was not well grounded: he gave into temptations all too easily, whether it was to take a swing at Hugh Lynn or make a pass at a college co-ed. It's what came next in the reading that piqued his interest.

The reading indicated that he, like Arthur Lammers, had once been a monk, suggesting that life in a cloister had not only fostered his interest in Catholicism, writing, and scholarship, but also in music. In his most recent incarnation he had been a crusader in the Holy Land. The Source said that this was why he had an innate desire to see the Holy Lands and write about them—which, in fact, Tom had desperately wanted to do and later, after a Jerusalem pilgrimage, he would write a book about them.

Tom's most relevant incarnation was as a scribe in ancient Egypt when he had become involved in a conspiracy that pitted Edgar Cayce, then the high priest Ra Ta, against Hugh Lynn, who was the Pharaoh. Tom had taken the side of Edgar against Hugh Lynn, who was being influenced by Morton. Hence it was no small wonder that Hugh Lynn and Tom were prone to argue as they did in this incarnation. There was serious karma that needed to be worked out between them.

"The entity then [was] among those who rose in rebellion at the expulsion of the priest [Edgar Cayce], and led against that throne [where sat Hugh Lynn] . . . and the entity gained and lost in that period, yet much of the present urge is seen from that experience . . . That of the counsel to many for the definite stand for Right as must be taken, and the urge to write [about the teachings] . . . and in same will there be found in the present experience the greatest forces as may be manifest by the entity."

Hugh Lynn and Edgar interpreted this to mean that Tom was participating in the reunion of souls that were drawn together from their Egyptian sojourn and that he would find his vocation in writing about what he learned from the experience. As the Cayces and Gladys well knew, one of the great accomplishments that the team had taken on in Egypt was building what the Source called "The Temple Beautiful," which was a center for health and rejuvenation, similar in many ways to what the Cayce hospital would be in modern times. Only in Egypt, the endeavor had ended with the expulsion of Ra Ta, the High Priest.

This interpretation made perfect sense to everyone but Tom. In the days that followed, however, when Tom had a chance to study the other Life Readings, his own started to make more sense. Edgar understood what he was going through. "Becoming accustomed to the ideas [in the Cayce household] is . . . like living with jungle tribesmen who do not wear clothes," Edgar explained to Tom. "After a year or two you realize you are the funny-looking one with all your clothing."

Sugrue became an outright convert to the work on his second trip to Virginia Beach the following December when he received a medical reading. What he was told left him shocked and stunned. In trance, Cayce revealed intimate details of his personal life that a normal person could not possibly have known—not even Hugh Lynn, who by this time was sharing a dorm room with him. The reading indicated that he had contracted gonorrhea—a fact that Tom had never disclosed to anyone—and warned that there would be dire consequences if he did not follow a special diet, injections of medication into his urethra, and what the Source described as "clean and pure living." In trance, Cayce counseled him not to worry, "for worry will bring the greater disturbances for the system."

Everything changed for Tom once this reading was conducted. Hugh Lynn reported how his friend began to study what had now become a massive archive of readings and at night would join the family to discuss reincarnation, astrology, and medicine. Together with Hugh Lynn, they made a concerted effort to overcome their karmic past and learn to work together. Fights still took place, but they were over how the readings were best interpreted. Sugrue would further obtain trance counsel on publishers and editors to whom he should submit manuscripts, and when later given the opportunity to write Cayce's biography, trance counsel on how aspects of the readings and people in them were to be best presented to readers.

As construction on the Cayce hospital neared completion, Sugrue

Tom Sugrue's and Hugh Lynn Cayce's entries in the Washington and Lee University 1930 yearbook.

made the decision to devote himself entirely to the work in Virginia Beach. "I have decided [upon graduation] to enter into the work as a life career," he wrote Edgar. "And since I have full faith in it and in you . . . I should at this time put myself entirely in the hands of . . . [the Source] both physically and mentally."

He went to work immediately, first enlisting the help of his and Hugh Lynn's favorite college professor. Thanks to their coordinated efforts, the distinguished Washington and Lee psychology professor William Mosely Brown became intrigued with the work being done in Virginia Beach and would give the hospital dedication address on November 11, 1928. Morton, standing next to Edgar after the stirring address, was so moved by the moment that he leaned over to him and said, "[Here] rises our great oak, Edgar, from the earth heavenward."

Tom and Hugh Lynn's ongoing relationship with Brown would further bring the professor into the Cayce fold. A few months later, when Morton proposed building a college on the same campus as the hospital, Brown was chosen as its president and tasked with selecting the faculty. Atlantic University would be to the academic community what the Cayce Hospital was to be to medicine.

The first hospital planning session was a wake-up call to the challenges that lay ahead for everyone. The arguments began the moment everyone sat down to business. The initial disagreement was over whether a tin or shingle roof should be put on the twelve-car garage that was then being constructed for employees behind the hospital. Next came heated discussions over employee salaries, hospital patient fees, and other financial matters. As Morton was paying the bills, he invariably got his way, which Tom understood from his own study of the readings was not how it was supposed to be. Morton and Edgar had to learn to work together just as Tom and Hugh Lynn were endeavoring to do.

William Mosely Brown
(1894-1966).

"The rebel who tried to wreck things in Egypt seems to have an opportunity to put things together this time," Tom alerted Edgar. "Let's all hope he has developed the strength necessary for it."

VIRGINIAN-PILOT
MONDAY, NOVEMBER 12, 1928

CAYCE HOSPITAL AT VIRGINIA BEACH OPENS NEXT MONTH

Formal Dedicatory Exercises For New Institution Conducted Yesterday

THIRTY PRIVATE ROOMS CONTAINED IN STRUCTURE

Virginia Beach realized another ambition yesterday with the dedication of the new $150,000 Cayce Hospital at One Hundred and Fifth street and Atlantic boulevard. Owing to inclement weather the exercises were held

The opening of the Cayce Hospital was celebrated in Virginia Beach! (at 67th and Atlantic Avenue).

Such concerns were put on hold when, on February 11, 1929, the Cayce hospital admitted the first patient—Michigan furniture salesman Charles Dillman—who was suffering from a chronic sinus condition. Nine days later his condition was gone. Before his departure, the second patient had arrived, a thirty-six-year-old woman who had been suffering from digestive problems for over a year. Two others would arrive before the month was out: a fifty-eight-year-old man with a tumor in his bladder and the wife of a pharmacist who had asthma, bronchitis, and gall bladder disturbances. Over the next ten months, over forty more patients would be admitted including Sugrue, being treated for venereal disease. Though Sugrue too would experience relief from his symptoms while at the hospital, unfortunate events already in the works would conspire against him completing his treatment and would come back to haunt him in a most tragic way: he would spend much of his later writing career confined to wheelchair.

This eventuality, however, was not on anyone's mind when all pitched in to make the Cayce hospital and Atlantic University a success. Never before had Edgar given so many physical readings and never before had there been so many physicians on hand to treat the patients exactly as the readings recommended. During the first three months of the new year, Edgar gave over two hundred readings, far more than had ever been conducted before. Also for the first time, there was a waiting list for appointments which ran months into the future. The difficult days in Dayton appeared to finally be behind them.

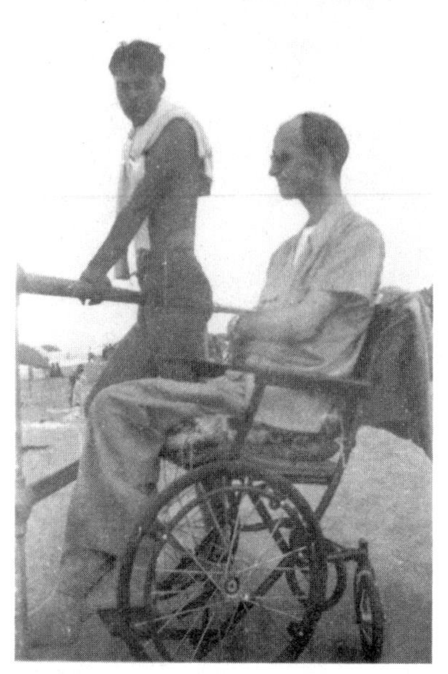

Tom would eventually live out his life in a wheelchair.

Morton shared Edgar's enthusiasm but quickly shifted his attention to Atlantic University. Although there would be standard courses in math, science and the arts, the college would offer what now might be termed a "New Age" curriculum. Inventors and engineers like Tim Brown and Marion Stansell would introduce students to new scientific concepts, and Morton and his brother would create a series of "cutting-edge" courses on philosophy, metaphysics, spiritualism, and the esoteric sciences suggested in the readings.

Tom and Hugh Lynn were equally excited, as they would both be employed at the university. Upon graduation, Tom would write PR copy for both the hospital and university and move into an apartment on the third floor of the hospital building. Hugh Lynn would be hired as the university librarian and in addition, take over the sports program. For young college graduates, the future truly held previously unimaginable possibilities. They were at the center of what promised to be a community unlike anything that had ever before existed—except, perhaps, in Egypt.

DR. WILLIAM MOSELEY BROWN HEADS NEW UNIVERSITY AT VIRGINIA BEACH, VA.

THE FACULTY AND STUDENT BODY ON THE OPENING DAY

DR. WILLIAM MOSELEY BROWN, PRESIDENT, (LEFT) AND MORTON BLUMENTHAL, CHAIRMEN OF THE BOARD OF TRUSTEES

SOME OF THE STUDENTS BEFORE ONE OF THE HANDSOME TEMPORARY BUILDINGS

ATLANTIC UNIVERSITY FOOTBALL SQUARD 1930

Dr William Moseley Brown, famous educator and formerly professor of psychology at Washington and Lee University, heads the faculty of eminent college professors of the new Atlantic University at Virginia Beach Va.

Classes are now in full session at this, America's youngest institution

ly, we do not expect the institution ever to reach a stage of completion,

beginning the program of studies offered this year will be granted a B. S

Article from *Alexandria Times-Tribune* (Elwood, Indiana) celebrating the opening of the Atlantic University, December 1, 1930.

Although Cayce and many others on the hospital board believed Blumenthal shouldn't try to launch a college before the hospital was self-supporting, they capitulated after Morton promised to personally fund and oversee all start-up costs. The board decided in favor of Morton chairing a newly formed Educational Board, composed of himself, Edwin, and Tim Brown, which would develop and operate a university with funds they believed would be forthcoming from the Stansell motor. The board would answer to no one but themselves.

This, as Sugrue would later chronicle, was another unheeded wake-up call. Edgar had no voice in the Educational Board's decisions, nor was he consulted or requested to give trance advice. And his lack of involvement was not a matter of his tight schedule. The truth, as later became apparent but not given voice to at the time, was that Morton didn't consider Edgar Cayce an educated man. He repeatedly pointed out that Edgar had no formal schooling, let alone a college degree, and that it was he, Morton, who had raised the psychic out of "obscurity." Such an attitude was in striking contrast to what was coming through in the readings about the partnership: that "mind is the builder" and that proper thought must be given to how the institution was to be operated. "Be not dictatorial, nor lording in thine own activity," Morton was told.

Edgar was again slighted in a newspaper story which outlined Dr. Brown's proposed Atlantic University curriculum. In addition to mainstream courses as found in other liberal arts colleges, psychic phenomenon would be studied, but purely from the scientific perspective. "The same general methods will be used as are utilized in all of the other sciences," Brown told reporters, [but we are] most emphatically not interested in spiritualism, mediumism, clairvoyance, or any of the other commonly known quackeries."

The inference that "quackery" was taking place across the street from the proposed site of Atlantic University shocked Edgar. He also found it disturbing that the partners' work in Virginia Beach was being separated into two discrete endeavors.

The same scenario, Sugrue would later detail, had taken place back in Egypt when Edgar, as the priest Ra Ta, was marginalized and then driven from the Pharaoh's court. A community of like-minded souls operating in partnership was what the readings called for. Unfortunately for Sugrue, and to a lesser degree Hugh Lynn, by virtue of their age and relative inexperience, their roles in the unfolding drama were played only from the sidelines. Tom's role was to chronicle what took place and not actively participate in the decision making.

"It looks like you will stand as chief guardian at the gate to the hospital, I at the gate to the university," Morton said of his and Edgar's respective roles. By way of apology for not including him in the decision-making process, Morton said: "I have never lost my affection for you, yours, or the work, nor do I want to usurp any bossy power that in any way would seek to take advantage of anyone. Yet, be patient until I can completely find my own self, which is not so easy in the terrific strain and pressure that is constantly upon me"

However much Morton was feeling the strain of running a brokerage company in New York and building a university in Virginia Beach, Edgar, too, was under considerable strain. By default, he was the acting administrator at the hospital, while at the same time giving readings and explaining them to the patients. Moreover, with Morton and his accountants preoccupied with building a university campus, no one was in charge of the hospital bookkeeping, a subject that caused considerable friction when Morton demanded a detailed accounting of expenses.

Unhappy with what he received, Morton requested that expenses be cut and efforts be made to keep the budget in line with revenue. As soon became evident, no single person was in charge of business affairs nor was any one individual in charge of purchasing supplies. To make matters worse, half the patients who had been admitted into the hospital didn't have the money to pay for their visits or were not keeping their accounts up to date.

Edgar promised Morton to put the books in order. Overwhelmed with other tasks, he handed the responsibility over to his father, who was temporarily hired as a central purchasing agent until someone else was found to take charge. Leslie, who had a long track record of business failures, was even less equipped than Edgar to take on the responsibility.

Tom Sugrue and Hugh Lynn saw the writing on the wall. There was no teamwork, a subject the Source expounded upon at length. When the situation had reached a crisis point, the readings were once again interrupted by a heavenly presence, only this time by the Master Himself. In language that could easily be mistaken for a passage from the Bible, the "entity" speaking through Cayce stressed the urgency of cooperation before their endeavor foundered.

> Let each be mindful of that place, that niche, that [purpose] each is to fill. Cooperate with other individuals, working in their individual capacities, that the whole [purpose] may be as one, even as the Father and I are one in you. I speak not of myself, but that ye may know the truth, even as delivered in the day when I walked among men and became known as the 'son of man' and the savior . . . Here, my brethren, ye are come again to fulfill, in this place, a

glorious principle, a glorious article of work among the sons of man.

Despite the admonitions, there is no evidence that the hospital board members acted on the advice given. Dave Kahn was sending his monthly payments to Virginia Beach as he had promised when the governing association was formed, but his checks were written personally to Edgar, not to the hospital account. Gertrude conducted all the readings but stayed at home, rarely venturing into the hospital itself to visit with patients. Linden Shroyer, apparently jealous of the role that Gladys played as Edgar's chief confidant, blamed her for the cost overruns and failure to maintain the books. Edgar, the chief administrator, was ultimately responsible for the overall functioning of the hospital, but as Tom and Hugh Lynn noted, his health and eyesight were deteriorating under the stress. He wasn't a businessman nor had ever pretended to be one. Yet increasingly, this was the role he was asked to perform.

Financial matters gradually became the focus of all the discord. And looming over them, like storm clouds, was what would become the Great Depression. By the end 1929, patients at the hospital weren't paying their bills, and in the first year of the university's operation, more than 40 percent of the incoming students would be unable to pay the tuition.

How much money the Blumenthals lost during the Depression varies dramatically depending on whom one believes. Tom Sugrue claimed that the Blumenthals lost over $1 million. Morton claimed that their losses were closer to $100,000 and further, that he and his brother rode out the Depression in style, during which they took expensive vacations.

That Morton and Edwin didn't lose their seat on the exchange until 1937 and that they respectively took trips to Europe and Cuba after the stock market crash suggests that their losses weren't as devastating as Sugrue believed. Yet Morton's account of the events that transpired immediately prior to and following the crash are in striking contrast to the extant records.

Morton and his brother would claim that the trance readings gave them no hint of the events to come, which was the primary reason they would later give for becoming disillusioned with Cayce and were unable in good faith to continue to take his trance advice seriously or continue to support the hospital effort.

"I have often wondered if the money-crazed era of the twenties didn't have some effect on Cayce," Blumenthal would later write. "People were making fortunes overnight, and Cayce himself had moved rather quickly from the edge of poverty into a world of money and material plenty. It is just possible that this was the cause of some of his inconsistencies. At any rate, his psychic gifts seemed never to benefit his benefactors, and they let me down at the moment when they could have been the greatest help."

Blumenthal would particularly reference events on and around October 29, 1929, what has been called "Black Tuesday," when prices on the exchange dropped ten points in the early morning, and by the end of the day lost thirty points. According to Morton's account of what happened that day, he called Virginia Beach and requested that Edgar come to New York to be at his side so that readings could be conducted on an hourly basis. Further, according to Morton, the subsequent information that came through in the New York readings indicated that the worst was over. The market would stabilize and soon start to rise.

The archival record does not support Blumenthal's claims. Not only were Morton and Edwin warned of the crash in the readings so were David Kahn and Tim Brown, who received readings consistent with those received by the Blumenthals. And unlike the Blumenthals, Kahn got out of the market. Brown was unable to do so because he had put a portion of his portfolio in Morton's hands to oversee as he saw fit.

References in the readings to the upheavals to come were most notable in the summer of 1929, and by the fall, Morton and his brother were so concerned by what was coming through that they traveled to Virginia Beach for the express purpose of clarifying the warnings of impending disaster. During their last Virginia Beach session, conducted just prior to Black Tuesday, the Source said that one of the Blumenthals' largest accounts could be "wiped out" the next day. "Best to sell, and then buy back at a lower price at a later date," came the recommendation.

Edgar's next contact with the Blumenthals was by telephone in Virginia Beach in early November, after Black Tuesday, at which time

Morton requested confirmation that he should be "out" of the market. The advice was the same as given earlier. Morton was told to stay out of the market until instructed otherwise.

The trip Edgar made to New York, referenced by Morton as having taken place at the end of October, didn't actually occur until November. The reading had a particularly spiritual tone: a reminder to Morton and Edwin that the "union" they represented with Cayce would be "envied by many" and that it was their responsibility to "honor" the trust that had been given them by remaining steadfast.

"He that furnisheth bread for the brothers shall control many cities," the Source said. "He that honoreth his God shall not go without full recompense, saith the Lord. For him that I have loved, him will I also raise up. Him that teacheth his brother the right way, shall not go unrewarded."

The Blumenthals received several more readings before leaving New York on extended holidays. Morton and Adeline went to France and North Africa, and Edwin and his wife went to Cuba. None of their correspondence hints that they felt betrayed by Cayce or that the readings had failed them when they were most needed. All that is clear from the record is that the upheavals in the market had shaken Morton and filled him with fear. And instead of turning to Edgar Cayce for help, he invited another psychic into his life.

To Sugrue, the drama being played out was more than two millennia old. Ra Ta was out. Morton had chosen a High Priestess to install in The Temple Beautiful.

Cayce Hospital in January 1929 and then on their Christmas card that year. So much gained, so much to lose.

PATRICIA DEVLIN:

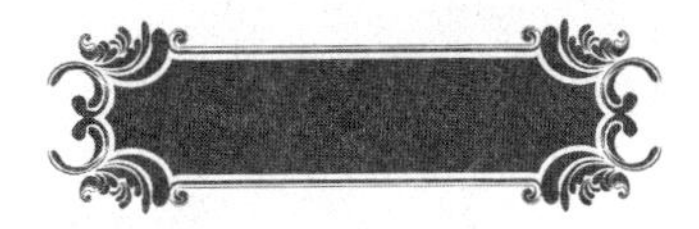

THE HIGH PRIESTESS

The Cayce hospital was still in the planning stages when Morton's wife, Adeline, had a disturbing dream she wished Edgar to interpret. She saw the number 32, and then experienced the following:

> [I] saw Morton being married to another girl, deserting me. I appealed to his mother, Freda, and she said, 'No, I see no reason to stop him if he wants to marry her.' 'But, I love him,' I replied. She was homely and a big blond. Morton married her and I attended the wedding. Then I wanted Morton to divorce her and remarry me because I simply adored him. But that was not consented to. I saw her sit in a chair [and] smoke a cigarette as she prayed to God. She was despicable to me.

Edgar had previously given Adeline eighteen dream interpretation readings. There is no record that one for this dream was ever conducted. In retrospect, given how accurate and insightful Adeline's other dream readings were, most notably about her and Morton's "weak-minded" son, it gives one pause to wonder what future difficulties might have been avoided had Edgar conducted the dream interpretation.

The number 32 may have been a reference to 1932—the year that former members of the Cayce hospital's board of directors squared off in court, Atlantic University closed its doors, and Morton would leave Adeline for another woman. That woman was indeed a homely, blond chain-smoker. According to Gladys she was "chubby" with streaks of strawberry red in her hair. Though Adeline desired to make peace with Morton and resume her marriage, their relationship ended in a bitter custody battle.

The other woman who figured into the drama was twenty-five-year-old Patricia Couglin Devlin, a former switchboard operator in the Broadway building where the Blumenthal brothers had their New York brokerage company. No record details the circumstances of what transpired between her and Morton behind closed doors, but whatever took place was more complex than a husband leaving his wife for another woman. Devlin was married when she met Morton. And as Morton's marriage unraveled, she intermittently lived with both Morton and her husband in a variety of apartments and homes as well as also living briefly with Morton's brother, Edwin. All that can be said with certainty was that Morton considered "Pat" psychically gifted and sought to help her develop her gifts. He and his brother eventually put her in charge of their Virginia Beach business affairs.

That Devlin was a switchboard operator in the Blumenthal office building may or may not have "enhanced" her ability to provide detailed psychic information. Gladys, who spoke with Morton's office three to four times a day, was convinced that she eavesdropped on their conversations. Regardless of the source of her information, however, there is no question that she had an intimate knowledge of Morton and Edgar's personal and business affairs before Morton hired her as his personal assistant in 1929. Devlin herself claimed her source of information was the same "psychic channels" that Edgar Cayce tapped into and told Morton that she had only to close her eyes to enter a self-induced trance state that permitted her to subconsciously travel to Virginia Beach to see what was going on at the hospital. Morton's correspondence only reveals that he "discovered" in Devlin what he had seen in Edgar Cayce back in Dayton and as he had with

Switchboard operators at work.

Cayce, he took credit for helping Devlin develop the "precious gift" she possessed.

No records exist of when her relationship with Morton passed beyond that of employee and employer. The Cayces knew only that she began accompanying Morton to Virginia Beach in early 1929, helped him to prepare lectures he gave at the hospital, and was subsequently put in charge of Atlantic University's business affairs. The following year she would give her own lectures at the hospital and would become the chief source of psychic information for Stansell Motor. Just as entity DeWitt Clinton had previously spoken through Edgar, he now spoke through her, though not with the same detail. To the surprise of Tim Brown and Stansell, the entity Clinton now claimed that Patricia's unemployed husband, Paul Devlin, could both solve the motor difficulties and help them construct an antigravity device.

Edgar expressed only mild interest in what he termed Morton's "protégé" when they were first introduced in Virginia Beach. He, too, encouraged her to develop her psychic talents. Though she and Edgar don't appear to have had any discussion about their respective responsibilities regarding the Blumenthal brothers' on-going desire for psychic information, it soon became clear that she was not only giving

Morton and Edwin psychic stock market advice but was also consulting on matters related to the hospital accounts. The only thing she apparently couldn't do was the medical readings.

Given that virtually all employees of both the hospital and university had been vetted by the Source, it is noteworthy that no dedicated reading was requested on Devlin's suitability. The first significant reference in the readings is a single question put to the Source in February 1930 when Edwin was apparently concerned about problems he was having staying "attuned" while working with Devlin in trance. In a particularly revealing response, the Source said that he should not put his "trust in powers made with hands." As disagreements arose between board members the following September, Kahn decided for the best interests of the partnership to conduct a reading to ask if Morton, as the President of the Association, was being properly served by his "spiritual advisor" Patricia Devlin. This time the Source simply came back, "Let them [the partners] answer for themselves."

The only trance session entirely dedicated to Devlin was a physical reading conducted on January 11, 1931, to diagnose and recommend treatment for pains she was having in her back and solar plexus. Cayce—in trance—prescribed a standard treatment that consisted of a change of diet and the application of Epsom salts and castor oil packs, indicating that should she follow the recommendations her pains would disappear within two or three days.

Edgar may well have been relieved not to have to give readings to the Blumenthals while simultaneously working at the hospital. Giving stock market advice had not been to his liking and was viewed by him more as a means to keep the hospital afloat. And Morton did seem to be receiving genuine help from her. As Edgar remarked in a letter to Tim Brown, "[There] certainly [have] been some wonderful things that Morton has been able to get through his helper and assistant there at the office."

Devlin's trance sessions were different from Edgar's. She could remember the information that allegedly came through her, and she spoke in her normal voice using clear distinct sentences without the repetitious use of pronouns, adverbs, and biblical language that sometimes made Cayce's readings difficult to understand. Morton clearly saw this difference as a great advantage and likewise her availability to meet with him at a moment's notice. Friends of David Kahn would report seeing Morton coming and going from her apartment at all hours of the day and night, which worried him more than it apparently did the Cayces. "It will probably end in a dangerous shooting," Kahn wrote, "but it's no business of mine."

Atlantic University's president Mosley Brown had the first serious run-in with her. In early October of 1929, while Devlin was reviewing university correspondence, she discovered that unbeknown to Morton, Brown had hired two more professors than they had agreed upon in an earlier meeting. While Morton was justifiably upset, Devlin was ready to go to war. As Morton later said, "Pat nodded her pretty red head, put on her hat, and left, returning with a lawyer."

Devlin played an increasing role in overseeing the hospital accounts. Soon after her run-in with Brown, she and Morton were visiting the hospital and took Edgar aside, informing him that expenses had to be cut and that it was up to him to see that employees abided by the new rules. What upset Edgar most about this meeting was her and Morton's request that Edgar cut back on giving "freebie" readings and concentrate on paying customers.

After the stock market crash, when Morton and Edwin took their trips abroad, Devlin was placed in charge of overseeing all of their Virginia Beach interests. Edgar himself didn't object to the arrangement as it removed the responsibility from his and Gladys' shoulders. Edgar's challenge came in January 1930 when she informed him of a decision that had been made, presumably with Morton's blessing, to limit the number of readings given to patients who were unable or unwilling to pay for them.

Edgar, stirred into action, immediately wrote Morton informing him in no uncertain terms that the only power to limit who would receive help was a higher power than either of them. "[No one] you or anybody else . . . can control the readings," he wrote. "[You and I] may be able to control the times when we will give the readings, but who they are going to be for, and when they are going to be given—the minute we do that, we have lost the very . . . foundation of the whole work . . . Remember the Master didn't refuse to heal the whole ten lepers, though only two came back and said 'thank you.'"

Morton didn't press the matter when he and Adeline came home from Europe, but Gladys and others noted a change that had come over him. As Gladys later reflected, "Mr. Blumenthal was never the same after his return. Somewhere along the line he lost that magic contact which had protected him." In this regard she was not only referring to his money-making ability but to his health as well. While Devlin was increasingly providing stock market information, Morton was turning to Edgar for stress-related health advice.

At this point the readings were pleading for the partners to begin cooperating. Where the Source described cooperation as a "need" when the partners first came to together, it was now indicating that "all would be lost" unless cooperation became their central "task" and "purpose." The message was nearly identical to that given for the Edgar Davis and Frank Seiberling partnership: "Unless there is a coalition of the interests . . . much of that which has been as a dream . . . will be lost. Rather than . . . magnifying the differences that have existed [act] in the manner of brotherly love . . . The law of the Lord is as the two-edged sword."

On February 16, 1930, Devlin reported to Morton what she described as the "disillusioning" news that Edgar was in the midst of taking him for a "financial ride." Spending hadn't been cut at the hospital, as had been promised. Moreover, Devlin's personal investigation had revealed what she determined to be an excess of nonpaying guests living in the top floor of the hospital, whose contributions to the bottom line she declared to be marginal. Among the culprits were Tom Sugrue, Leslie Cayce, Edgar's sisters, Annie Cayce and Sarah Cayce Hesson; and Gladys' cousin, Mildred Davis. She also named Booker Avery, the hospital's handyman and driver who, according to Devlin, used the hospital automobile for frequent all-night excursions.

Morton called an emergency hospital board meeting. When everyone arrived and Devlin led Tim Brown and Morton up the hill to the meeting room, one of her high heels caught on something buried in the lawn. They discovered a pipe. Tim Brown traced the pipe and found that it ran from the hospital water line to a neighbor's cottage. When asked to explain the arrangement, Edgar admitted that he had let the neighbor tap into the hospital water line rather than have him go to the expense of digging his own well. And no, the neighbor was not compensating the hospital accounts for the water.

There was one further problem which cast a pall over the proceedings. Shroyer, the hospital records keeper, couldn't find the ledger which detailed disbursements. Try as he and Gladys did, the ledger couldn't be found until Devlin "psychically" led the search into the hospital basement where the missing book was discovered under what Morton termed a "pile of debris." Devlin now had her smoking gun—this ledger revealed excess payments for food, extraneous hospital equipment, and many personal expenditures by the Cayce family and hospital staff. Further irregularities were reportedly discovered when Devlin consulted merchants from whom large purchases had been made.

"I'm [just] not that good a businessman," Edgar admitted when confronted by the ledger and Devlin's accounting. "It certainly does get my goat to do my level best and then find I have fallen far short of what should be done."

A subsequent reading did indeed put blame on Edgar. "This present discord . . . has been . . . the extravagant expenditure by . . . Edgar Cayce." Although the Source, when asked for specifics, suggested that this might only be viewed as an extravagance in material terms: "[his extravagance can only be] judged by individuals. [But] not from here." In this regard, Edgar had been extravagant, but his was an extravagance characterized by charity, not a lavish lifestyle.

Another special board meeting was held on September 16, 1930, in which Morton and his brother assumed total control of the hospital. Edgar would have no authority to pay bills or accept new patients without prior approval. Only the nursing staff, with a cut in salary, would receive room and board, and a device known as a "governor" would be placed on the hospital automobile to record and restrict its unauthorized use. Further, the hospital physicians, henceforth, were to report directly to the Blumenthals, and not to Edgar. The final crushing blow for Edgar was Morton demanding that David Kahn receive no further readings.

Devlin herself presented the case against Kahn to the board. As she had discovered in her investigation of hospital records, Kahn had not only been delinquent in making his contractual contributions to the hospital fund, but he had also charged the hospital account for $7,000 in furniture from his own New York factory. Upon cross-examination Edgar admitted that he, too, had been surprised to have received an invoice from Kahn for the furniture, but he had paid it without question. No one, he believed, should feel obligated to make donations. They were to come from the heart.

Despite Edgar's plea for understanding, Morton remained adamant. Kahn was to receive no more readings. Edgar was furious. "As much affection as I have for you, and as much as I appreciate all you have done for me," Edgar told him, "on the day that I cannot give a reading for Dave Kahn or any member of his family or anyone, is the day 'little Eddy' will be six feet under the ground."

On February 28, 1931, the hospital doors closed forever, and a month later a board meeting was held in New York during which the Association was disbanded. A few months after that, the university also closed its doors. Unlike Edgar, who signed whatever papers were put before him by Morton's attorneys, David Kahn put up a fight and was then served by Devlin with a subpoena. She sued him on behalf of Morton and Edwin for notes that he had countersigned for the hospital property and for stock options he had purchased on margin before the crash. Then Morton and Edwin, again using Devlin as a go-between, sued Edgar in another civil suit for several hundred dollars they claimed Edgar had drawn in unauthorized expenses in the final months of the hospital's decline.

David Kahn's arrest instigated by the Devlins in 1933 put him at risk of losing his businesses and going bankrupt.

D.E. KAHN IS ARRESTED.
New York Times (1923-Current file); Sep 7, 1933;
ProQuest Historical Newspapers The New York Times (1851 - 2011)
pg. 4

D. E. KAHN IS ARRESTED.

Ordered to Turn Over His Interest in Suit Against Brokers.

David E. Kahn, president of the David E. Kahn Wood and Metal Products Corporation, was arrested yesterday by Deputy Sheriff Leo Goldstein on the recent order of Supreme Court Justice Alfred Frankenthaler fining him $250 for contempt of court and directing him to turn over to a receiver of his property his interest in a suit against Blumenthal Brothers, brokers. He will be released when he pays the fine and turns over the property.

The application to punish Kahn was made by Paul Devlin, who sued here on an assigned claim of the Pennsylvania Secretary of Bank-

Edgar was permitted to return to the hospital to collect the records of the trance readings, a clock that had been given to him by the carpenters who built the hospital building, and a picture of his mother, which had hung over the fireplace at the entrance. The problem was that he soon had no fireplace of his own over which to hang it.

Morton, again using Devlin to act as his agent in Virginia Beach, dispatched a sheriff to serve the Cayces with an eviction notice. The home that the Cayces believed had been given them by the Blumenthals was ultimately determined to belong to the hospital association and like the hospital building, went into receivership. They were eventually turned over, by court order, to the Blumenthals. Had Edgar put up a fight and not signed documents giving Morton authority over the association, the circumstances might have turned out differently. But as he explained to Hugh Lynn, the hospital had been a shared dream, and without Morton the dream was merely bricks and mortar.

Unfortunately for Sugrue and so many others the Cayces considered to be family, there wasn't money to keep him or anyone else on staff. Tom would return to his home in Connecticut and eventually land a newspaper job which would launch his writing career; only without the nurses in the hospital reminding him to adhere to his medical treatments, the virus had lodged in his joints. By the time he returned to the Cayce fold and eventually wrote Edgar's biography, his joints had swelled to the point that a wheelchair was necessary.

Gladys, again without salary, was sleeping on a cot in a drafty bedroom in a rented Virginia Beach cottage shared by the four Cayces. Hidden under her cot were the file boxes of readings she had collected since her days back in Selma. That Morton saw no long-term value in them was a hidden blessing, for otherwise he might have claimed them as property belonging to him, just like her hospital typewriter.

As Adeline's dream had forewarned, Morton would divorce her. In the years to come, she suffered a nervous breakdown, as would her son. The woman who had once been married to one of New York's wealthiest stockbrokers, would first become a nurse and then a maid.

As these events unfolded, the Blumenthals wasted no time in liquidating what remained of the hospital. Devlin fired the hospital's doctors and therapists, and for pennies on the dollar, dismantled and sold the equipment. Days later a crew of carpenters arrived to turn the hospital building into a hotel. The new Temple Beautiful indeed had its High Priestess.

The Princess Pat Hotel, named in honor of its manager Patricia Devlin, had a grand opening complete with a bandstand and champagne but would close its doors after four years for lack of guests. Later still, the old hospital building would be sold and turned into a nightclub, then an officers' club, country club, and eventually a Masonic Temple. A decade after Edgar's passing, Hugh Lynn would take great pleasure in finally reclaiming the property to further the Cayce

Terrace Beach Club, 1938 and the Hillcrest Beach Club, 1949.

work. "Like troops retaking ground lost in an earlier skirmish, its spiritual soldiers enjoyed a sense of triumph," Hugh Lynn's biographer would write.

In a strange twist of fate, the Blumenthal brothers, who shared a home with Devlin—and intermittently with her husband—would live in relative close proximity to the Cayces for the rest of their lives. After the failure of the Princess Pat Hotel, the Blumenthals declared bank-

The Blumenthals moved in with the Devlins and worked with their printing company.

ruptcy and in 1946 moved permanently to Virginia Beach. Years before their respective deaths in 1954 and 1980, Morton operated the Patricia G. Devlin Printing Company, which sold specialized greeting and post-cards on Atlantic Avenue. After Devlin's passing in 1951, Edwin worked as a short-order cook on the boardwalk.

Despite the Blumenthal brothers involvement in Patricia's life, she and her husband Paul were buried together in St. Mary's Catholic Cemetery in Norfolk, Va. upon their deaths in 1950 and 1951.

Had it not been for the intervention of David Kahn and a handful of grateful recipients of the readings who formed what became the Association for Research and Enlightenment (A.R.E.), the Cayces might have found themselves headed back to live with Gertrude's family in Hopkinsville. But this was not to be. Funds were raised to buy the Cayces a home of their own on Arctic Circle, and with it, the readings were begun once again.

As Virginia Harding, a woman who would suffer hardships not unlike the Cayces would later counsel Edgar, "Those who have awareness must go on as did the trail blazers of old . . . There is so much dead wood which has to be cut away before the light of truth may be revealed."

Mitchell Hastings (1910-1994) in Arizona, 1933.

MITCHELL HASTINGS:

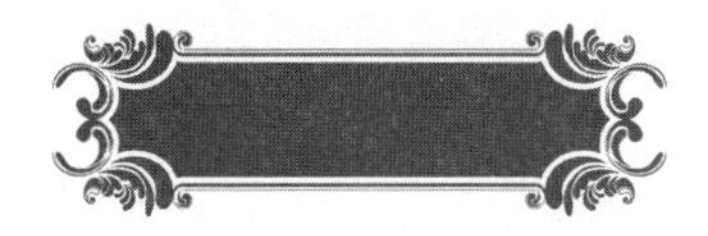

MISSING IN ACTION

Despite the support of A.R.E. members who bought a home for Gladys and the Cayces to inhabit and whose membership fees provided income for them to continue conducting readings, the demise of the hospital and the stress of starting over brought Edgar to the verge of a nervous breakdown. Now fifty-four years old, he felt as if his life was over.

Gladys described her twin soul as "listless" and "unable to concentrate." Friends were disturbed to see him "bewildered" and "uncertain." They had every reason to be concerned, for his physical being was clearly reflecting his inner turmoil: Edgar temporarily lost his voice once again; he suffered from neuritis and severe constipation; he now required glasses, and a simple cold took him weeks to overcome. In less than three months, he was twenty pounds lighter and his usually tanned face was drawn and waxen. "Unless changes are made, this might become a very serious condition," a physical reading warned.

Friends and family were thus seriously worried when, without advance warning, Edgar asked Gladys to cancel scheduled readings, and on February 27, 1934, he left Virginia Beach for Arizona. How long he would be gone and whether or not he would continue readings when he returned was anyone's guess. All Edgar told his family was that he and Mitchell Hastings, the twenty-three-year-old son of new A.R.E. members from New York, would be traveling together and that he would write home when they had a chance.

Hugh Lynn was mystified by his father's behavior and immediately tried to figure out how Hastings fit into the greater story, and the young man's relationship with the core team of people drawn to the Cayce work. Hastings had been connected to the team in previous lifetimes, but his role was more closely identified with what had happened in Atlantis than back in Egypt. The future of the work, he suspected, was now being driven by different group of individuals from those who had previously come together to build the hospital. Atlanteans were taking charge.

Mitchell hadn't been present for the first reading he received, which was conducted in New York on November 14, 1933, while Mitchell was an undergraduate at Harvard. The Cayce family had been on a trip to Manhattan to raise funds for the fledgling A.R.E. The request for a Life Reading had come through Hastings' parents, Theodore and Carolyn, wealthy Park Avenue socialites and theosophists who received their own readings the following day.

Cayce—in trance—suggested that Mitchell was a deeply talented and spiritual individual who had much to offer the world should he focus on scientific matters related to electrical energy. Further, he was identified in a previous incarnation, along with Edgar Evans Cayce, as one of the scientists in Atlantis who had highly developed psychic powers and who had helped to construct the "firestone" in the Atlantean power plant which had led to the destruction of that continent. This Life Reading was especially convincing to the Hastings family, for unbeknown to Cayce in his waking state, young Mitchell had already been recognized as a budding genius in the field of electromagnetic energy and was conducting experiments at Harvard using crystals to alter electrical frequencies.

The following month, when the Cayces were back in Virginia Beach, Edgar received a request to give Mitchell a second reading. A physical reading conducted on December 13 described severe back and abdominal ailments related to an injury in which Mitchell had fractured several of his ribs. This, too, was convincing evidence of Cayce's clairvoyance, since Edgar had not been told that Mitchell had seriously injured himself playing football and had indeed fractured three ribs. The diagnosis proved accurate in every detail, and after following the prescribed treatment plan, Mitchell was soon on his feet and would go on to win several amateur golf and tennis championships.

At Edgar's invitation, Mitchell traveled to Virginia Beach for Christmas vacation in 1933 where he and Edgar met in person for the first time. They enjoyed one another's company so much that Mitchell was invited to stay through the New Year, and unusual for a new A.R.E. member, was given an unprecedented fourteen readings over the next two months. As part of the prescribed treatments for Hastings' back injury, the readings recommended that he spend time in Arizona where he could get out in the sun and dry air to mentally and physically recuperate. A physical reading Edgar received for himself that December had also recommended that he get out in the sun and dry air. Hence, it was only natural that the two men—one a psychic, the other a scientist—decided on the spur of the moment to take a vacation.

As it would later be revealed, Mitchell was under as much stress as Edgar, not only the result of his injury, but also from the criticism of his professors who did not share the young man's radical theories of electromagnetism. They were attempting to steer him to what they believed was a more conventional direction. Hastings had been able to extend his Christmas holiday because he had decided to drop out of Harvard.

Just like two schoolboys playing hooky, Edgar and Mitchell hurriedly bid friends and family goodbye and left Virginia Beach in Mitchell's Pontiac, accompanied by Edgar's secretary, Gladys Davis, who was hitching a ride to Selma to visit her family. After dropping Gladys off in Alabama, they drove west through Mississippi, Louisiana, and Texas, arriving in Willcox, Arizona on March 10 where Edgar received a wire from Gladys requesting that he give an emergency reading for a family friend who had suffered a heart attack. As Gladys only knew that Edgar was headed to Arizona, the telegram had been forwarded from Alabama to Texas and finally to Willcox, where it reached Edgar. Mitchell conducted and transcribed the five-minute trance session, which is the only reading on file as having been conducted during what would be Edgar's month-long excursion. The pair then drove to Bonita, outside of Bisbee, Arizona, where they set up camp at the "76 Ranch", which would become the base of operations for their subsequent expeditions, including a journey into Mexico.

A typical guest house at the 4100 acre "76 Ranch", owned then by famed cattle rancher Wilfred Taft Webb.

The "76 Ranch" dates back to 1870s and was the site of the Apache Indian battle of KH Butte in 1881 and of the Wham paymaster robbery of 1889. The ranch was a noted "dude" ranch in the 1930s when Edgar and Mitchell were there.

Many years would pass before details of their adventure became known to family and friends, and even then, it is only through Mitchell's later correspondence with Edgar, brief comments Edgar made to Hugh Lynn, and an interview with Mitchell's son that the greater story is now known.

In all likelihood, Edgar didn't speak candidly about the trip as he didn't wish to draw attention to his nervous exhaustion and the sudden abandonment of his family and responsibilities. All he would later write to friends about the trip was that he had "some quite interesting experiences." Mitchell also did not discuss their daily activities, but for other reasons. They would be difficult for most people to believe. He was already troubled by what fellow students and his Harvard professors thought of him and his work. The trance readings he had previously received from Cayce on engineering and electromagnetism were the only positive feedback he had received concerning what his professors believed to be fundamentally flawed theories.

In addition to soaking up the sun and dry air, Mitchell and Edgar had gone in search of "talking stones." Most specifically they were prospecting for lapis linguis, or azurite, a dark blue mineral that occurs in either crystals or dull mushroom-shaped masses. According to readings Hastings had received earlier in Virginia Beach, psychically inclined people could hold azurite in their hands for five or ten minutes or wear it against their skin in the form of a pendant and potentially raise their psychic vibrations to such an extent that miraculous things could happen.

A spectacular example of layered azurite with malachite from Brisbee, Arizona. It is a deep "azure" blue.

This was not an entirely new concept from the Cayce readings. In many instances Cayce had recommended that an individual surround himself with a particular rock, mineral, or gem, which would influence a variety of physical, mental, and spiritual conditions. Bloodstone and rubies, for example, were recommended to a woman from Cuba for help transcending negative influences from past incarnations. A woman born in Argentina was told to wear topaz, as its beauty, purity, and clarity would bring her strength. Knowledge of how these rocks and minerals are to be used, the readings make clear, was a highly developed science in Atlantis and ancient Egypt but sadly, in more modern times, had been corrupted or lost altogether.

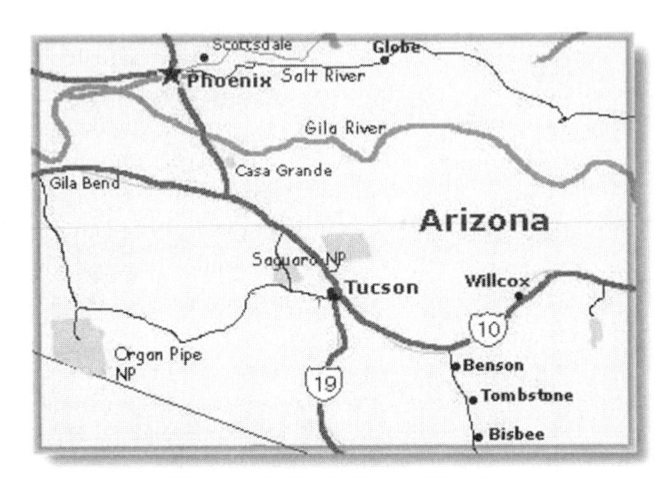

Edgar and Mitchell would end up in rockhounding territory.

Azurite holds special significance in the larger body of the Cayce readings. It was this mineral and possibly other gemstones that Cayce suggested were the "Urim and Thummim" mentioned in Exodus 28:15-21 which were placed on the breastplate of the high priest Aaron and which were used by him to determine the Lord's will for his people. In addition to unspecified things that might happen when a psychically inclined person handled or "listened" to the mineral, the readings suggested that azurite, when exposed to or charged by sunlight and held in the hand or against the skin, could enhance an individual's ability to follow more closely their vocational path.

As both Cayce and Hastings had important career decisions to make, it only stood to reason that prospecting for azurite was their primary activity on this field trip. Beyond wanting to bask in the sun and breathe the dry air, this explains why they specifically chose to visit Southern Arizona and would, on day trips, venture into Mexico. Edgar was open to the possibility that handling the mineral could help him decide whether or not to stay in Virginia Beach and continue his work. Mitchell could use it similarly to help him decide whether or not to return to Harvard and pursue a career as an electrical engineer.

Despite complications throughout their journey—they had numerous mechanical problems with the car along with flat tires at regular intervals along the way—they successfully found azurite in copper mines in and around Bisbee and Douglas, Arizona, and further south, in Mexico, outside of what is presumed to be Nogales and Agua Prieta—border regions noted for high quality lapis. On one particular fieldtrip, they ventured several hundred feet underground into an abandoned mine shaft, carrying with them pickaxes and lanterns. Prospecting readings were presumably given, similar to those Cayce gave to Texas oilmen a decade earlier, but these never found their way back to Gladys Davis and the Cayce vault.

After selecting particularly large and colorful specimens, Cayce and Hastings washed and cleaned their azurite samples and placed them in the sun to dry. What happened next could easily be described as the stuff of fiction. They had visions—what Hastings called "mirages" in which dreamlike images of people would ride toward them on horseback, and strangers would approach them to impart a curious bit

Edgar's mother, Carrie Elizabeth Cayce (nee Major).

of information or advice. In Mitchell's case, he encountered a "red-haired beauty," who presented herself to him, vanished, and would later appear in flesh and blood when he returned home to New York.

Perhaps the most astonishing and revealing of these visions was one they had in a field in New Mexico. An apparition of Edgar's dead mother appeared and spoke to Edgar about the future. She urged him to not give up hope and to not worry about his precarious financial situation. And he should not doubt the power and veracity of the information coming through him. In previous visionary experiences, Edgar had only seen or heard spirit visitors. But in New Mexico, perhaps aided by Hastings' own power of mind and the increased vibration of the azurite they carried with them, Edgar reportedly received a more tangible manifestation of the visit. His mother handed him a silver dollar, and when she had faded from sight, the coin remained in the palm of his hand.

On Easter Sunday, April 16, Cayce returned to Virginia Beach with the lucky silver dollar in his pocket and a renewed enthusiasm, as he said, "to be of greater service to his fellow man." Mitchell, carrying bags laden with a variety of mineral samples, remained at the "76 Ranch" for an additional month before returning to Harvard where he would graduate with honors and would eventually meet and marry the "red-headed beauty" of his visions.

This was not, however, the end of the story. Just as Cayce would deliver ever more insightful readings in the years to come, Hastings also had an exciting future ahead of him. His first major innovation, inspired by the Cayce readings, was on crystalline "static eliminators" which would revolutionize the electronics industry and earn him a well-deserved reputation as one of the foremost electrical engineers of his generation. Also with Cayce's trance counsel, Hastings would pioneer FM radio at NBC and play a pivotal role in the development of computer technology at IBM.

Beyond his many scientific accomplishments and how they relate to the trance advice he received, Hastings was also significant to the Cayce story in that he was one of the rare individuals Cayce trusted to conduct private trance sessions. He also produced the only existing voice recording of Cayce giving a reading. For reasons not understood then or now, Edgar and Mitchell had only to be in close proximity to one another for Cayce to experience heightened powers of conscious clairvoyance. The same, apparently, was true for Hastings. Atlanteans, it seemed, somehow operated on a different psychic level from the team who had been together in Egypt. As had been foreshadowed by the Stansell motor reading, Atlanteans could and would use science and technology to transform the planet.

Mitchell Hastings, Hugh Lynn, Edgar, Gladys Davis, and Carolyn Hastings atop the Empire State Building, 1934.

Thanks to the gem and mineral readings provided to Hastings, many students of the Cayce work would descend upon the Morgan Wing of New York's Natural History Museum where, the readings said, a particularly enormous block of nearly pure azurite was housed. Such a specimen, nearly five feet tall, weighing four-and-a-half tons, and mined in Bisbee, Arizona, was indeed on display at the museum where

The 4.5-ton block of azurite-malachite ore from Arizona at the Museum of Natural History in New York City.

it is today. This particular specimen was long known as the "singing stone" because so many museum visitors reported hearing a humming sound when they stood beside it. Strangely, the stone stopped singing a decade ago. As Cayce researchers have subsequently discovered, the stone's silence coincided with a museum renovation. The stone was removed from a prominent position in front of the gallery windows where it stood in direct sunlight and was placed in the back of the room where it is bathed in artificial light. Perhaps one day an enlightened curator will position the massive specimen back in the sunlight, and it will sing again.

Cayce's silver dollar also became a subject of further research. Hugh Lynn eventually liberated it from his father. Desirous of delving deeper into an altogether unbelievable story, he sent the coin to the Federal Treasury for examination, setting into motion a chain of events that nearly resulted in his arrest. As FBI agents duly informed him, the silver dollar was perfect in just about every way. It just didn't have a mint mark. Hugh Lynn, then in his thirties, escaped prosecution for counterfeiting by pleading innocence: If he had produced the coin himself, why would he have risked calling attention to himself and his family by sending it to federal authorities? Hugh Lynn's only regret was that nothing he said could convince the FBI to return the silver dollar.

The type of mint mark Carrie's silver coin was missing.

Psychic Eileen Garrett, c. 1930.

EILEEN GARRETT:

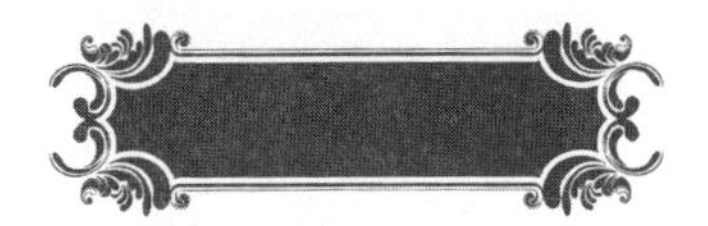

A TALE OF TWO PSYCHICS

Only once did Edgar Cayce request a trance reading from another psychic. Part of the reason was because his circle of trusted friends didn't include practicing psychics and also because Edgar preferred to use his free time fishing and working in his garden. Besides, why ask someone else for psychic advice when you could provide it for yourself? Conversely, Hugh Lynn, who assumed management of the A.R.E. after the demise of the hospital, received readings from many famed psychics of his day, attended their lectures, and compared their experiences with his father's.

Hugh Lynn went a step further on February 3, 1934, when renowned London psychic Eileen Garrett was visiting New York on a U.S. tour. With the help of Mitchell Hastings' mother, Carolyn, he arranged for his father and Garrett to meet at the Staten Island home of A.R.E. members Ernest and Margaret Zentgraf. Cayce, considered by many to be America's greatest psychic, gave Garrett a reading in the morning, and Garrett, Europe's most famous psychic, gave Cayce a reading in the afternoon. What these readings revealed about their respective work not only provided unique insight into how and why psychic information was made available to them but also the respective sources of their information.

The Irish born Garrett, sixteen years Cayce's junior, had much in common with her Kentucky-born counterpart. Both had spirit playmates with whom they shared childhood adventures. Garrett called hers "the children." Both saw colorful auras around people and plants—what Garrett described as "surrounds." They also saw and conversed with dead people. In Garrett's case, her first encounter was with her Aunt Leon, who appeared early one morning carrying an infant in her arms. She told adolescent Eileen that she would have to "go away" and "take baby with me." Only later was it revealed that Aunt Leon and her infant had died that morning during childbirth. Eileen, too, like young Eddy, had difficulty acclimating to school and was routinely scolded for reporting on what others considered lies and fanciful storytelling.

Cayce's hardships, however, pale by comparison with Garrett's. Her parents, one Protestant and the other Catholic, married in secret and then committed suicide rather than face what would surely have been sectarian ridicule in the Irish farming community where Eileen was born. She was shipped off to boarding school in London, wed at fifteen to a man twelve years her senior, and gave birth to three sons who would not outlive adolescence. Her first husband compelled her to visit a psychiatrist because he considered her visions evidence of insanity. Her second husband was killed in battle in World War I. A subsequent fiancé succumbed to sudden illness before vows could be exchanged.

Painful as these tragedies were, each served as a catalyst for further development of her psychic abilities. In the case of her first born, Garrett was pushing her infant in a stroller when she heard a discarnate voice telling her the child would not be with her for long. Months later he suddenly took ill with meningitis. As he lay dying in her arms, she would see the child's "surround" envelope of color rise like a nebulous cloud and leave his body. She would not grieve in the conventional sense as she knew for certain, as she would write, "that death was not an end but led to other states of being."

Forward onto her path to becoming a practicing psychic, she would talk to the dead, provide advice and consolation to the sick and infirm, and predict future events. Like Cayce's, her trance sessions were not conducted in darkened rooms nor accompanied by theatrics. There was no levitation of tables, otherworldly playing of musical instruments, and no vaporous manifestations of phantom ectoplasm. Garrett would put herself into a self-induced hypnotic trance, and entities would speak through her.

Unlike Cayce, Garrett's entities introduced themselves at the onset of the reading. They were described as her "controls" through whom she could obtain psychic information or converse with other spirits. Her most frequent controlling entity was Uvani, who purported to be a fourteenth century Arab soldier. Abdul Latif, a seventeenth century Persian physician, dealt primarily with diagnosis and healing. Entities calling themselves Tahotah and Ramah claimed no earthy incarnations.

During Garrett's most widely reported trance session, conducted in London in 1930, Uvani introduced Flight Lieutenant Irwin, Captain of the R101 dirigible which had crashed two days earlier in France. Garrett

The R101, the largest aircraft at that time weighed almost 260,000 pounds empty and was 777 feet long and 131 feet wide. It took 400 people to move it. (Some of whom appear in this photo.)

Flight Lieutenant Herbert Carmichael Irwin, AFC, Royal Air Force spoke through Eileen, reporting what had gone wrong with the aircraft when it crashed two days earlier.

Garrett provided such a comprehensive and technical account of the disaster that Scotland Yard became involved.

Morning Post

R101:

REMARKABLE

SEANCE

ONE PENNY

provided such a comprehensive and technical account of the disaster that Scotland Yard become involved. Investigators couldn't explain how Garrett could possibly have obtained such accurate and detailed information, nor was this all. In what became a series of R101 readings, crewmen and passengers would also come through Garrett to share uncannily accurate details of their lives along with first-person accounts of their last moments in the burning wreck.

Thus her career was launched. Though both she and Cayce would give readings for celebrities, world leaders, and corporate executives, neither would trade on these associations. Like Cayce, Garrett didn't charge for giving trance counsel, believing that psychic information was not to be used for personal enrichment, but for the betterment of mankind. Also similar to what came through in the Cayce readings, Garrett believed that with training, anyone was capable of clairvoyance, telepathy, and what she termed "psychic mediumship." There was no magic involved, only sensitivity to the inherent power of the unconscious mind.

The area where Garrett and Cayce most differed was how they believed their respective talents ought to be used. While Cayce primarily devoted his career to giving health and spiritual readings to individuals who came to him for help, Garrett gave herself over to teams of scientists and researchers. Traveling extensively, she willingly let herself be tested, analyzed, and interviewed more than any psychic before or since, and by subjecting herself to intense scientific scrutiny, her work became largely responsible for the creation of paranormal research programs in universities and study centers the world over. She would also found a publishing company, magazine, and philanthropic foundation that would promote and widely disseminate scientific and scholarly studies of the paranormal. Today, the A.R.E. Cayce library in Virginia Beach is just one of the many beneficiaries of her largesse.

In 1934 when forty-one-year-old Garrett was introduced to fifty-seven-year-old Cayce in the Zentgraf family's sprawling Staten Island home, Garrett was already on her second U.S. tour. Described by those who knew her as "attractive in a commanding and lusty way," the full-figured Garrett, with closely cropped brunette hair, was richly dressed and wore a variety of her trademark bangles, bracelets, and rings. Accompanying her on tour was her eighteen-year-old daughter, the fu-

The Staten Island Home of Ernest and Helene Zentgraf (built: 1908-09).

ture Eileen Garrett Coly. That she should bring her daughter was providential, as Edgar was accompanied by twenty-seven-year-old Hugh Lynn. Just as Hugh Lynn would steer the A.R.E. in the future, Eileen Coly would carry on Garrett's legacy as President of the Parapsychology Foundation, and their respective children, Charles Thomas Cayce and Lisette Coly, would preserve their legacies into the next century.

Although the Staten Island summit was an experiment and not viewed as a duel between the world's leading psychics, an element of friendly competition was naturally on the minds of the thirteen friends and family members who witnessed what took place. Which psychic would provide the most compelling insights? By virtue of Cayce frequently staying with the Zentgraf family—their residence was the equivalent of an A.R.E. New York Center—the Cayces had what might be termed the home-team advantage. Still, unusual circumstances leading up to the main events kept the participants on edge. The morning that the readings were to be given, Cayce received by mail, addressed to the Zentgraf home, a package sent from India. The parcel contained a crystal ball. No one in attendance claimed to know who had sent it or why.

Had the crystal ball been delivered to Cayce's home in Virginia Beach, it wouldn't have received quite the same degree of attention.

A crystal ball from the Cayce household, possibly the crystal ball received that day. It is 3 inches in diameter and has no imperfections.

Here in Staten Island, however, the circumstances were substantively different. The package, which contained no accompanying letter or identifying card, must have been mailed in advance of when Hugh Lynn scheduled the meeting between Garrett and his father. How would someone have known that Edgar would be staying with the Zentgrafs this particular day? Equally perplexing was the possible connection between the crystal ball and unexplained events that had taken place on Cayce's last visit to the Zentgraf's home.

The past October, when Cayce had stayed with the Zentgrafs while giving readings to New York A.R.E. supporters, a turban-wearing East Indian had mysteriously arrived on the doorstep asking to talk to Edgar. Edgar met with the exotic stranger and before the visitor's abrupt departure, delivered a verbal message known only to Edgar. Gladys Davis, who had been present, believed that the turbaned man was some spirit guide in disguise. Adding to the mystery was the fact that this same East Indian had visited Cayce at several important turning points in career, including a day, more than two decades earlier, when Cayce had entered into the ill-fated business agreement to conduct readings in Hopkinsville.

On another occasion, the East Indian—who apparently didn't age—had appeared to him on a New York sidewalk, knelt before him, and offered him blessings and a warning about a meeting he was scheduled to have in a hotel thirty minutes later. The most recent appearance of the East Indian, the previous October, had coincided with Edgar having contracted a life-threatening case of pneumonia.

Was the delivery of a crystal ball, mailed from India, somehow connected to what might be a reappearance of the mysterious turbaned man? Could the crystal ball somehow be connected with the reading Cayce was about to give Garrett or the reading Garrett was to give him?

Hugh Lynn, seated in a hardback chair in the Zentgraf's spacious second-floor living room, must have had these questions in mind when he guided his father into what would be a thirty-five minute trance session. He wouldn't, however, ask for information about the crystal ball until later that day. First on his agenda was to find out how and where Garrett obtained her information.

"What is the source of Mrs. Garrett's psychic information?" Hugh Lynn asked soon after the session had begun.

Cayce—in trance—responded in nearly an identical way as when Lammers asked a similar question. "A portion is from the soul . . . that has made and does make for a channel through which spiritual or psychic forces may manifest in a material world . . . Also from those influences from without that are . . . teachers, instructors, directors, or those that would give to those in the material plane the better comprehension."

Also consistent with information that had previously come through, Cayce said that the purpose of Garrett giving the information was an opportunity for soul growth and that when such information is used for self-indulgence, the results would be contention and strife. When used for good, the results would bring the uplifting fruits of such activities.

"How can Mrs. Garrett develop her ability to the highest degree?" Hugh Lynn enquired further.

"By keeping self in accord in the inner self with that which is the highest that may manifest itself through the abilities and faculties of the soul body. Thus may it give to the seeker, thus may it give to those that would knock."

Again, this information was nothing that hadn't previously been given in readings. Garrett was described as accessing her psychic information through subjugation of her conscious mind. Also similar to previous readings on Cayce, Garrett was described as having developed her psychic abilities in previous lifetimes. The most relevant previous incarnations had been in the Middle East, what was then Persia and Arabia, when she was said to have contributed much to the hearts and minds of the people as a teacher.

When Hugh Lynn followed up by asking who her spiritual guides were, the Source surprised them by foreshadowing what would be revealed when Garrett had her turn to give a reading for Cayce. "Let them rather speak for themselves. For their names are rather in *her* experience, in *her* seeking."

Hugh Lynn and others would interpret this and later references to mean that various spirits or entities were working through and with Garrett to obtain information. Further, those spirits or entities might reasonably be understood to be consulting the same records as accessed by Cayce. The defining or perhaps limiting factor was the intent or degree of soul development of the seeker. When asked, "Is Mrs. Garrett contacting the highest possible sources for information in accordance with her development?" the Source responded: "As the soul seeks, higher and higher, [there] may be those influences . . . in the experience for the *development* of others in *their* approach to such realms. When the soul seeks for self, for self's own protection, and self's own activities, it [only] reaches the highest that is for that soul's development. When the self is open to those that would question or would counsel with, [it is] dependent upon the desire, the purposes, the aims, as to from what source or channel . . . "

In other words, Cayce was suggesting that when one is seeking for self only, then the highest possible source is limited to what is necessary and sufficient just for that soul's development. When one seeks for the development of others, then the source or channel they reach depends upon their desires, purposes and aims, and could feasibly be higher sources than they would otherwise contact.

Hugh Lynn would a little later pose this question about his father, not Garrett: "If Edgar Cayce has ever had controls, does he know who they are?" This was an understandable question as only on rare occasions did who or what was speaking through Cayce stop and identify itself. But when it did happen, who or what coming through made a special point of interrupting the reading to do so.

The response and subsequent exchange was particularly insightful. "Anyone may speak who may seek, if the entity or the soul's activities will allow same; or if the desire of the individuals seeking so over commands as to make for a set channel."

This suggested that who or whatever came through Cayce in trance could depend upon the seeker. More intriguing was the response when Hugh Lynn asked about Cayce's power of clairvoyance. The Source said that Edgar didn't have to enter a trance to access psychic information but that he actually was "more [psychic] in the normal or physical state than in the hypnotic state." What was required for Edgar to exercise this presumably latent ability was for him to cleanse himself of his "carnal influences." Further, that "with the regeneration that should come into the experience of the entity, this then may be the manner, the channel, the way through which much of constructive forces may be given."

This response surprised Hugh Lynn as it did the others. But Gladys and the Cayce family on some level understood that this statement had merit. Edgar already experienced a wide range of paranormal talents in his waking state—more so with each new year. He just didn't talk about the experiences or choose to explore this side of his waking self. Critics already considered him to be "freakish." There was no telling how the Cayces and their lives might be negatively affected if it were discovered that, in addition to what Edgar could do when "asleep," he could consciously read minds, intuit future events, and converse with discarnates.

Also noteworthy was the reference to rejuvenation. Ever since the demise of the Cayce hospital, Gertrude and Gladys Davis feared for Edgar's health. That he would somehow need to "rejuvenate" himself was a distinct possibility. Gladys and the Cayces had only to consider Edgar's last visit to the Zentgraf home when the East Indian had appeared. Edgar had contracted a case of pneumonia so severe that an ambulance had been called to take him to the hospital. Against everyone's advice, Edgar had inexplicably gone into an upstairs bedroom with Hugh Lynn and locked the door. He told Hugh Lynn that he had to cure himself, which is what he did. Had Edgar discussed this event with his family, their lingering concerns might have been mitigated. But he stubbornly wouldn't talk about it. Nor did he reveal what the East Indian had told him.

Had the mysterious turbaned man warned Edgar not to go to the hospital? Had he told Edgar to heal himself instead? Edgar had not satisfactorily answered either of these questions. He had simply gone upstairs and locked himself in one of the bedrooms and hours later, drenched in sweat, exited the room, having cured himself of pneumonia. The latest reading now suggested he might have to heal himself again. If that was so, how soon would it be? Would there be another appearance by the turbaned man?

Who or what was speaking through Cayce in this reading was Hugh Lynn's final question of the session. Just as the previous remarks his father had made in trance, the answer came as a surprise, and not a pleasant one: "Being directed . . . from the records through Halaliel."

The mention of Halaliel's name was enough to send shivers through everyone in the room. This was an entity who had only recently made appearances in the readings. In the entity's first appearance, five months earlier, Halaliel was introduced as "a new initiate" offering his services to become Cayce's channel or control dedicated to enhancing his psychic ability. Halaliel would later pay an unexpected return visit in a reading requesting information on Germany's new chancellor, Adolf Hitler.

In a thunderous and altogether ominous voice, this is what had come through: "The weakling, the unsteady, must enter into the crucible and become as naught, even as He [the Master of Masters], that they may know the way. I, Halaliel, have spoken."

Halaliel, the readings indicated, was an angel of the highest order who, alongside Archangel Michael, had fought Ariel, the defender and companion to Lucifer. Halaliel was what might reasonably be described as the Lord of Karma, whose power would make paths straight and correct human faults and weakness by bringing immediate or forced "understanding." Only the price one paid for such "understanding," the readings made clear, would be "heavy." In Hitler's case, that understanding would come with one nation making devastating war on others.

Halaliel was now back, hovering somewhere in the room or in some other dimension and speaking through the sleeping Cayce in a reading intended for Eileen Garrett. Only the reading somehow didn't seem to be so much about a fellow psychic as about Edgar and the future of the Cayce work. Did Edgar need a designated control? And if so, was it to be Halaliel?

This made what would follow in Garrett's reading both frightening and all the more compelling. Hugh Lynn conducted the hour-and-twenty-minute session with Garrett seated on the same couch where Cayce had previously lain down. The dialogue commenced immediately after Garrett nodded off into a trance and Garrett's control introduced himself.

"It is I, Uvani, I give you greeting, friends. Peace be with you and in your life, and in your work, and in your household. I give you greeting, my friends. What is it you would have of me, please?"

Hugh Lynn asked Uvani what he could tell them about Cayce's work.

"Little more than you yourselves know," Uvani replied, then proceeded to describe how Cayce was particularly sensitive and intuitive, hence his ability to ethereally travel and bring back psychically derived information. As expanded upon later in the reading, Edgar was said to pass through several or more planes to obtain necessary records of an individual's life. His etheric passage, Uvani declared, was slow and dangerous, for Cayce failed to request assistance when journeying and was expending much "strength" to reach beyond himself.

In what appeared to be an invitation for Cayce to turn to some other entity for help, Uvani described an onerous weight on Edgar's shoulders. "It makes a great drain [for him] . . . using his full etheric leverage and is also drawing upon his own spiritual light for your assistance. While it may be said, therefore, that ever did he use this without help [in the form of a control], he is giving you something of his own life."

Hugh Lynn also wanted to know if his father actually met someone or something on the other side when he went to collect psychic information.

Uvani said that he suspected that Cayce was not alone when he arrived to consult the Akashic records, what Uvani called the "hall of wisdom," but admitted that he couldn't see who was waiting or helping Cayce to obtain the desired knowledge. As this reading suggested, and a later reading would elaborate upon, Uvani himself could not go to the same destination as Cayce did or rise through as many planes as Cayce was described as doing. In so traveling, Uvani maintained, it was difficult for Cayce to translate what he found into easily comprehensible language or into what Uvani described as Edgar's own "understandings," and so better or more clearly convey the information he found. Uvani seemed again to be inviting or tempting Edgar to seek help from someone or something who would presumably be doing the heavy lifting on his behalf.

As successful as Uvani said Edgar was in his etheric journeying and as Cayce himself remarked in the reading earlier that day, Uvani said that Cayce was capable of doing much more in his waking state than he was doing in his subjugated trance state. Among the gifts available to Edgar would be the laying on of hands to heal the sick, whether it was people who came to him for medical help or medical help Edgar himself required.

Uvani further remarked that Edgar was not willing to go the extra distance required to access this latent ability. Edgar had convinced himself that he had to be in hypnotic trance to accomplish what he did and that this was how he wanted it. For Edgar to overcome what might be termed his mental hurdle, Edgar had only to ask for help, which was clearly Uvani's way of extending yet another overture for Edgar to invite a controlling entity into the equation. However, as Uvani also said, "If he is happy in his own state, it is also good, for what *is* good for him, as *he* knows and understands . . . is probably the right interpretation."

Consistent with readings Cayce had conducted for himself, Uvani described previous incarnations which had led to Edgar's psychic development. The difference, in this case, was Uvani's expansion or elucidation on a past life Cayce had in India, which he said Edgar had been suppressing. It was in this lifetime, Uvani said, where Edgar had been tortured and was the reason that Edgar had suffered throat-related problems. "For he evidently has suffered, been tortured, been hurt; and you will find, my friend, that sometime if you like I would speak with you of these many things that have held him up in life, the . . . [propensity] almost to choke, the inability sometimes to be able to get the words clearly."

These remarks resonated with Hugh Lynn as they did with his father. An Indian incarnation had been referenced before in Cayce's Life Readings, but it had never been more than a footnote. Details hadn't been forthcoming as they had for his lifetimes in Egypt and Persia. Yet, as was known to everyone in the Cayce family, Edgar had an unexplained affinity for artwork from India, especially work featuring elephants. He had photographed circus elephants when he first became a photographer and collected miniature carved and glass elephants, which he kept on a shelf behind his Virginia Beach office desk.

Most relevant to what Uvani was saying, Edgar had had many throat-related maladies over the years, not the least was his year-long debilitating case of laryngitis. When he had chosen to ignore or suppress his psychic gifts, he always seemed to lose his voice. Was it only

Just a few of many in Edgar's Elephant Collection.

a coincidence that the debilitating laryngitis of his youth was described in previous readings as both physiological *and* psychological? What Uvani now seemed to be suggesting was that if Cayce were to embrace his previous incarnation in India, he would not only overcome the difficulties he had with his throat, but that many new insights would also be revealed to him and greater psychic powers would result.

"I will tell you what to do, and do it with great earnestness and great care," Uvani said, again extending an invitation. "With your cooperation . . . [I will] ask and insist upon that strength through someone else who will help you, free you, and give you greater ability to reach these things."

The reference was not to Uvani himself. Yet Uvani claimed to know of the entity of whom he spoke, saying: "There are those around me who often speak, who know him well."

Hugh Lynn asked if this was the same entity who had spoken through Edgar in the reading he had given for Garrett. Uvani wouldn't say: "I was not present, my friend, at this experience; also I have not your father's permission to speak of this."

At this point in the reading, Edgar himself, seated beside Hugh Lynn, interjected: "You may speak of it."

Uvani replied, referencing without explanation someone or something which was Edgar's "parent" and presumably was the actual or primary source of Cayce's information. In so doing, however, Uvani continued to be evasive about who the entity was Uvani wanted Edgar to take on as a partner:

> A man of strong and ardent physique . . . he knows . . . much of the Mosaic law, he knows the law of Chaldea and the law of the Egyptian . . . and has on more than one occasion revealed himself. Now why do you not let him come and break down some of the darkness . . . If you . . . allow this one to come into being, you will loosen a whole fund of ability and give to him the greater clarification with all his work, taking away much of the exhaustion and confusion . . . [of entering a hypnotic trance state]. If you knew the infinitive power for good that you have behind you, you would not be discouraged at this moment . . . If you open your arms to the loving help that this one would give to you, it would renew a virility . . .

When pressed by Hugh Lynn, and having received Edgar's permission to speak more on this subject, Uvani still would not reveal the entity's name, only tantalizing clues.

"Do you connect in any way with his work the name Halaliel?" Hugh Lynn asked.

"We do know the meaning of the name, my friend," Uvani came back. "It is connected so definitely over a period of time that we just spoke of . . . one who has responded, one who has been scorched, one who has overcome, one who has survived."

Was the reference to the Indian incarnation? Was Edgar's throat burned in this lifetime, perhaps for speaking of things that were outlawed? Or was this one who was scorched Halaliel in his heavenly battle with Lucifer's Ariel? Uvani didn't say. He only continued to issue an invitation:

> I rather hope, my friend, you will permit this dweller to come very close. . . . Because . . . you do not always know how to use that illimitable fund that is yours, I would say to you it would be so well worthwhile to permit help, that there may be much beauty and understanding, much more humility and much more healing, from your experience in the Indian incarnation . . . Is there anything more you would like to say to me before I leave?

This was Uvani's cue that Hugh Lynn should wrap up the session. He would likely have time for just one or two final questions. "Can you tell us anything regarding this crystal sent my father from India?" Hugh Lynn asked. "Do you know who sent it to him?"

Uvani replied:

> I am very certain there is a definite connection between that and . . . [Cayce's] own experience, and I feel very definitely certain that it is after all what you call the looking glass. Look within it, my friend, and see the thing that has been troubling your life . . . I do not think that your father [Edgar Cayce] desires to look within the crystal at all, but I'm sure that if he does he will see this [India] experience that he is avoiding. It is given to him as a symbol.

The message here, as Uvani's response suggested, was that Halaliel had somehow sent the crystal ball and further, that he could be the East Indian who had mysteriously appeared and disappeared at pivotal moments in Cayce's life. Perhaps this was such a moment.

Edgar was being invited to do what Garrett had apparently done years earlier by permitting Uvani to control or act as her etheric agent. The entity in this case, Halaliel, could potentially move Cayce's work to an all new level—one in which the total sum of his psychic powers would manifest or be released in his conscious state. Miracles might be his to perform.

To begin the journey Cayce was told he had only to look into the crystal ball where would be revealed images of the Indian incarnation which he had been suppressing. Would he see, by chance, his tongue being torn out by its root or visions of being tortured for revealing hidden mysteries of the universe?

Always courteous, Uvani signed off. "And I thank you, my friend, for this opportunity to speak with you. May the good Lord in His infinite mercy, Lord of all the universe, inspire and bless you and keep you."

Here the reading ended.

Eileen Garrett and Edgar Cayce would say good-be and would not cross paths again. But this would not end the relationship between the A.R.E. and Garrett's Parapsychology Foundation. Relations would always remain cordial. Before Garrett's death in France in 1970, she would deliver a keynote lecture at an A.R.E. conference and was introduced by Tom Sugrue.

Edgar apparently never looked into the crystal ball. Nor did he invite Halaliel into his readings. Tempted though he must have been, Uvani was perhaps correct in suggesting that Edgar wasn't ready, willing, or desirous of exploring his Indian incarnation or having an intercessor or control. Even though giving the readings ultimately proved to be too great a strain—by all accounts hastening his premature demise—Cayce preferred to do his own etheric heavy lifting. Nor was he eager to experience the kind of soul development and "understanding" that might come hand-in-hand with inviting Halaliel into his life. Edgar believed, and the readings would later confirm, that he was being directed by no less than the Master of Masters, Jesus himself.

While Halaliel was not invited to join the party, so to speak, the crystal ball remained property of the Cayce family, though it was not used for its intended purpose. Grandson Charles Thomas Cayce would fondly remember playing with it as an infant. He would take it from his grandfather's office shelf and roll it down the hallway. For bowling pins he would use his grandfather's collection of miniature elephants.

Ernest Zentgraf (1877 to 1960).

Ernest Zentgraf:

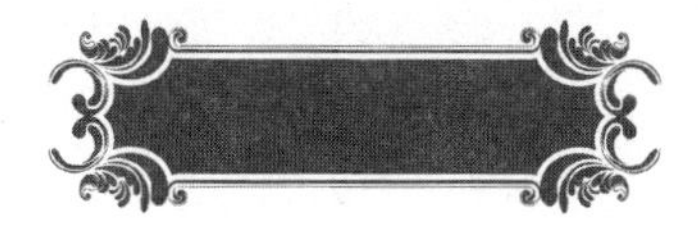

Contemplating Suicide

Edgar's relationship with Helene and Ernest Zentgraf went far beyond their provision of a safe haven on his trips to New York. Three family members had been successfully treated at the Cayce hospital and Ernest had been the first chairman of the A.R.E. Board of Trustees. They and their six children, extended family members, and employees would collectively receive nearly two hundred spiritual and medical readings. To Helene—whose love of life, dedication to the family, and generosity were an inspiration to all who knew her—Edgar would pay a most magnanimous compliment: "If I had to choose one woman out of the world to pattern my life after, it would be you."

Gladys Davis and the Cayces were thus deeply saddened by a telephone call from Helene's seventeen-year-old daughter Margaret on April 19, 1934, less than three months after Edgar had given the reading for Eileen Garrett. Ernest had disappeared from home, taking with him a pistol. He was last seen at a small coffee shop in Reading, Pennsylvania where he had mailed a postcard indicating that he was about to take his own life. Knowing what they did about Ernest—once he made up his mind about something, he invariably followed through—Helene and the Cayces feared for the worst.

Ernest had suffered a nervous breakdown, the result of a depression stemming from his belief that he was a failure as a businessman, husband, and father. Margaret didn't share the specifics, but as would later be revealed by others, fifty-six-year-old Ernest had been the trustee for a $2 million family trust, most of which he had lost in the stock market and on other bad investments. Just before his disappearance, Ernest's sister, Marie, a trust beneficiary, had severely criticized Ernest for his handling of the family accounts.

Edgar had suspected something of the family's financial plight because Ernest had previously requested a series of business readings relating to the sale of a large tract of property in upstate New York and difficulties he was having at his Staten Island paper-products manufacturing plant. The readings had repeatedly counseled Ernest to stay calm and not do anything rash; his business challenges would eventually take care of themselves. Edgar was also aware that mental instability ran in the family. Ernest's sister had to be temporarily hospitalized for obsessive and irrational behaviors.

Edgar, appreciative of the family's desire for privacy, asked no further questions. At Margaret's request a reading was conducted the same afternoon and one the following morning to determine if Ernest was still alive, and if so, where he was and what could be done to return him home.

The message that came back was not hopeful. No information could be given without Ernest or his higher-self requesting that help be given. Further, as indicated in the reading, Ernest had built a veritable mental "wall" separating him from outside help. No family member, or even Edgar Cayce in trance, could directly interfere in what was a matter of Ernest's free will. If Ernest chose to kill himself, the decision was his alone. As the Source made clear:

> Each soul must seek . . . within itself. Ernest's desire builds as great a wall of resistance between the known and the unknown as may be built by any desire on the part of individuals. For each is the test of that they hold as their ideal. And, as given, there should not be sought through such channels that which would prevent any soul

> from meeting that which is its own cross to bear.

Edgar explained this concept to Margaret over the phone and also in a letter he wrote to Helene: "This is one of those things that is hard to understand . . . The readings are given wholly from the mental and spiritual angle, as we have been told not to use these channels for forcing a person against his will . . . or to override another's desire . . . Even in a case like this where the man means so much to us, we are helpless. A man's will is supreme."

Still, Edgar was not about to give up. Ernest was too dear a friend and the consequences of his committing suicide too horrible to imagine. Previous readings given for individuals with suicidal tendencies indicated that suicide, except in rare instances, was a supremely selfish act which degraded the soul and defeated the very purpose of life. The premise in the readings is that suicide essentially deprives the soul of lessons it needs to encounter and at some level, has chosen. Not only was suicide seen as an act of selfishness, but the Cayce information states that the soul will simply have to encounter again the same issues that led to the suicide in the first place.

"Why is the thought always with me to kill myself?" a Broadway showgirl, suffering from anorexia, asked Cayce. "Self-condemnation" came the response. "Why is suicide considered wrong?" asked a Michigan housewife and mother. "So long as there are those that depend upon the body . . . No man liveth to himself, no man dieth to himself. No man hath been so low that some soul hath not depended upon, relied upon same for strength."

The recommendation that consistently came through Cayce was for the individual to strengthen his will by putting his fears aside, doing good for others, and letting God take care of the rest. "When desire for death and the desire for life is presented . . . make thy life one with His love! When such desires . . . [take hold] look about self and see the struggle so many souls are making to keep body and soul together. How hast thou in ANY manner ministered to making THEIR burden lighter? In lightening the burden of another thine own is lightened twofold." Cayce—in trance—also offered a prayer that would help calm the suicidal urge. "When this thought occurs, let thy prayer be as indicated: Lord, Here am I—Thine! Use me in those ways and manners as

FEAR STATEN ISLAND MAN SUICIDE HERE

Son's Search Fruitless; Locates Auto

Following a fruitless search for his father, Ernest Zentgraf, jr., Staten Island, N. Y., left Reading yesterday.

Police will continue their search today for Ernest W. Zentgraf, sr., 57, president of a glazed paper and book-bindery company, who it is feared by the family may nave contemplated suicide after mailing a claim check to his wife for his automobile, stored in a Reading garage.

A check revealed the manufacturer had registered last Tuesday at a hotel here, placed his suitcase, hat and topcoat in his automobile, and had driven to a garage for storage. That was the last seen of him, police said.

The missing man's son, accompanied by a friend, arrived here yesterday, after members of the family had communicated with New York police. The son recovered the car with the claim check mailed to Mrs. Zentgraf. The suitcase and clothes were in the car.

1934 New York newspaper article on search for Ernest Zentgraf.

thou seest, that I may ever glorify thee."

How to convey this message to Ernest? He had left for parts unknown, taking his pistol with him. Helen and the family chauffeur had already driven to Reading and had searched for him everywhere they could think of. They had shown a photograph of Ernest to shopkeepers, police, and strangers on the street. There wasn't a clue as to what had become of him.

The plan which Edgar and Helene conceived was for Edgar to use his psychic gifts so that it would not interfere with Ernest's free will, but rather, through prayer and direct communication on a soul-to-soul level, strengthen and support Ernest in a time of obvious need. The Zentgrafs in Staten Island and the Cayces in Virginia Beach would open a psychic channel through which they could receive whatever advice or insights the Source would have for the family, and through which they could send their prayers directly to Ernest. Thus began what became the first of thirty-three trance sessions conducted between April 19 and June 11, 1934, during which the Zentgrafs and the Cayces sent their love and prayers to Ernest and perhaps also opened a psychic soul-to-soul dialogue.

The second reading in the series, conducted on April 20, began not with a question but a statement of intent: "You will have before you the Ernest Zentgraf family at 400 St. Paul's Ave., Staten Island, N.Y., in their seeking to manifest His love during this hour of trial. You will give them that needed to enable them to carry on in the way He would have them."

The Source came back with a prayer which would be similar to how virtually every subsequent reading would begin and end:

> God, thy will be done! Thou knowest the weaknesses of the flesh. Thou knowest the purpose of every soul. Be thou the guide. Direct our words, keep our hearts, make that burden in his soul clean through the promises thou hast given in thy Son that if we cast our burdens on Him, He will be faithful to succor and aid in the hour of trial and temptation. Be with us, with him, and let the words of our mouth and the meditations of our hearts be acceptable in Thy sight, my Lord, my Redeemer, the Christ! . . . Keep the faith. Pray the prayer, and mean it.

During the third reading the family received a hopeful sign: Ernest, they were told, was "still among the living." In this same session, the Source counseled against an individual taking one's life: "To desecrate the body that is the temple of the living God is to belittle self . . . To destroy same is to be weak and unworthy of those privileges that have been thine in thy relations in the earth . . . Put thy burden on Him, and He will sustain and guide and guard thee."

On April 24, during the sixth reading in the series, the family asked that through Cayce they be permitted to "urge him to have faith in his desire for his home." Cayce—in trance—sent the prayer but indicated that Ernest was resisting, and now apparently ill. A strange discourse followed, as if the Source had stepped aside, and an angelic spirit entity was speaking directly to Ernest through Cayce's open channel, only those listening to the reading could hear the Spirit's half of the conversation:

> "Why dost thou rebel against those impulses that arise? Why dost thou continue in subjugating the better self, in making for those effects that will weaken those desires? . . . Yield not to self, but rather to that desire that is growing in thee to be with and among those that love thee best."

Similarly, on April 25, the Spirit was apparently speaking again directly to Ernest, or his higher self, imploring him to listen. "Let *Him*, thy Master, thy God . . . have His way with thee . . . For, through thine efforts may yet come *joy* in the knowledge that He lives in spirit in the hearts of those that would worship as a brother, as a friend. For, He will walk with thee and talk with thee, wilt thou but open thine inner self to hear His voice! Harkin to those promptings—now!"

The reading conducted the next day, the eighth in the series, reflected what appeared to be another step backwards for Ernest. Though still alive, he was resisting further contact. The Spirit, through Edgar, implored—almost demanded—Ernest's attention. "You have seen the way out! *Come!* You *will* come! You will let those [who love you] know, and keep that promise to self that you will let them know! Let them know!"

The message, that Ernest contact home, was apparently received. On April 28, they were told that he had written the family a letter. The next day, however, Ernest had apparently taken another step back. There was no way to know if the letter had been mailed. The Spirit again carried on a dialogue but conveyed, through Cayce, only fragments of what was being said. "Where is it? . . . This backs away!" Neither the Zentgrafs nor Cayces had a clue what was taking place except that Ernest must be undergoing some new tribulation. The only positive news came at the end of the reading: "Still in body!"

On May 2, during the twelfth reading in the series, there was indication that Christ was waiting in the wings, hovering about Ernest, anticipating a response to the pleas of His spirit messenger: "The Christ! Yes! Be thou willing that He, the God, the Christ, the love, will guide thee!"

Did Ernest respond? There was no indication in the reading the following day, only a curious reference: "Lot of water about the body this morning!"

Had Ernest now gone to the seashore? Atlantic City? There was no

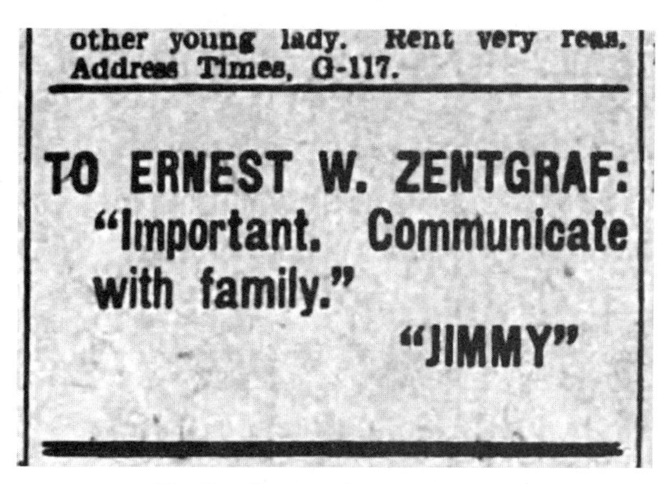
other young lady. Rent very reas. Address Times, G-117.

TO ERNEST W. ZENTGRAF: "Important. Communicate with family." "JIMMY"

The family was also attempting to contact Ernest through newspapers.

way to tell from the readings. But time was running out. "Come!" the Spirit commanded two days later. "Come while ye may."

The Spirit continued to beseech Ernest on May 7. "He knocks at the door of thy consciousness. Wilt thou not let Him in?" Then, the next day, "Be not afraid." And the following day: "He has promised to hide those in the shadow of His wings. He has promised and does put His loving arms about those that seek to let Him have His way with those hearts that are weary or burdened with the cares of the earth."

The eighteenth reading in the series, in which the Source presumably spoke through Cayce, confirmed that Ernest was still alive but that he had now changed location again. On May 12 came a similarly upbeat message. "Everything much lighter about the body, about the activities of the soul in the present." On May 14, Cayce—in trance—said that more "spirituality" was coming into Ernest's understanding of himself and that he was "surrounded by green." Ernest, at this point, appeared to be outdoors, maybe in a forest. As would later be revealed in a subsequent reading, Ernest was standing in a wooded cemetery glen.

On May 19, there appeared to be another setback. "Hindrances" had returned to haunt him. The Spirit was again beseeching Ernest to ask the Christ for help. "Let Him in. Let Him guide. Praise through thy soul

GOOD NEWS AWAITS MISSING ZENTGRAF

Son Hopes It Will Bring Father Back

Ernest W. Zentgraf, Staten Island, N. Y., manufacturer who has been missing for a week, has good news in store for him if he communicates with the members of his family who have been searching through three states for him.

Philip Zentgraf, a son who is directing the search which is being carried on by police in and around Reading—the last city in which the paper manufacturer was known to have been in—said that officials of the paper company announced business to be better than it has been for a long time.

"I know that father was worried greatly about the business," the son said, "so I know that he would be happy to learn that things were picking up."

Knowing his father enjoyed farming, the son hoped yesterday that he might be found on a Berks county farm.

The family tried to lure Ernest with good news about their business.

will make for the breaking away of those things that would hinder. Be not a stumbling block to self."

Finally, on May 25, in the twenty-seventh reading, Ernest seemed poised for a breakthrough. "There is the desire being made . . . "

Progress continued to be shown four days later. "Thou hast made the way open."

On June 2 there were no further developments that came through in the reading, but Gladys Davis had a premonition in the form of a vivid dream that Ernest had returned home. Edgar didn't want Gladys to share the dream with Helene, as it might give her false hope. Gladys thought otherwise and over Edgar's objections, wrote Helene:

> I think... [Edgar] was afraid the dream might be true. And yet I have known all along that you'd rather know. Men are so different; sometimes the very thing they think is protecting a woman is the very thing that hurts most. You see, ever since Mr. Zentgraf went away, I've been praying that I would have a vision in order to help ... This is the first thing that has come, and I don't know whether it is real or not; yet I do know that it affected me the same as the few other *real* visions I have had. It is a marvel to all of us, and especially Mrs. Cayce and me, how strong and self-reliant (rather God-reliant) you have been through this situation which has 'hit home' to the very core. Yet, it makes me feel and know what the ideal woman should be: 'Mighty in battle—serving the Lord.'

On June 9, Ernest was on the move again, walking through fields of grain, which was apparently a farmer's field. The reading on June 11 opened on a very positive note, "More hopeful . . . better conditions." Yet frustratingly, no details were given. Had Ernest finally extended his hand to the Christ?

Strangely—but very exciting for all involved—the greater message came through minutes later, just after the June 11 reading ended. Without prompting, after Gertrude gave Edgar the suggestion to come out of trance, the Source exclaimed: "How beautiful the face of those whom the Lord, the Christ, smiles upon! He would walk and talk with thee, my children."

Ernest Zentgraf returned home that night from Philadelphia. He had visited the seashore, walked in a farmer's field, and spent time in a cemetery. He had also written a letter, as referenced in the readings. After much consternation, he had finally mailed the letter in Philadelphia, and it arrived in Staten Island the day after he himself had arrived home. The letter chronicled his trials and tribulations as well as his eventual turning to Christ for help in his time of need.

Helene referred to the letter as a "holy thing," for it showed to her "the birth of a soul." Here, in part, was what it said:

> Five months ago my affairs seemed so hopeless, the tangle so muddled, that I could not see my way out . . . I made such a mess of my own affairs . . . I had been living in a 'Fool's Paradise' and needed this shock to cleanse my soul. I have confessed my errors to God and I know He has forgiven me, for wonders have happened.

The trance sessions had also touched Helene. As she wrote Edgar: "I have through this experience learned much: the necessity of living every hour of life as clearly as possible. I am surer of God as Presence and Power than ever in my life. The Divine Law must be manifested through us, and this now is my work."

Ernest Zentgraf with a grandchild, c. 1930s.

The Warshawsky home in Detroit where Gladys Davis and the Cayces stayed, conducted readings, and were arrested!

MAURICE MITSHKUN:

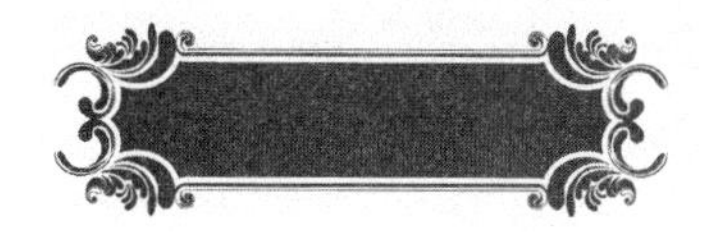

ARREST CAYCE!

Cayce was fifty-eight years old when he accepted an invitation to visit "Motor City" in mid-November 1935. His intentions were to give readings for the Detroit area A.R.E. members as well as to meet with local physicians and chiropractors desirous of learning more about his trance-inspired health treatments. Thanks to the outreach efforts of Cayce supporters Harry Bonelli, General Manager of Detroit's massive Buick manufacturing plant, and Charles Dillman, the furniture salesman in nearby Dearborn who had been the first Cayce hospital patient, a wide and divergent group of A.R.E. members awaited his arrival. Among them were Abe and Bessie Warshawsky, who were hosting Edgar, Gertrude, Hugh Lynn, and Gladys in their Webb Avenue home.

Edgar gave thirteen readings over a four-day period when on the afternoon of November 21, he was requested to give a health reading for twenty-year-old Betty Ruth Mitshkun. As was the customary practice, Edgar was not told the woman's condition, only her name and the address on Waverly Avenue where she could be found at the time that the reading was being conducted. The forty-five minute trance session that resulted was unremarkable when viewed in the greater context of the estimated fifty-two hundred health readings Cayce had previously delivered, but it bears noting as startling events would later unfold.

Betty Ruth Mitshkun suffered a respiratory condition that Cayce—in trance—said was caused by an injury at her birth or in early infancy. Recommendations included spinal manipulations, an alkaline-producing diet, and treatment sessions with a "wet-cell," a device which uses a low-voltage battery to stimulate the glands to promote eliminations of poisons.

The atypical aspects of the reading were that Betty Ruth herself had not requested the reading, applied for A.R.E. membership, paid the requisite dues, nor was she likely to have been aware that the reading was even being conducted. Technically this was breaking the cardinal rules of the fledgling A.R.E.'s bylaws which were intended to provide a legal firewall between Edgar Cayce giving trance counsel and statutes governing healthcare providers.

In this particular instance, however, the Cayces weren't concerned because membership dues were paid by a Mitshkun family friend, and Betty Ruth's father, Maurice, who had requested the reading on her behalf, had filled out the application. In addition, he had already witnessed one trance session. It was assumed that he understood the nature of the readings and the means by which they were given. The desire to jump ahead and help a critically ill young woman trumped standard operating procedures.

Over the next nine days, eighteen more readings were given including one which was witnessed by upwards of forty people—many of whom were physicians and medical practitioners. The only early warning sign that anything was amiss was the unexpected arrival, on the twenty-eighth, of a man identifying himself as "Mr. King," who claimed to have a child in desperate need of Cayce's medical help. As no A.R.E. members had referred him to the Warshawskys for a reading and he was unwilling to pay dues or sign membership papers, no reading was given.

Two days later on Saturday, November 30, just before 2 p.m., four police officers, including a Michigan health officer, arrived at the

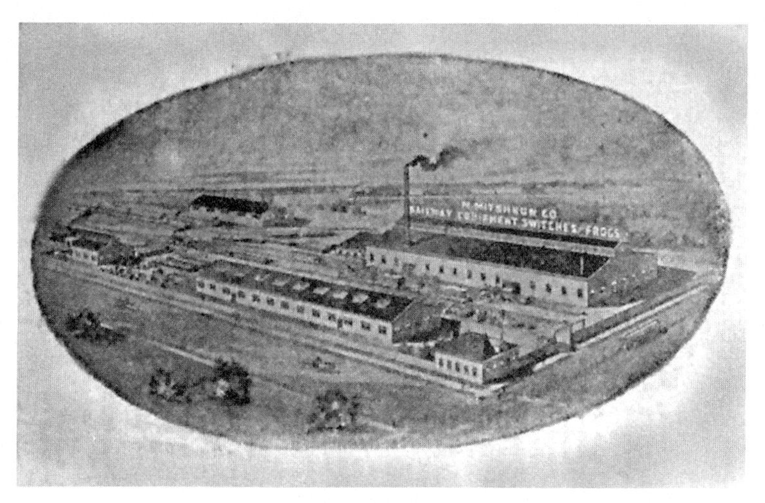

The owner of M. Mitshkun Co. Railway Equipment Company, Maurice Mitshkun, had thought that although his daughter was not present for the reading, that somehow treatments had been rendered. He complained that she had not been cured.

OFFICE OF THE
PROSECUTING ATTORNEY
COUNTY OF WAYNE

Detroit, Mich. Nov. 30, 1935.

Hon. John P. Scallen,
Judge of the Recorder's Court of the City of Detroit

Dear Sir:—I recommend the issuing of a warrant for

Practicing medicine without a license.

Betty Ruth Mitshkun

Date of Offense Nov.21,1935 - Nov.22,1935.

against Edgar Cayce, Hugh Lynn Cayce, Gertrude Cayce, Gladys Davis,

Address 3046 Webb Ave.

upon the complaint of Maurice D. Mitshkun

Address 2940 Waverly Ave.

Respectfully yours,

Prosecuting Attorney.

BRB

The arrest warrant for the Cayce family and Gladys Davis, November 30, 1935.

Warshawsky home and arrested Edgar, Gertrude, Hugh Lynn, and Gladys on charges of practicing medicine without a license. The arrest warrant was signed by Maurice Mitshkun and included charges that health treatments for Betty Ruth had been recommended—which was true—and that treatments had been given—which was false.

Maurice Mitshkun, as it soon became clear, hadn't adequately understood the membership form he had signed or the nature of the trance advice he had received. He apparently believed that Edgar Cayce could "cure" his daughter by simply going into trance and did not find her cured when he next saw her. Moreover, his daughter's physician had declared the reading "worthless." Without first meeting or speaking to Edgar or giving the reading to one of the physicians familiar with Cayce's methods, this physician had recommended that Mitshkun file charges.

Police detectives took Gladys' stenography notebook for evidence. They then escorted her and the three Cayces to the county jail where they were processed and locked up pending arraignment. Following standard police procedure, their clothes, wallets, purses, and keys were taken, leaving each with $1.50 for cigarettes and candy.

The timing of their arrest on a Saturday afternoon when the courts were closed and the previous visit by Mr. King, who was later revealed to be an undercover policeman, didn't bode well. The plan from the start, apparently, was for the prosecutor to assemble a case against the Cayces and Gladys Davis and to keep them behind bars for the entire weekend. Had they been arrested the day before, or even earlier the same day, the "out-of-towners" would have appeared before a judge and been released pending a formal hearing.

Edgar was baffled. Having long straddled the thin line between offering trance counsel and providing medical advice, he could understand how this might have happened to him, but having his family and secretary treated as common criminals was beyond comprehension. Later he looked on the incident as a blessing in disguise, for it revealed the good that could be done in a jail cell.

Gladys and Gertrude were taken to the women's section of the jail and each put in a narrow cell furnished with a bunk and toilet. Edgar and Hugh Lynn, however, were locked inside a "holding tank" with some twenty to twenty-five inmates awaiting arraignment, sentencing, or transfer to another facility. As twenty-eight-year-old Hugh Lynn recounted the story, as soon as the jail door slammed closed behind them, fellow inmates gathered in a menacing circle around him and Edgar. The leader of the group—no doubt an individual capable of physically enforcing his will—demanded the three dollars that they had been given, and they promptly handed it over. As other extortion demands were surely about to be made upon them, a remarkable event occurred.

The leader asked Edgar why they had been arrested, and in answering, Edgar displayed his rarely exhibited power of conscious clairvoyance. Without entering into a trance state, he told his fellow inmates the real reason that they, the other inmates, were there.

"Like all of you, there is the back of what you are accused of, the real cause, the real reason for your confinement," Edgar said. He then looked directly at the jailhouse leader. "You are accused of hitting a child with an automobile. That's why you are here. But the real reason for your confinement is a conflict with your wife that's been going on for a long time. You were very, very angry after an argument with her. Because of this anger you got into your car and pulled out quickly without being very observant and struck a child."

Hugh Lynn described the jailhouse leader as turning white and the other inmates, upon hearing their "back-stories," gasping at the "truths" Cayce revealed to them. As might be expected, Edgar and Hugh Lynn were given the two best mattresses in the holding tank, along with overall preferential treatment.

Fortunately, Edgar and Hugh Lynn didn't actually have to sleep on the mattresses, as they, along with Gertrude and Gladys, were released on bail through the timely intercession of people who had attended their Detroit trance readings. Half their bail bond was put up by Harry Bonelli, who had just the week before received a successful reading for kidney stones, and the other half by Charles Dillman. Instead of a night in jail, they were taken to a restaurant and the theater.

In a plea-bargain agreement the following March, charges against Hugh Lynn, Gertrude, and Gladys were dropped, and Edgar, on the advice of his attorney, pled guilty to reduced charges. The judge was satisfied that Edgar had not physically examined or treated Betty Ruth, but under a strict interpretation of Michigan law, Cayce—not licensed

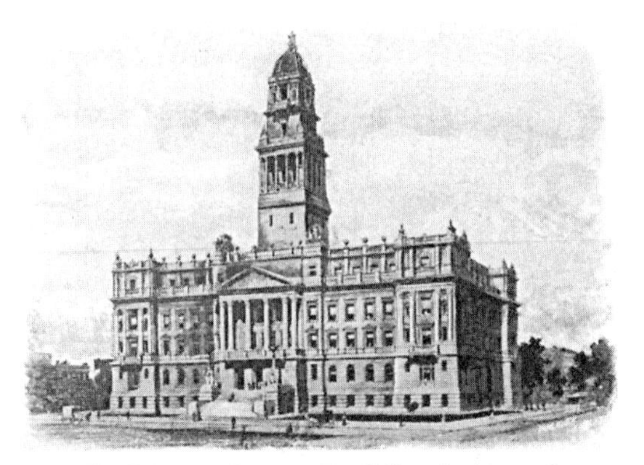

The Wayne County Building in Detroit where the Cayces most likely went to trial.

A. Mrs. Warshawsky, Mr. and Mrs. Cayce and Miss Gladys Davis.
Q. During this evening at your home did Mr. Cayce, Mrs. Cayce or Gladys Davis make any promises to Mr. Mitshkun regarding cures for his daughter?
A. I did not. After Mr. Mitchkun stated that he did not have funds to carry out the reading Mr. Cayce offered to recommend to the Association for Research and Enlightenment, Inc., that whatever ~~treatments necessary for his daughter~~ expenses necessary in checking the information of the reading be met by the Association without cost to Mr. Mitchkun.

Note: The point might be stressed from the above testimony that Mr. Mitchkun received from Mr. Warshawsky and Mr. Lasky the impression that Mr. Cayce made promises regarding curing his daughter, but that no such claims were made by any one connected with the Association.

Questioning Hugh Lynn Cayce

Q. Do you know one, Maurice D. Mitchkun?
A. Yes.
Q. When did you first meet Mr. Mitchkun?
A. On the afternoon of November 21, 1935, at the home of Mr. Warshawsky, 3046 Webb Ave.
Q. Give the subatance of your conversation with him

A snippet of the transcript of the trial in March of 1936.

to practice medicine—had given information that constituted a medical diagnosis. Because no one other than the Cayces and Gladys Davis had been harmed or inconvenienced, no fine or jail time was warranted.

Cayce was sentenced to a short period of probation in Virginia Beach. By chance, serendipity, or the universal forces at work, the Norfolk parole officer assigned his case was the brother-in-law of an A.R.E. member whom Edgar had helped overcome injuries sustained in a debilitating automobile accident. The officer enjoyed making routine checks on his Virginia Beach parolee during which he received medical, vocational, and business readings, including advice on taking out a home loan.

Cayce's impromptu jail-house trance counsel was one of several examples of his conscious clairvoyance which appeared to increase after the demise of the Cayce hospital and "stewardship" of the Atlanteans who were now working with Cayce.

In another notable instance, which took place when Edgar and Hugh Lynn were dining at a hotel restaurant, Edgar stopped a woman as she was about to step out the door. He politely excused himself for intruding, explained briefly who he was, and urged the woman—a perfect stranger—not to ride in a car that day. The conversation lasted no more than a few minutes, after which Edgar bid the woman goodbye and returned to his meal. The next day Edgar and Hugh Lynn returned to the same restaurant where they found the woman waiting for them. She was nearly "breathless" as she hugged and blessed Edgar for saving her life. Only hours before she had received news that a relative, with whom she had intended to take a car trip, had had a fatal automobile accident. Because of Edgar's warning she had decided to stay home and had urged the driver—to no avail—to do the same. The woman carried with her a telegram confirming the accident.

Edgar's trip to Detroit is also relevant to an aspect of his work which has long intrigued students of the readings: his predictions of future world events. On March 3, 1936, after sentencing and on his return train trip from Detroit to Virginia Beach, Edgar dreamed he had been reborn in the year 2158 in Nebraska, which, due to earthquakes or war, had become a coastal region. While just a boy in this dream, he insisted to his elders that he had been Edgar Cayce in a previous life and had been arrested in Detroit. He said that if someone would take him back to the city, he could find the actual police records.

Would America eventually self-destruct as had Atlantis? This was how many people chose to interpret the information that came through in the dream. It should be noted, however, that this came through in a dream and not in a reading. In addition, nearly all the so-called "predictions" said to appear in the Cayce readings aren't actually presented as fact but as statements regarding what might be given the current circumstances. The future, as Cayce repeatedly said, was not set in stone. It's what was held in a person's heart and mind that determined his or her future, both individually and collectively. Further, the earnest prayers and intercession of just a few dedicated souls could change the course of mankind.

As Cayce would say a few years later to Sherwood Eddy, the influential Protestant missionary and author who touched the lives of millions:

> "The prayers of ten may save a city, the prayers of twenty-five may save a nation, as the prayers and activities of one may! But in union there is strength."

The photo of 16-year-old Anne Neumark (center), her twin Sara (Sadie), and sister Goldie (Dolly) on their US Passport obtained while living in Petrograd, Russia. They were born in the USA to Latvian parents, left as young girls with their parents, and returned to Boston in 1923.

Anne Neumark:

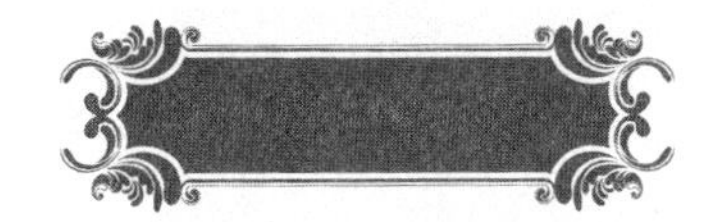

Artist in the Asylum

The closure of the Cayce hospital had made it all the more difficult for the ill to find Cayce and obtain readings. There was also the added problem of locating physicians willing to treat patients as the readings recommended. Even celebrity A.R.E. members such as film producer Jessie Lasky and composer George Gershwin couldn't locate doctors willing to act on the treatments recommended–despite the fact that in Lasky's case his physicians deemed Cayce's diagnosis of heart disease as "perfect." In Gershwin's case the physicians didn't consider Cayce's dietary treatments as being relevant to the "mental depression" for which he sought relief. Gershwin died from a brain tumor five years after his reading, and Lasky later dropped dead from a heart attack.

For thirty-two-year-old Anne Neumark, strapped to a gurney at the Ward's Island Hospital, New York City's largest insane asylum, the challenges were much greater. Her mental condition was considered hopeless, and her physical state deteriorated to the point where she was down to 80 pounds. And without funds to obtain private care, she had to rely solely on a staff of doctors and nurses whose case

**View of Ward's Island
Lunatic Asylum from Manhattan.**

loads didn't permit any more than a cursory examination more than once a week. How she found Cayce in 1938 and received trance recommended medical treatment the following year was nothing short of a miracle.

Dr. Frank Dobbins, the private practice physician who came to Anne's rescue, was one of only three physicians in all of New York who had dedicated himself to using the Cayce trance readings to treat his patients. By this time, it wasn't only the failure of the hospital but also the bad press that ensued which turned other doctors away from the holistic type of medicine suggested by the readings. The discovery of penicillin in 1928 had already set into motion a popular abandonment of natural approaches to medicine. By 1938 the media was portraying physicians as "scientists" who would eventually provide cures for whatever ailments and diseases plagued the human race in the form of a simple pill. The innovations Cayce recommended in terms of diet, preventative therapeutics, and holistic health were viewed by the medical community as antiquated or worse still, a dangerous alternative to "modern medicine."

Before discovering the Cayce readings, Dr. Dobbins himself had conformed to the more fashionable dictates of his colleagues. Then, just as Dr. House before him, he was touched by the readings in ways that made it impossible for him to turn his back on the methods pioneered in the Cayce hospital. An osteopath, he had moved from Maine to New York in 1932 to try and expand his practice. Then a day came when a New York housewife arrived at his office and handed him a Cayce reading she had obtained at the hospital in Virginia Beach, expecting Dobbins to treat her daughter based on what it said. Dobbins had obvious misgivings but having just arrived in the city and having very few patients, said that he would take the reading under consideration after first examining the patient himself.

Before studying the reading, he gave the child a complete physical examination. Later that night, he investigated the reading, and to his shock and surprise, the diagnosis tallied exactly with his own. When he got to the end of the reading, his shock turned into incredulity. Dobbins nearly fell out of his chair when he came to the part where Cayce—in trance—was asked where the mother should take her daughter for treatments in New York: "Find Dobbins!" Had the reading been given later, once Dobbins was more established, he might not have been so astonished. When the reading was given, his name was not even listed in the phone book. Dobbins soon became a devoted fan of Cayce and used the readings to diagnose 95% of his cases.

Another dedicated convert to Cayce's view of medicine was Dr. Harold J. Reilly, a physiotherapist who would, more than any single physician in the two decades after the hospital's closure, popularize the value of the medical readings and thereby provide the Cayce family with a steady inflow of new A.R.E. members.

Using trance advice and his own considerable charm and medical expertise, Reilly was able to relocate his practice from a small gym in the Bronx to a suite of rooms at the Rockefeller Center, where his clients would come to include a number of famous business and professional people in New York and Hollywood. Eventually he would specialize in all forms of drugless therapy, using techniques he had learned at the American School of Naturopathy and the American School of Chiropractics. His unique medical knowledge and emphasis on physical fitness had been everywhere evident in his small gym, which offered a complete line of exercise equipment as well as many types of hydrotherapy, electrotherapy, and other forms of manipulative therapeutics. "It is an old cliché to say that Americans take better care of their cars than they do their bodies," he told patients. "But it is none the less true. Less wax on the car and more peanut oil on the body should be the rule in households for a stronger, healthier country."

A third New York physician, Henry Hardwicke, took a particular

Dr. Harold Reilly
1895 to 1987.

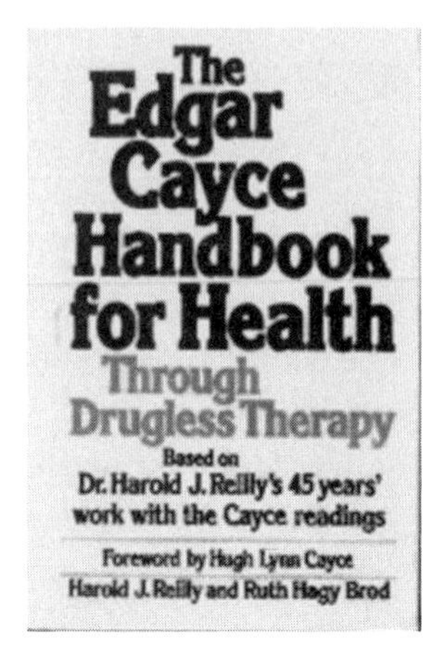

Original cover of Dr. Reilly's book (still in print today).

interest in readings referring to nutrition and its relationship to the freshness of food and how it is prepared. He would lead the way by conducting studies referencing the negative effects of smoking cigarettes and inhaling automobile and other toxic fumes. He even addressed subjects that were increasingly taboo, such as the chemical imbalance which resulted from taking antibiotics. Like Dobbins and Reilly, he viewed all of these factors as "dangerous traps" that conspired to make it more difficult to stay healthy and avoid disease.

Anne Neumark, the patient confined at the Manhattan Psychiatric Center on Ward's Island, would need the combined wisdom of all three of these physicians, along with Cayce, to truly effect her cure. By sheer coincidence—Divine intervention fans of the Cayce work would later say—the three doctors, accompanied by Edgar, were on stage at the Hotel McAlpin in New York on the night of December 6, 1938, lecturing on the holistic health practices pioneered at the Cayce hospital. Among other topics covered was alternative therapy for the mentally ill—something that perhaps had never before been discussed in such a public forum outside of medical school. A sudden and thunderous downpour of rain sent a thirty-two-year-old seamstress, Anne Neumark's twin sister, rushing into the hotel lobby for shelter. She might not have paid attention to what was taking place in the hotel

McAlpin Hotel at 34th and Broadway (Herald Square) in New York City.

conference room had it not been for the dramatic appearance of a second unexpected visitor at the hotel that night.

As rain was pounding the sidewalks outside the hotel, Dr. Dobbins was on stage sharing the story of a former New York postal employee who had been sent to an upstate mental institution. Physicians had diagnosed him as suffering from a stress-related mental illness but were unable to ascertain what had actually caused his condition. An otherwise normal and well-adjusted forty-six-year-old husband and father, he had returned home from work one evening and exploded with sudden rage, beating his wife and nearly killing one of his three children. The police had been called in, and he was subsequently remanded to an insane asylum, placed in a padded cell, and could not be safely examined for several days without wearing a straight-jacket.

The postal worker's wife knew about Cayce from her sister, who was a nanny for David Kahn's two young boys. With Kahn's help, she obtained a Cayce reading and thanks to Dobbins, treatment. The reading identified the root of the problem as an accident in which he had slipped on a patch of ice in front of the post office and injured his spine. Dobbins administered the osteopathic treatments recommended in the reading, and after fourteen sessions, the patient recovered completely. This came as a revelation to those in the audience as it illustrated how instances of apparent mental illness could have physical causes. "Postal rage" hadn't yet been given a name.

As Dr. Dobbins told the story, he had no idea that his former patient, Thomas Scanlon, who wanted to meet Edgar Cayce in person, was sitting in the audience. To everyone's great surprise, Scanlon, described as a giant of a man, stood up at the back of the room and announced: "I am that man, and everything that the doctor said was true!"

Scanlon hadn't ever before publically identified himself; mental illness was one of those conditions that was only discussed in private among family members and with physicians. As Scanlon stepped up to the podium to shake his hand and tell his own story in his own words, Edgar began to cry, as did audience members. Among them was Neumark's twin sister.

Unbelievable as the story seemed to her, there on stage was Scanlon himself, returned to his former position at the postal service, substantiating the treatment provided by Dobbins that had been recommended by Cayce. Moreover, in the audience was Kahn, who had paid for Scanlon's osteopathic treatment and Hugh Lynn, now working full time for his father, who had been instrumental in coordinating their efforts. After the lecture ended and the participants gathered to leave the hotel, Anne's sister begged them to stay and listen to her sister's tragic story.

Anne, a Boston art student, had moved to New York with the dream of becoming a professional portrait painter. The first public showing of her work, at a prestigious Manhattan gallery, had been extremely well received, and she was poised to gain a foothold in a difficult and highly competitive profession. Then, inexplicably, she began to act irrationally. She would suddenly burst into tears and become violent. The next moment she would laugh uproariously and fall into a stupor. She injured herself, and then others. Physicians didn't know how to help.

For her own sake and those around her, Anne was remanded to the

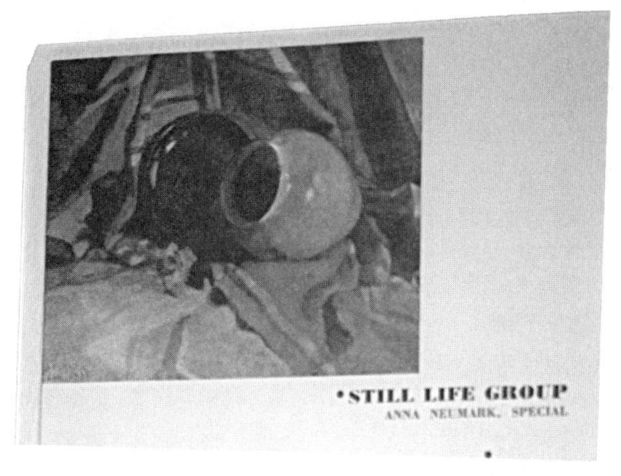

Anne's work as featured in the 1933-1934 brochure for Designer's Art School of Boston, Massachusetts.

psychiatric hospital on Ward's Island, adjacent to Randall's Island. Her condition continued to deteriorate. After an episode in which she tore her mattress in half with her fingernails, restraints had been put on her. Unable or unwilling to eat, she was now just skin and bones. She no longer recognized family members, nor could she communicate in any comprehensible manner. Electroshock therapy was ineffective; she was considered so weak from anemia that any sudden shock to her system might result in her death. At the rate at which her sister was losing weight, Sara believed that she might not live out the New Year.

After hearing her story, Cayce took hold of Hugh Lynn's arm and told him to set up an emergency appointment. Kahn volunteered to pay for her membership in the A.R.E. and to visit Ward's Island in order to consult with her physicians to ascertain the veracity of the story. He would do much more by interceding on behalf of the indigent Neumark family for Anne to be given special care and wrote letters to several well-heeled A.R.E. members to raise money to pay for her treatment.

The first of six medical readings, conducted on January 13, 1939, suggested that her condition was indeed dire, but that recovery was possible. Similar to postal worker Tom Scanlon, the cause of her mental illness was linked to a spinal injury in her lower back in the lumbar

Application For Associate Membership
IN THE ASSOCIATION FOR RESEARCH AND ENLIGHTENMENT, INC.
VIRGINIA BEACH, VIRGINIA

The undersigned hereby applies for Associate Membership in the Association for Research and Enlightenment, Incorporated, and agrees to pay the required membership dues as follows: $20.00 Cash herewith.

I wish to avail myself at this time of the privilege of receiving through Mr. Edgar Cayce the psychic reading which is offered me through this membership and of the kind indicated below:

☑ Physical ☐ Life

In requesting this psychic reading I understand that I am taking part in an experiment conducted by the Association for the purpose of ascertaining the value of psychic information and extending the knowledge of the laws governing its transmission. I understand that no claims or promises are made in connection with this reading.

Date Dec. 27, 1938 (s) Sadie Neumark
Witnessed By
Recommended By David E. Kahn
Approved By
(Membership Committee)
Samples of Publications Will Be Sent Upon Request.

Name Anne Neumark
Address Manhattan State Hospital
Wards Island - Rooms 14A on Surgical Ward
Age -32- Date of Birth May 3-1906
Place of Birth Boston Mass
Occupation Artist Position
~~Married or~~ Single?
Name of Husband or Wife
No. Children Names
Name of Father and Mother Helene Le Neumark
Sister - Sadie Neumark

NOTE: Send applications, together with payment of dues, direct to the ASSOCIATION FOR RESEARCH AND ENLIGHTENMENT, INC., Virginia Beach, Va.
Appointments for readings will be made in order of receipt of application, except in emergency cases.

Anne Neumark's application for membership in the Association For Research and Enlightenment, signed by David Kahn, 1938.

and coccyx area. No explicit reference was made in this first reading to how she had suffered the injury—a curious thing considering how often commentary was provided in most other readings of this kind. All that was said in this regard was that she had experienced trauma which had caused both physical injury, resulting in her impaired mental state, and emotional injury that had shattered what, Cayce said, were her "hopes" and "aspirations." Whatever the cause, her higher self had become detached from her earthly physical self. She had entered what Cayce called "the borderland" and strongly recommended that great care needed to be taken as she was "so near possession."

Foremost on the list of recommendations was to remove her from the hospital and place her in an environment Cayce described as one of "gentleness, of kindness, of patience." A full-time constant care attendant was necessary— someone who was physically able to control her, but also to do so in a "loving, kind, and patient manner." Malnutrition, not anemia, was at the root of her weight loss, a condition which could be remedied with plenty of nutritious whole foods. In addition to osteopathy, which would help repair her cerebrospinal system, she was to undergo treatments with a "wet-cell," the device developed at the Cayce hospital and built by Tommy House which transmitted a mild electrical current through the body. In Anne's case, the appliance was to be used in conjunction with a solution of gold chloride which would modify the current to a particular frequency which would supplement the body's ability to heal itself. Although any number of physicians could conduct the treatments, Dobbins was identified by name as being the most suitable.

In closing, Cayce encouraged everyone working with her that the

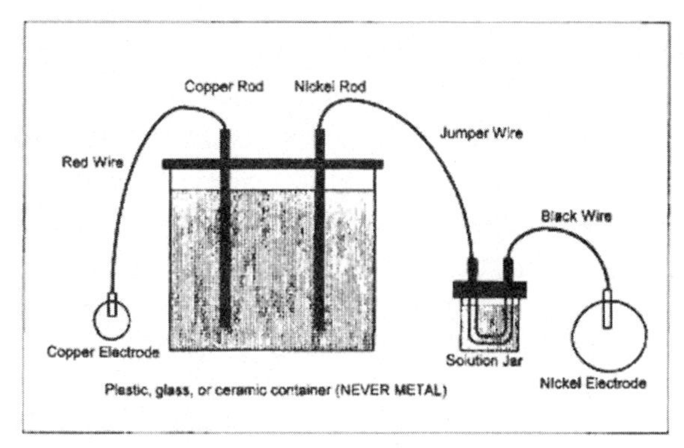

Figure 1. Wet cell battery and solution jar.

A subtle energy device, the Wet Cell battery recommended by Cayce and built according to his in-trance specifications.

results would be well worth their efforts. "The beauty of this soul, its abilities as a creative influence in the lives of those who may bring it back . . . from the very borderland, is worth all the effort, all the love, all the kindness one may give."

Kahn, who visited Anne several times before the reading was given, confirmed everything that had been conveyed in the readings. Anne had the appearance of an anorexic, and her body was covered with black and blue marks from efforts the staff had made to restrain her. And this was putting a positive spin on the brutal manner in which she was being treated in a hospital where a small staff of physicians and nurses was caring for a population of over three-thousand mental patients. The last "bout" with her caretakers had somehow resulted in the bones of one of Anne's feet being broken. It thus came as no surprise that that the first recommendation that came through in the reading was to remove her from the hospital.

Kahn took the opportunity to conduct interviews with the hospital staff, Anne's mother, and two sisters. His sleuthing, combined with references in subsequent readings, suggested that there had indeed been some undisclosed physical as well as mental injury which had brought on her mental illness. Specifics wouldn't be discovered for several weeks, but from what Kahn had learned, immediately prior to her mental collapse she had made an appointment with a man who was interested in buying her artwork. Anne's mother and sisters didn't know whether or not she had visited the man, but it seemed too great a coincidence that the scheduled appointment had coincided with her outbursts. They hadn't been able to query her on the matter because by that time she had begun raging and was incomprehensible. Strangely, she would rant about a man carrying a black umbrella.

As Kahn continued to investigate this matter and Dr. Dobbins began daily osteopathic treatments, funds arrived from A.R.E. donors willing to help move Anne to another care facility. This was one of several topics covered in the next reading that Cayce gave her. The news was hopeful. Her condition was improving; treatments as specified in the first reading were to continue. Further, the arrangements being made for Anne to be moved into a private care facility were fundamentally right. The most important determining factor was the care provided by the person hired to be with her. "Willing for hire is one thing," Cayce cautioned. "Willing because of the love and the human element is another. Willing because of the physical, mental, and spiritual experiences is still another."

Anne was moved into a private home in close proximity to Dr. Dobbins' Staten Island office, so that he could more easily visit her. Here, she improved remarkably. She still couldn't communicate in any comprehensible way and wasn't at the point of being able to feed herself, but the outbursts were fewer and farther between. A straightjacket was no longer necessary.

When Cayce conducted his fourth reading on May 4, 1939, there had been so much improvement that a full-time professional caregiver was no longer necessary. Her mother took over, aided by her siblings. Anne was now able to communicate in full sentences. Though she couldn't remember events prior to her hospitalization, she hadn't lost her painting skills, and though there were periods when she merely stared blankly at her easel or wouldn't go near it at all, she gradually began sketching. As Kahn would report, "On my visit . . . she was as quiet and demure and sane as any person you have ever met. The past is an entire blank to her. She does not understand how she is in her present surroundings except that, as I told her, it was for rest, quiet, and proper care in a convalescent hospital for people who have had shocks."

The fifth reading in the series, conducted on July 26, confirmed what the family knew to be true: Anne continued to improve in just about every way. The only unusual thing about this reading was a curious remark in which Cayce—in trance—revealed details of her mental condition that, the reading clearly stated, were not to be shared with the patient. She was too emotionally fragile; the injury which had led to her mental illness had left scars that were not physical and still needed healing. This was indeed a most unusual thing to come through in a reading and was repeated in a subsequent reading: "There's so much to withhold . . . This had best not be given just now. There are too many turmoils still within the experiences . . . "

With the help of family members, the Cayce readings, and eventually Anne herself, Kahn ferreted out the truth. Anne had been asked to bring samples of her artwork to the apartment of a potential customer. She did so and was brutally attacked. In the struggle to free herself she had injured her spine. The nervous shock coupled with the injury had brought on her insanity. No mention was made of the mysterious umbrella, but one could only imagine.

The physical healing, and then emotional healing, continued. Though at this point she wasn't aware of the trance readings being used to treat her, or even who Edgar Cayce was, she knew something strange and unusual was taking place. A man named David Kahn gave her a job in his office, and some of his friends from faraway Virginia Beach were helping her family.

Kahn continued to note her daily improvement, as did Dobbins, who reported in July: "She looks perfectly marvelous, is much more active, laughs a great deal more, and I caught her singing several times. We try to find excuses for anything that is funny. I think there's nothing better than good hearty laughing to loosen one up."

Over time she started asking who Edgar Cayce was. When she found out that he was the source of the medical help she was receiving, she wrote him a letter and he in turn wrote her back, offering encouragement. He received a response back from his letter several days later. "Dear Mr. Cayce: Thank you very much for the letter. I appreciate your interest in me a lot. I too have heard so many nice things about you; it seems so strange to write to you and have you all [in Virginia Beach] like me without ever having seen me. I trust someday to be able to do something for you in my own work."

Her ongoing pen-pal relationship with Edgar would result in her obtaining a Life Reading, which proved to be most revealing. In the incarnation before being born as Anne Neumark, she had been a woman named Mana Smyrth, who lived in Salem, Massachusetts, during the witch hunts when she had suffered persecution and been

A Neumark pastel courtesy of Nancy Membrez.

brought "under submission" by being repeatedly dunked underwater. From this incarnation she had developed a fear of men—a condition exacerbated in the present. Her love of art and talent as a painter had been developed in the incarnation before this, when she had been a student of Peter Paul Rubens, one of the greatest artists who ever lived.

"Hence in the present we find that the entity's activity should follow in this line [of artistic endeavor], whether in oil or in the water color," the Source recommended.

Neumark followed the advice in the readings. She would go on to become a highly accomplished New York portraitist with paintings in several museum collections. Today, after Neumark's passing at age 91 in 1997, her reputation is still growing. The portrait she painted that Edgar personally prized was one she did of him when Edgar visited her New York studio in 1940. He hung the portrait over his desk in Virginia Beach, not only for the beauty he found in it, but also as a constant reminder of the good that could come from the readings.

A signed and dated etching by Anne Neumark recently donated to the Edgar Cayce Foundation archives.

Anne Neumark's portrait of Edgar Cayce, 1940. What a remarkable gift coming from a (former) student of Rubens!

Virginia Harding and five-year-old
Faith Hope Charity Harding, 1940.

Faith Harding:

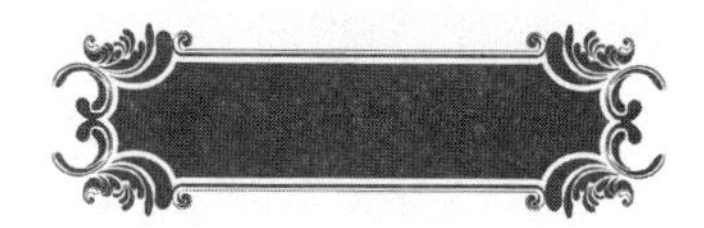

The Little Prophetess

Edgar took increasing joy and delight in the company of children whose parents had received life-saving readings. Though it would still be several years before he and Gertrude would themselves have grandchildren, there were more than enough Cayce babies—as Edgar liked to call them—to fill the void. One had been born to a couple who had been patients at the Cayce hospital. The mother had previously been told that she wouldn't be able to have children and was considering adoption when a reading told her she would give birth to not one, but two children, which indeed turned out to be the case. Earlier there had been Edgar Cayce Jones, named in honor of Edgar for the love, fellowship, and trance readings he had given the child's parents, Alva Jones and husband Lamar. Gladys' brother and his wife, who had both had readings, gave birth to Thomas Jefferson Davis, called "T.J.," who would come to live with Edgar and Gertrude off and on throughout his childhood. Then there was Caroline House, born to Tommy and Doris House. They were practically like family.

Edgar's readings for Caroline House and the other Cayce babies made it clear to him and Gertrude just how important the home environment was to health and spiritual growth. This became even more evident in readings for four-year-old Faith Harding, whose psychic abilities were purported to rival Edgar's own.

Edgar first learned about the child in a letter he received on February 22, 1940, from Leila Learned, an A.R.E. member in Connecticut who had been hearing curious and altogether fantastic reports about Faith from the Wyoming Valley region of eastern Pennsylvania. Two days later Cayce would receive a letter from another member, Josephine Buchanan, with equally intriguing comments: "She is the child prophetess who has been giving, verbally, the most amazing prophecies since she was six months old—when she began to talk. Perhaps you know about her. Faith Hope Charity Harding is the name."

Leila Learned (1915, Fort Wayne Sun, Indiana) and her husband, Arthur, became god-parents of little Faith when she was 4½ years old.

The "Little Prophetess," as Faith was called, had been born in Trucksville, Pennsylvania, the child of typewriter-pad inventor Harry C. Harding and his wife, Virginia. According to popular legend, Faith could speak in complete sentences at just eighteen months and was credited with remarkable powers of clairvoyance. Doctors who examined her were said to be confounded by her astonishing vocabulary, frequent biblical references, predictions of future events, and the highly unusual messages of love and hope she delivered.

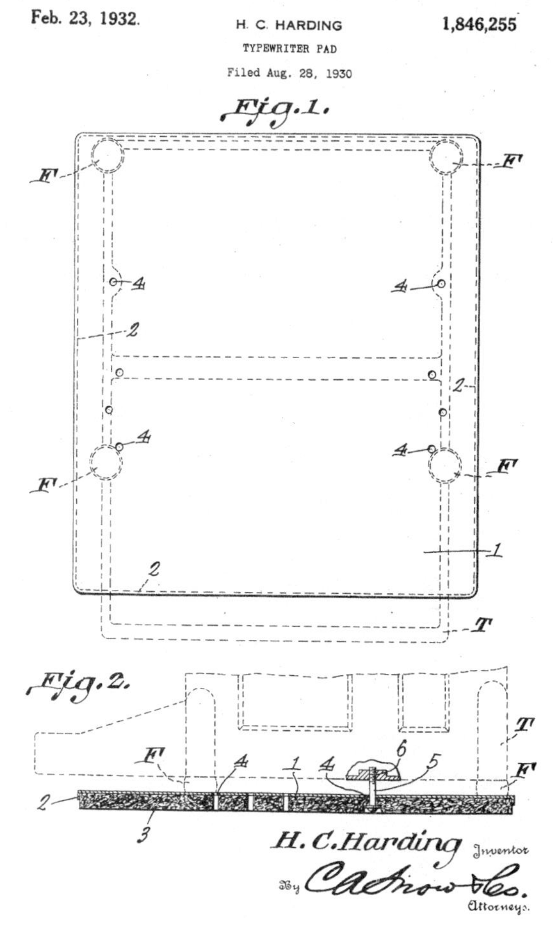

1932 Typewriter Pad patent by Faith's father, Harry.

According to popular legend, Faith could speak in complete sentences at just eighteen months and was credited with remarkable powers of clairvoyance. Doctors who examined her were said to be

In one reported incident of precognition, Faith burst into tears and demanded to be taken off a bus only minutes before it exploded into flames. In another, she had a vision of her elementary school catching fire, as indeed turned out to be the case. There were also examples of spontaneous healing, as when Faith had wandered out of her house and spent the morning sitting under an apple tree with an immigrant Greek laborer's son, suffering from polio. Inexplicably, the boy's polio had vanished the next day.

Faith Hope Charity Harding, 1942-43.

A local newspaperman investigating the claims had witnessed the child prophesying. Overwhelmed by what he had seen, he reportedly quit his job and began recording her words for posterity. With Virginia Harding's blessing and the agreement of "The Entity"—that which was said to be speaking through Faith—her words were shared with the greater community in a series of weekly newspaper columns. One

OCCULT SUASION

GODLY MESSAGES
FROM THE ENTITY

—By—

Faith Hope Charity Harding

Faith's weekly newspaper column in the *Nanticote Daily Press*, 1939.

"Goeth ye out and meditate, on the oneness of the earthchildren. And knoweth ye not their boundries nor their creed nor their color. But, sayeth within thine hear's We are all Gods, and are as one out of the Godhead. And we worketh our ways aback unto a oneness."

A snippet from a message from little Faith in October 1939 in the weekly column.

such communication, when Faith was only four, began with a phrase in Latin, another expounded on the Epistle of Paul, and a third quoted verbatim an extensive passage from the Book of John.

Faith's "otherworldly" communications so impressed Leila and Arthur Learned that they became Faith's devoted godparents and hosted her baptism in a Shinto temple they had imported to their Connecticut home. This was the same temple where talks had been given by Alice Bailey, a noted theosophist and writer, the Catholic archbishop William Francis, and Khalil Gibran, the Lebanese poet and author of *The Prophet.*

Less than a month after Edgar received his first communications about Faith, Josephine Buchanan was back in touch with Edgar asking that Faith be the subject of a Life Reading. Buchanan reported visiting the child in Pennsylvania and seeing in her "definite proof of the [Divine] guidance." She described her in nearly angelic terms: "lovely . . .

natural, sweet, happy, and good and just radiating light and love. You simply must meet her!"

In early 1940, Faith delivered a message just as relevant today as it was then, at the time of World War II.

> " . . . ye hath sat in judgment upon thine brothers . . . And taketh apart their intentions and turneth about their purposes . . . "This country or that country beeth without reason and I wouldst that they beeth overcome!" . . .
>
> First, there must be peace within your hearts. Love for all . . . irrespective of creed, color or nationality. For God hath breathed into ye all, the Breath of Life . . . If ye loved one another as strongly as ye hateth . . . ye would be of victory. Looketh upon thy brother with . . . a concernment for his welfare . . . Knowest not that hate, doubt, envy and superstition, lived and passed on, generation to generation, createth a monster and reflects unto ye, all ye hath poured forth upon races and mankind? . . . And it centers within a Leader who calleth it up and showeth unto ye the picture ye hath portrayed of him and his . . . And when ye tasteth unto such, [ye] calleth upon God . . . "Oh God . . . Slay mine enemies . . . that I may of revenge!" Nay, sayeth the Creator, ye are not without blame and ye suffereth also along side of thine brother from whom ye hath withheld the light . . . Think ye the Creator loveth one child and despiseth the other? Thinketh ye that [ye] . . . beeth of all goodness and thine brother's hateful unto His sight? . . . [That] ye and ye alone shall enjoy the favored smile of the Creator, of which ye are as much a part as the leaf is unto the tree? Within your . . . temples . . . ye worship dogma more than the Spirit. And ye would have that all earthchildren so worship –and maketh a pattern after ye. Therein lieth the sin . . . resigneth thine desire of selfishness . . . Loveth all mankind as ye loveth thineselves. And asketh that ye be loved of Him. Then seeketh ye out a brother . . . whom ye hath so hated . . . and sayeth, "Thou art mine brother and we hath one Father and He loveth us alike. Leaneth upon mine arm . . . [and] I taketh your arm when I suffereth a weakness. And so we walketh together . . . "

Difficult as it was to believe that a four-year-old girl had delivered such a missive—and the above just some of a 1,000 word recitation—Faith was doing much as Cayce did in some of his own readings.

Faith's mother had turned down numerous requests to have Faith "psychically" tested, but after finding out what Cayce did, and how he did it, and with the urging of the Buchanans and other A.R.E. members, she agreed to have Edgar do a reading. A thirty-minute trance session was conducted in Virginia Beach on March 30, 1940 while Faith and her mother were at home in Trucksville.

The Source astonished listeners by saying that the entity known as Faith Harding was "a chosen channel which the Father hath bestowed upon the children of men," and that she was "a vessel through which the Prince of Peace would bring encouragement, assurance, and . . . messages of hope and of light to . . . those who are not only mentally but physically sick . . . to those who are ill at ease, rather than the diseased." Faith Harding would do this, the reading stated, by her own psychic ability to communicate with "patience," "love," and "kindness," and through the "laying on hands," a talent she would develop as she grew older.

"He hath promised to stand in the places of those who are discouraged, disconsolate, who have lost a vision, lost hope," the Source said. "So may this entity be that channel through which many may take hope, many may be aroused to the awareness that the Lord is nigh, that He standeth at the door of thy consciousness, that ye may be awakened!"

According to the reading, Faith had been through many previous incarnations, and this fact would continue to serve her in the years to come. Most important were her incarnations as Elizabeth, the mother of John the Baptist, and as Saint Cecilia, who, during the Roman era, had bought much to the world through her divinely inspired music. Little Faith represented a powerful female energy that ushered in, what Cayce said, the "fruit of the spirit of truth."

However gifted this child was in her present incarnation, the Source also admonished Faith's parents and those around her to nurture and carefully watch over her, to provide her with love, kindness, and gentleness in those things that bring "constructive, hopeful, helpful forces into the experiences of others," and to not let her experience

A pen and ink drawing of the Holy Family with St. Elizabeth (standing), by Raphael, (1507-08).

St. Cecilia and Saint Augustine with St. John, St. Paul, and Mary Magdalene, (1516-17). Painting by Raphael. (Interesting that the artist placed St. Cecilia with Paul, John, and Mary whom she would have known in an earlier incarnation as St. Elizabeth.)

"distrust," "envy," "malice," or "jealousy." The reading stated that given her "special nature," she would never experience "a normal world or normal environment," but that nevertheless the child should be provided with as typical a childhood as possible. Further, because of various astrological aspects and sojourns in other realms, Faith would, if left without guidance, desire to marry young. Better that she fully embody her gifts, the reading suggested, before sharing herself with another in matrimony. In closing, the Source said, "Let there not be a worshipfulness as of the body of the entity, but rather as of its abilities to arouse in the hearts and minds of others the knowledge that the day of the Lord is at hand!"

Edgar had an opportunity to meet Faith and her mother on April 16, 1940, at the home of A.R.E board member Milton Harrison and his wife Irene in Bronxville, New York. At the time, Faith and her mother, Virginia, were on their way to Tryon, North Carolina, to meet with the board of a foundation interested in helping to develop Faith's gifts.

At their brief meeting, Edgar characterized the child as "darling" and found the mother extremely knowledgeable about psychic phenomena and the spiritualist movement. According to Virginia, Faith's psychic talents had first come to the family's attention when, at barely over a year old, she would wake up in the middle of the night, reach for a crayon, and scrawl words on loose sheets of paper. The words eventually became messages, which were recognized by the Harding's friends and neighbors as prophetic. By the time she was two, she was communicating in the form of automatic writing, which she did in the evening on long rolls of plain wrapping paper. Eventually she was prophesying without the need to write words down. She would sit quietly and then fall into a state of spiritual ecstasy in which the Entity took over.

Although Edgar himself was convinced of the integrity of both mother and daughter, there were certain aspects of the mother's approach that caused him concern. Like a typical Hollywood stage mother, Virginia Harding was all too eager to promote her daughter. Dave Kahn had beat the drum for Edgar in much the same way as Mrs. Harding did for her daughter, but there was an important difference in addition to their ages.

Apart from the stories Mrs. Harding told about her child, she carried with her a scrapbook of newspaper clippings and a file folder of signed affidavits from people who had witnessed her marvels. She also had a photograph purported to have been taken during Faith's baptism, which she claimed to be evidence of a Divine presence. Hovering near the head of the child were the shadowy and indistinct images of Mother Mary, Christ, Buddha, and a number of other images that Edgar recognized as holy men and women. Despite the fact that Edgar himself had once experimented with double exposures and that Arthur Conan Doyle had been publicly humiliated by Houdini for having been fooled into believing in the authenticity of similar pictures, Edgar gave Gladys and Gertrude the impression that he believed the photo to be a genuine vision of Divine spirits gathered to bless Faith during her baptism.

While Edgar was in Bronxville, he gave a second reading for the child, and again the Source directed a warning to those "privileged to have the care, the attention of this entity in this material experience."

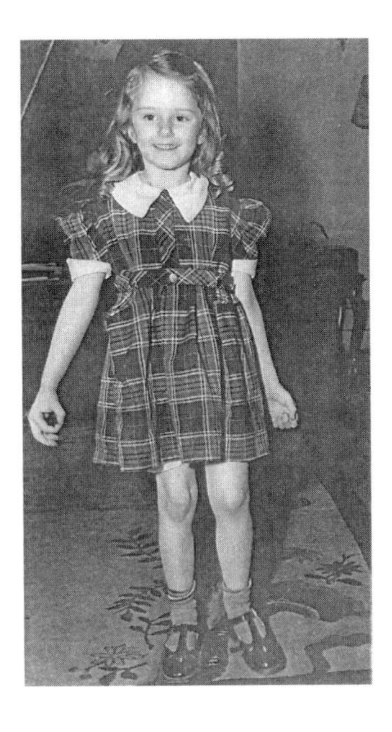

Faith is starting to grow up ... all arms and legs! c. 1940.

The reading requested that the parents "heed those warnings indicated" and reminded them of the specialness of their child. Faith Harding, the reading stated, expressed the "voice of nature itself . . . in the laughter . . . in the look of its eye, in the movement of its body, in the patter of its feet, giving expression in a manner that brings to the minds and consciousness of those who seek to know God and God's ways with the children of men."

Near the end of this second reading, Cayce was asked if anything else could be said about this child. "Worlds might be filled with that as might be given!" the Source said. "But let each of you here so live the Christ consciousness as manifested in the Master that you may be counted worthy to be even as those who would gather the crumbs of wisdom that will be manifested through this entity!"

At this point in the reading, Gladys and others in the room became aware of an unearthly presence, just as they previously had when there was an angelic visitor. Though the windows were closed, a wind blew through the room, sending a stack of Gladys Davis' typed stenographic notes cascading across the floor. A vibration rattled the windowpanes.

"*HARK, YE FRIENDS*!" Cayce suddenly announced in a voice that witnesses said had more force and fury than at any other time they could remember. "*I MICHAEL, LORD OF THE WAY, WOULD GIVE THEE WARNING*!" Cayce continued. "Bow thine heads, ye vile ones of the Earth! Know what has been entrusted to thee! Live the life, lest ye be counted accursed for being unworthy of the trust given thee!"

Everyone in the room sat in stunned silence as Archangel Michael, the angel who stands before the "Throne of the Father," spoke in and through Cayce. As Gladys later described it, there was such energy in the room that she felt as if the steno pad in her hand was being pulled away from her.

It is not known how much or little Gladys and the Cayces knew about the circumstances surrounding Faith Harding or her parents at the time this reading was given, or whether they grasped the full import of this admonition from the Archangel Michael. However, soon after Faith and her mother left Bronxville, and in the months that followed, it became clear to everyone involved that the child's life was taking a tragic turn for the worse. Though Edgar would never again

St. Michael Vanquishing Satan by Raphael (1518).

see Faith, reports about what was happening filtered in from friends.

Edgar, Gertrude, and Gladys soon learned that Virginia Harding had erected a temple in Tyron, North Carolina where initiates of "The Cross and Circle Foundation" would devote themselves to the "Little Prophetess" and her teachings. Thousands of dollars had been raised to install Faith and her mother in what has been described as a Greek temple and to have them driven around in a station wagon with the Little Prophetess' logo painted on its doors. Faith, in short, had become a psychic celebrity. And there was more to come the following year.

"Faith Hope Charity Harding . . . is either the greatest oracle of all

Strange Workings of a Child's Mind, Manifestations of "Second Sight" and the Occult...

PROPHET IN Pigtails

...and a Tiny Girl Stumps the Experts on a Subject for Which Science Has No Answer —Yet

Faith was getting a lot of press, even outside of their home state. Here is a full page spread in the *Albuquerque Journal* in March 1940.

times or . . . the cutest hoax this side of Delphi," a reporter announced on *We the People,* one of most listened to radio shows in the nation. A *Time Magazine* story about her would follow and then a movie deal from a Hollywood studio. At the height of her renown she was reportedly offered $10,000—the equivalent of what today would be $162,000—for her to prove her prophetic abilities to a self-styled committee called the Universal Council of Psychic Research.

Faith's father, inventor Harry Harding, was infuriated by the attention given his daughter and enraged at his wife's behavior. He accused her of exploiting their child for her own personal fame and notoriety.

In letters and divorce court declarations, Harry Harding detailed Virginia's misdeeds, including an allegation that she had embellished her daughter's psychic messages before they reached the public. He then hired a physician who suggested his wife was delusional and sought a court order to retain sole custody of the child until the mother could undergo psychiatric therapy. Virginia Harding countered, casting her husband as cruel, insensitive, and incapable of understanding or appreciating the gift that had been given them in Faith. In a letter to Edgar, Virginia claimed that Harry "would see to it that nothing [about Faith] would ever reach the public's ear again."

Despite the difficulties that were raging on around the "Little Prophetess," her predictions of future events proved uncannily accurate. Faith described how and when the war in Europe would begin and the battle that would determine the outcome of hostilities. She also described, in the fall of 1940, how America would be pulled into the war by what she said was an "act" of aggression by a small but unnamed Asian nation—a prediction that was similarly made in one of Cayce's readings.

On January 3, 1941—nearly a year before the surprise attack on Pearl Harbor—a message would come through Faith to be presented to President Roosevelt and was immediately couriered to the White House. "Ye thinketh ye hath friends to the southwinds, but they are few," the Entity announced. "And they besiege ye along with Spain, Mexico, and Japan . . . Knoweth this and watcheth for the fulfillment—as was a warning given to the House in a telegram concerning Hawaii, watcheth yet even so the warning."

Edgar himself was the subject of one of her last predictions. He was told by Virginia Harding that the Entity had said that unless he immediately stopped giving readings and left on an extended retreat to "fast" and "rejuvenate," his dreams of his own death would become a reality, and mankind would sustain a "deplorable loss."

The Harding divorce and custody battle reached its climax with the testimony of a psychiatrist who declared that Faith's mother was certifiably insane. The judge declared that unless Virginia Harding agreed to undergo a lobotomy, he would grant sole custody to Harry. Unwilling to undergo the procedure, Virginia gave up custody. It would be Harry who set about raising her and her three older siblings, doing everything he could to put the past behind them.

Virginia, however, desirous of remaining close to her children, moved into the house next door. In what was a strange and perhaps altogether spooky twist of fate, which took place after the judge's ruling, a fire broke out in her husband's basement workshop. A spark leapt across the room where Harry had his hands immersed in a tub of flammable solvent. He was burned head to foot. His screams brought Virginia from next door, whose nursing experience may have saved his life. The dynamics of their relationship are unclear, but she would care for him until he regained his health. Today Virginia is remembered as both a nurse and poet.

As for Faith, her life changed greatly. The publishing arrangement made with the local newspaper ended, the movie deal expired, and nothing more was written of her or her talents. With the help of her father, she did everything she could, she later said, to block out "dreams, visions, and voices" and anything pertaining to the spirit world. As she later confided, this was not an easy thing. She would wake up with what she termed as "nightmares." Later, with her father's encouragement, she was hospitalized where she underwent psychiatric treatments typical of the day. By her late teens her "cure," as a neighbor described it, was complete. Faith married young, shortly after meeting her husband. Her marriage had been foretold in a dream she could not block out. Her dream included such details as whom she would marry, the number of children they would have, and where they would live.

Edgar never learned what had become of Faith and the Hardings, but he nevertheless understood that the chaotic environment of Faith's family life had destroyed her incredible gift. Perhaps he now appreciated more than ever the love and protection his parents and grandparents had provided him back on the farm in Beverly. How many other children, he naturally wondered, had been born with such gifts as himself and Little Faith Harding?

The readings had made clear that every home should manifest the experience of God in the earth. "In the establishing of the home, make it as that which may be the pattern of a heavenly home," the Source had advised a young woman about to marry. "Not as that set aside for only a place to sleep or to rest, but where not only self but all who enter there may feel, may experience, by the very vibrations that are set up by each in the sacredness of the home, a helpfulness, a hopefulness in the air about the home . . ."

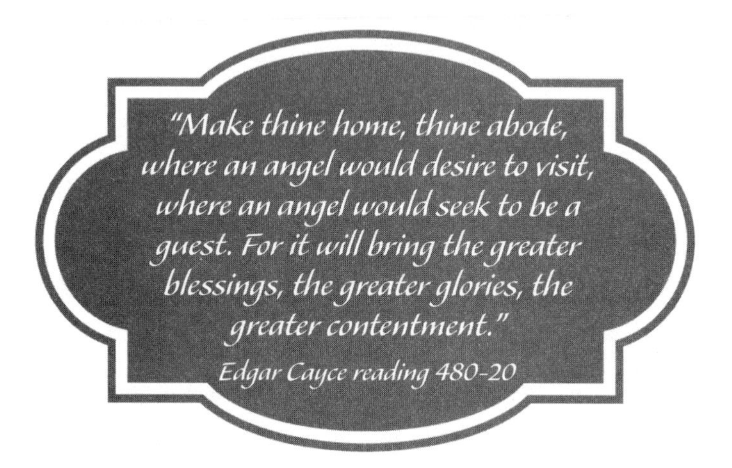

Burton Wheeler (1882-1975) on the front cover of *Time Magazine*, June 18, 1923.

BURTON WHEELER:

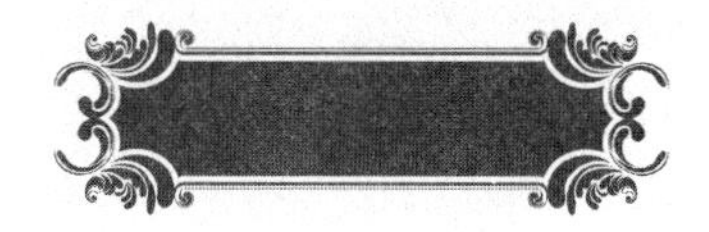

PRESIDENTIAL CANDIDATE

Leadership, integrity, diplomatic skills, voting record, and party affiliation are all considerations when casting a vote for the U.S. Presidency. Into this equation Edgar Cayce added astrological influences and experiences gained in past-life incarnations. This was the primary reason why Cayce—in trance—endorsed third-term Senator Burton Wheeler over incumbent Franklin Delano Roosevelt in the 1940 race for the presidency, and why A.R.E. campaign volunteers worked hard to put him into the Oval Office. Having lived as a Roman centurion turned Christian and later as a freedom-loving Viking explorer, Wheeler was uniquely suited to meet the leadership challenge.

"None of the other individuals who have been suggested for the office have as near the ideals and purposes of the entity Burton Wheeler," the Source declared on November, 26, 1939. Along with this bold endorsement came an ominous and prophetic warning: "Unless there is such a one with those principles as we find are present in the intent and purpose of Wheeler, a sad experience will be for this land through forty-two and three ('42 and '43)."

Wheeler was reported to have accompanied director Frank Capra to the opening night of *Mr. Smith Goes to Washington* in 1939.

The "sad" experience was America's entry into WWII, in which over 400,000 Americans and over sixty million people worldwide would lose their lives. How Wheeler, the "fighting progressive" from Montana, an anti-draft, anti-war, anti-big business defender of civil liberties might have handled diplomacy differently on the lead up to war and what was revealed in the readings requested by him and A.R.E. campaign workers is only part of the intriguing story of what might have been had Wheeler and not Roosevelt sat in the Oval Office.

Though Wheeler's name has all but disappeared from our nation's political discourse, movie fans today will know him as the inspiration for the now classic *Mr. Smith Goes to Washington*, the 1939 film which made Jimmy Stewart into a star. Based on the book *The Gentleman from Montana*, it tells the story of an idealistic young senator from a small unidentified western town who heads to Washington and suddenly finds himself single-handedly battling ruthless and corrupt politicians out to destroy him. What the film fails to show is what would become of Stewart's character when his notoriety brings him to within one small step of becoming the next U.S. President.

Standing six-feet tall with a trade-mark dented Stetson, expressive hands, and a purposeful stride, Wheeler was not a polished speaker, but by "natural force of will" and "his gift of idiom," as journalists described him, he was an effective one. Born in Massachusetts to a family of dedicated Quaker pacifists, he began his career by working his way through the University of Michigan Law School by going door to door selling cookbooks. Customers took to him immediately, as later would voters. Having obtained his law degree, he set out for the West Coast but got only as far as Butte, Montana where he lost everything he owned—a suitcase of clothes and a train ticket—in a poker game. With no money to continue his journey, he hung out a shingle and opened a law practice. His decision to represent lowly Montana immigrants and mine workers, and the mode of transportation in which he had arrived in Butte, earned him the nickname "Boxcar Burt."

A young attorney, Wheeler didn't know what lay in store for him when he went head-to-head with Anaconda Copper, which was Montana's largest employer and the state's largest landholder. As Wheeler soon discovered, Anaconda also "owned" the state's political parties, legislature, governor, and local officials down to the county level. Though he won numerous smaller battles on the local level, he felt powerless to stop what he viewed as the degradation of the environment and subhuman working conditions in the mines. With wide support from labor, he ran for state legislature. "If elected, I will not put Anaconda out of business," he swore, "but I will put it out of politics."

Anaconda Copper Mining Plant, Great Falls, Montana.

Riding a wave of populist sentiment, he served as a state representative from 1910–1912 and as the Montana U.S. district attorney from 1913–1918. When Anaconda discovered that Wheeler couldn't be bribed, they resorted to all manner of underhanded ways of ridding themselves of the young upstart. The maneuvering backfired. He succeeded in winning important health and environmental concessions—later emulated by other states. He touched the hearts of immigrant constituents by defending the rights of ethnic Germans and brought to light what he declared to be the near total misrepresentation of events leading up to America's entry into World War I. Although he was an avowed pacifist, his antiwar sentiments were more nuanced than isolationists of his day. He believed Americans were being sold a false bill of goods by special interest bankers and industrialists whose desire was not to make the world free for democracy, but free for the spread of imperialism. Constituents wouldn't soon forget his prophetic remarks, nor would A.R.E. supporters two decades later when they joined his campaign staff.

Elected to the U.S. Senate as a Democrat in 1922, Wheeler used his first major speech to take on corruption in what would become the "Teapot Dome" bribery scandal. The subsequent findings won Wheeler wide support but a vicious reprisal from the Attorney General's office, which indicted Wheeler on trumped-up charges of influence peddling. In the midst of controversy he was invited to run for Vice President on a third-party progressive ticket with Senator Robert La Follette, fighting what they termed "a government for sale to the highest bidder." Then, as later, party affiliation and ideological labels were secondary to the issues; he would team up with Democrats, Republicans, and Progressives, and as a result was praised or damned at various stages of his career for being both a liberal and a progressive, party stalwart, party renegade, and finally a revolutionary.

The La Follette-Wheeler platform was as radical as had ever been seen in U.S. politics. Their platform called for government takeover of the railroads, elimination of private utilities, the outlawing of child labor, the right of workers to organize unions, increased protection of civil liberties, an end to U.S. imperialism in Latin America, and a plebiscite before any President could again lead the nation into war. Highest on their agenda was doing away with what they termed corporate

U.S. Senator Burton Wheeler in 1922.

Wheeler with running mate, Senator Robert LaFollette.

Certificate for contributions to the Progressive Party for the 1924 presidential campaign in which La Follette was running for President and Wheeler for Vice President.

welfare schemes. Although La Follette and Wheeler lost the election, they decisively proved that a rural-urban populist coalition could be forged—a legacy which Franklin Delano Roosevelt used to successfully push through the New Deal.

Wheeler was initially supportive of President Roosevelt and would steadfastly remain a proponent of the New Deal reforms. Their relationship soured when decisions were made that he believed would inevitably lead the U.S. into World War II. On this point Wheeler was unbending. In the 1920s he had been an outspoken critic of the "dollar diplomacy" that had sent U.S. marines into Nicaragua and opposed those who called for war with Mexico. In the 1930s he vehemently opposed trade embargoes on Japan. This was not out of a desire that the U.S. remain isolationist, but because he believed that doing so would inevitably force Japan to declare war on the U.S. He was equally reluctant to provide lend-lease arms and U.S. dollars to Britain. Unless the U.S. went ahead and joined the war effort—which he believed wasn't necessary—this, too, would inevitably pull the U.S. into the war. "You can't put your shirt tail into a clothes wringer and pull it out suddenly when the wringer keeps turning," he passionately argued.

What was widely viewed at the time as Wheeler's final break with Roosevelt came when the President tried to pass measures which, in the name of "court reform," would limit the age of court justices and thereby permit Roosevelt to appoint six Supreme Court justices of his own choosing. Although Wheeler was in sympathy with Roosevelt's motives—the President wished to preserve his hard-fought New Deal reforms from being gutted by a Republican majority in the Supreme Court—Wheeler stood against the measure on principle. He viewed the proposed reforms as an anti-Constitutional grab for power which would destroy the Court as an independent institution. Risking his entire political future by leading the opposition against his own Democratic party, Wheeler successfully fought the bill in what has been described as the "fiercest battle in American history between two branches of our government over a third."

Progressives and conservatives alike applauded Wheeler's courage, which was why, in the late 1930s, there was a growing bipartisan movement calling for him to run for President. Among his many supporters was Milton Harrison, then a member of the A.R.E. board of directors, who would become its board president in 1941. It had been in his and Irene's Bronxville, New York, home where Edgar had met young Faith Harding and her mother.

A highly successful labor management mediator, bank president, and the Secretary of the American Bankers Association, Harrison came to know and respect Wheeler when testifying before the U.S. Congress in Senator Wheeler's Interstate Commerce Committee. Harrison's sen-

Milton Whateley Harrison (1889-1949) was an active member of the A.R.E. Board and served as President in 1941. During a reading Edgar gave for Milton he described having the following experience: When he approached the House of Records and asked for Milton's "book," the Keeper took it from a different section than usual saying, "This is from a special group, you see—and I must have it back." Then, when Mr. Cayce returned the book, it was open—and the Keeper took it, saying "I am loath to take it from you yet—so much more may be given."

timents were shared by his wife, Irene Seiberling, heiress to the Goodyear Tire and Rubber Company fortune who, like her husband, was close friends with Edgar and had received numerous business and spiritual readings. Though only tangential to what became a series of readings on Wheeler, both Harrison and his wife's Life Readings and interest in the Cayce work would contribute to their work with Bill Wilson and the creation of Alcoholics Anonymous.

In the second of the readings referencing Wheeler, conducted in 1938, Harrison came right out and asked if Wheeler would become the next President of the United States. "It's very probable that Burton Wheeler will be the next President if he chooses to accept" came the answer.

This response resulted in Harrison and his wife fully investing themselves in a drive to put Wheeler in the White House. To be certain that they were making the right decision, they put the question to Cayce in a follow-up reading. Harrison asked, "Am I following my best spiritual good, and the good of the country, in my activities and associations on behalf of Burton Wheeler for the Presidency of the United States?" The answer again was resoundingly positive. "As we find . . . in that entity Burton Wheeler, is the policy of there being a united effort for the country in all of its phases, in all of its undertakings and its problems, its faults as well as its virtues—more than there may be in any other individual that has, or as we find may be offered as one to fill that office."

As to why the others were unsuitable, Cayce was quite specific. "With every other one who has been mentioned . . . there are too many axes to grind by groups as well as sections of the country, as well as problems that are more of an international interest. Yet with the abilities of Burton Wheeler here is a basis for a *uniting* of these divisions that is not found in any of the others—not even excepting the present incumbent of that office [Franklin Roosevelt]."

Harrison was by no means the only A.R.E. member interested in Wheeler. Harold Sherman, a noted author on metaphysical subjects and a good friend of David Kahn, was negotiating with Wheeler to write his biography. Wheeler's strong antiwar and anticorruption stand resonated with both Sherman and Kahn, and they encouraged Harrison to approach Wheeler, telling him about Cayce's work. They also wanted him to see if he would agree to requesting a Life Reading. After talking to Wheeler about Cayce, Harrison reported that Wheeler was "very excited!" He wanted a reading, as Harrison said, "to know that he is doing the right thing." The subsequent reading, conducted on March 29, when Wheeler was in the Senate Office Building, bode well for him. Not only was he astrologically well situated to be in the Oval Office, his past-life incarnations were his strongest points.

Cayce—in trance—introduced Wheeler as a soul who had altered the paths of many, "not merely because of its historical value in the experiences of man, but because of the changes and the activities wrought by the entity's taking such a stand in the face of oppositions that might have been a part of the experience." Identified as a Piscean, he was described as having a rebellious nature which caused him "to be constantly in those positions where things and conditions are to be accomplished," yet also "tender, a lover of the beautiful, or art, or home, and all those things that make for the defense of same." Consistent with what his copper miner and immigrant worker constituents believed, Cayce said, "The entity is also considerate of those who supply the sources, or the means through which these may be accomplished; as well as to the freedom of thought, as to the manner in which individuals may worship . . . the dictates of their own conscience."

Other planetary influences were also important to making Wheeler a leader among men. Under the influence of Venus, Wheeler had developed "the love of the beautiful, the harmonious, and yet tempered with justice and mercy; and yet with that hardness which is an outcome of the application of discipline in such relationships. Under Jupiter's influence, he had developed a "rebellious leadership" as one who should have "influence upon the many, rather than the few." With the influence of Uranus, he had experienced extremes, "tending to make for that of leadership; not in the officious manner, yet . . . that bespeaks a conviction born of honesty, integrity, justice, mercy, truth, and the consideration of the relationships with the Creative Forces." These comments indeed reflected the makings of a soul prepared to lead the country. It was his previous incarnations, however, that most influenced his particular style of leading—what the readings suggested were his unique leadership capabilities.

In what Cayce described as being Wheeler's most important incarnation, one that "would be well were the entity to have the history of that sojourn in its fullest extent," he was identified as none other than Cornelius, "the first of the Roman officials to take an open stand with the followers of the Nazarene." Consistent with the story related in the Bible, Cayce described Cornelius as a centurion in charge of the Roman forces stationed in Caesarea, where he became associated with Jesus' followers, and through prayer and visions came to know man's relationship to God.

> Then there was the receiving of the vision as the warning that he, Cornelius, was to send for one [Peter] that would acquaint him with those truths which had been proclaimed by that representative of the heavenly kingdom. [This experience] . . . made for that *great* change which came in the governing of that land; and the modifying of the authority of those who were put in power

> through the activities of the authorities in Rome; making it possible, with those of its fellows, that there would come the great opportunities for man in every walk of life . . . Thus in the present may the entity, as one in authority, one in power, make for those activities in which there will be in the hearts of men and women . . . the opportunity of the peoples becoming aware more and more of their need to turn again to those tenets, those truths . . . For in such comes the power and the ability of the entity from those experiences to not only lead and direct men of many a position or status, but to be a voice heard among the nations of the earth.

This was all the endorsement the Harrisons could have hoped for. But there was more to be said, all equally positive. In another incarnation, Wheeler was identified Heth Erichlson, a Viking who had sailed with Leif Ericson, for whom he had built ships and helped to establish settlements. In this incarnation, the Source said: "There were the attempts made again and again to bring aid and help to that new-found freedom in a land in which there were plenteous opportunities of every nature, for not only the material attainments of the supplies for the physical but the opportunities for the mental and spiritual advancement." The Source went on to say that Wheeler, in the present, used these experiences by "daring to do that as the conscience bids as in relationships to making for freedom of thought, of activity, for others."

Other incarnations were also mentioned. He had been in Persia where he had sacrificed so that others might become better acquainted with the teachings of the leader of that time. Wheeler, at that time called Philon, had "cut short" that experience for the greater benefit of his fellow man, just as, Cayce said, he was doing in his present incarnation. The reference to being "cut short" was not expanded up, but Harrison and Sherman understood this to possibly be a reference to Wheeler's failed Vice Presidential bid. Only later would it take on a different significance, as would Cayce's reference to Leif Ericson.

"Before that we find the entity was in the land now called the Egyptian, among those who came into the land with those from the Atlantean land." It was there, Cayce said, that he had helped the Pha-

Leif Ericson on the shore of Vinland (Newfoundland) in approximately 999 A.D. (By Monro S. Orr).

raoh to "set things in order for a troubled, torn world; making it possible for a union of the activities with those of the land, . . . acting rather as one that would be called in the present a *messenger of peace*!"

In describing yet another of Wheeler's experiences he could draw upon in the present, Cayce said: "Again may the entity in the present find itself in that position . . . where it may stand not merely as a Pacifist, but as *conducting*, as *proclaiming*, as *carrying* peace through brotherly love and kindness and gentleness, and patience—even as was and is the great tenet of Him who was indeed the Peacemaker!"

Here, Cayce's recital of previous incarnations ended and a question and answer period, typical of the Life Readings, began.

"Am I following a correct life course in accordance with my experience?" Wheeler asked.

"Following in the correct life course in aiding, directing those of thy fellow man in a representative manner."

"Is it indicated that I will be the next President of the United States?"

"If there is the choice by the entity that it would desire to be, but that the entity would set that as would be its principles, and not someone else's, it may be, this entity, President."

"Is there a destiny consistent with the nation's destiny that I be the next President?"

"Unless there be one such as this entity arising to direct not only the ship of state but the destiny of the peoples of this land, *turmoils* and strifes must increase."

Along these same lines came Wheeler's final question. "Is there any advice that you can give me as to whether or not I can give my greatest life service through the Presidency of the United States?"

"Here is the greater service, even as ye rendered not only thy nation as the ruler in Caesarea as Cornelius, but to all of mankind, because of the stand ye took then!"

This final answer, "the stand ye took," had great relevance, not only to Wheeler, but personally for Cayce, a great reader of the Bible. Cornelius' faith and conviction in what he had experienced was so great that he—a Roman warrior—had put down his sword and become the first Christian Gentile. What the reading seemed to be suggesting was the strength and courage of Wheeler's pacifism. He was a warrior without a sword.

Did Wheeler find strength in Cayce's words? According to David Kahn he did, though the Senator left behind no written record of how it might have affected his decision making in his run up to the 1940 election. And decision making was what he was forced to do in what would become his most important meeting, held in private, with Franklin Roosevelt.

As the Democratic primary approached, there was no question that Wheeler was poised for higher office. He was trusted by both liberals and conservatives, labor and capital, and had brought together a powerful alliance of fellow pacifists, including Charles Lindbergh, while attempting to keep America out of the war. He had also appeared on the cover of *Time* magazine and was described by *Nation* magazine as going into the Democratic convention "with a cleaner political record than any Presidential Candidate." The undecided wild-card issue that would seal the election, however, was how American voters would view America's potential role in the war.

Even though Wheeler was a pacifist, he believed that the United

Baptism of Cornelius by St. Peter (Francesco Trevisani, 1708).

States, because of previous diplomatic mistakes, would inevitably be pulled into the war which he had lobbied so hard to avoid. He had seen it coming as far back as the Versailles peace treaty, which he believed almost guaranteed renewed hostilities. And if war was inevitable, he didn't wish to split the ticket by running for President and risking a reactionary Democrat or Republican stepping into the White House and undoing the lasting good that had been accomplished with Roosevelt's New Deal.

The A.R.E.'s Milton Harrison, however, knew what the press and public did not. There was no rift between Wheeler and Roosevelt. Though they had differed on what steps should have been taken to prevent the U.S. from being pulled into the war, the President acknowledged to Wheeler that this was "water under the bridge." Both Roosevelt and Wheeler wanted to move forward, and Roosevelt offered Wheeler the Vice Presidency. Wheeler had only to say yes.

In a private meeting with Roosevelt, Wheeler advised the President

"All the News That's Fit to Print"

The New York Times.

LATE CITY EDITION

NEW YORK, FRIDAY, APRIL 13, 1945.

THREE CENTS

PRESIDENT ROOSEVELT IS DEAD; TRUMAN TO CONTINUE POLICIES; 9TH CROSSES ELBE, NEARS BERLIN

U. S. AND RED ARMIES DRIVE TO MEET

Americans Across the Elbe in Strength Race Toward Russians Who Have Opened Offensive From Oder

WEIMAR TAKEN, RUHR POCKET SLASHED

Third Army Reported 19 Miles From Czechoslovak Border—British Drive Deeper in the North, Seizing Celle—Canadians Freeing Holland

OUR OKINAWA GUNS DOWN 118 PLANES

Franklin Delano Roosevelt
1882-1945

END COMES SUDDENLY AT WARM SPRINGS

Even His Family Unaware of Condition as Cerebral Stroke Brings Death to Nation's Leader at 63

ALL CABINET MEMBERS TO KEEP POSTS

Funeral to Be at White House Tomorrow, With Burial at Hyde Park Home—Impact of News Tremendous

TRUMAN IS SWORN IN THE WHITE HOUSE

Upon Roosevelt's death, Wheeler would have become President of the United States if he had accepted the invitation to become Vice President.

not to seek a third term. In the event that Roosevelt chose to seek his party's nomination, however, Wheeler said he would not stand against him on a progressive ticket as he had previously done with La Follette, as this would split the Democratic Party and inevitably result in rolling back the New Deal reforms. Wheeler also said he would not accept the Vice Presidency since the President was, despite his public posture otherwise, going to take the country into war.

Wheeler couldn't, in good consciousness, campaign for an office which would compromise his antiwar principles. This, in essence, was what the Cayce readings suggested might happen, but didn't put in the same terms as Harrison may have understood them to be. Wheeler might actually have become President (by virtue of Roosevelt's death in office) had he accepted the nomination for Vice President, which was on the table if Wheeler had not declined to serve.

"It's very probable that Burton Wheeler will be the next president if he *chooses* to accept," Cayce had said. True, too, as Cayce had referenced in regards to Wheeler's Persian incarnation, Wheeler had a karmic willingness to put the interests of a chosen leader ahead of his own. He had "cut short" his career for what he viewed as the greater good.

Wheeler did so again. By not joining the bandwagon of the Roosevelt administration and with the subsequent attack on Pearl Harbor, "Boxcar Burt" was pilloried in the press as "Bolshevik Burt." He would lose his seat in the Senate in a primary runoff with a candidate whose name ironically was Leif Erickson. Mention was not made of the fact that if Wheeler's repeated warnings had been listened to a decade earlier, America might not have been compelled to go to war in the first place.

The more important question in 1940, however, is whether or not Wheeler's decision to step aside was the correct one for him and the future of our nation. By Wheeler's decision not to compromise his antiwar principles, the U.S. was deprived of what in retrospect we now know would have been his presidency. Was Wheeler right in holding firm to his convictions and stepping aside, or should he have accepted the nomination?

No postelection follow-up reading was requested, so Cayce—in trance—wasn't asked to weigh-in. Based on the previous readings, however, the Source clearly said that Wheeler was the best candidate and would make the best President. He would ensure the safety of our nation and adhere to what must be its ideal: "In God We Trust." From this standpoint, it's reasonable to conclude that Wheeler shouldn't have let his pacifist convictions prevent him from joining the Roosevelt administration.

"Take things, conditions and circumstances where they are, not merely where you wishfully think, hope or desire that they are," Cayce had advised in a reading for a young woman facing a similar but less consequential dilemma. He also repeatedly said that the greater good would come in leadership. As Cayce indicated in many readings before and would again, "service is the measure of greatness," and "in service alone may any soul find advancement or development." Better that Wheeler had been in the White House where, Cayce told him, "is the greater service."

This advice was clearly stated in Wheeler's own reading: "stand not merely as a Pacifist, but as *conducting*, as *proclaiming*, as *carrying* peace through brotherly love and kindness and gentleness, and patience—

even as was and is the great tenet of Him who was indeed the Peacemaker!"

" . . . that nation that hath even set on its present monetary unit "In God We Trust . . . That principle [is] being forgotten . . . and that is the sin of America." (From Cayce reading 3976-29 in 1944.)

Louise Brigham Chisholm (1875-1956) featured in the *National Magazine*, (Volume 37 Oct. 1912-March 1913).

Louise Brigham:

The Innkeeper's Daughter

Among many other accomplished people who found their way to Edgar Cayce in the 1940s was Louise Brigham, a celebrated New York social worker and conceptual artist whose globetrotting adventures were as remarkable as the spiritual journey that led her to Virginia Beach. Thanks to a generous donation by Brigham, a fireproof vault was built in the Cayce's house to preserve and protect the readings. Also thanks to Brigham, Gladys was given a small tract of land in Virginia Beach where she built her first and only home.

As would become sixty-year-old Brigham's custom, twice a year she would vacation at the Martha Washington Hotel on Atlantic Avenue, a short walk from the Cayce house. Each morning she would sit quietly in Gladys' office and study the now extensive archive of Life Readings; the remainder of her day was spent writing her autobiography. Unlike the memoirs of her contemporaries, hers didn't begin with her birth, which was in Boston in 1875. The opening chapter of the Brigham story chronicled events nearly two millennia earlier when, in a previous incarnation, she had been the daughter of a Bethlehem

Gladys was able to build her very first home on the land that Louise helped her to obtain.

innkeeper. Though today the whereabouts of Brigham's memoirs are not known—she died without family at age eighty-one in a New Jersey nursing home—the details of her extraordinary story can be gleaned from her other writings, the fourteen Cayce readings she received, and her correspondence and conversations with Gladys and Edgar.

The story that Brigham most enjoyed telling was how her commitment to social work and artistry came together in the summer of 1906. At that time she was living seven hundred miles north of the Arctic Circle in a coal mining camp on the Norwegian island of Spitsbergen where the primary source of food was whale, polar bear, and reindeer meat. How Louise—an orphan from Boston who had studied art in New York—came to be living on a remote island with eighty men and one other woman is something of a mystery. Louise never adequately explained the details, leaving Hugh Lynn with the mistaken notion that Brigham was the widow of the U.S. Consul of Norway.

Longyearbye, known as Longyear City until 1926, is located in the valley of Longyeardalen. The town was established by and named after John Munro Longyear, whose Arctic Coal Company started coal mining operations there in 1906.

Brigham was the guest of mine developer John Munro Longyear and his wife, Mary Beecher, whom Louise may have known from Boston where her father once owned an apothecary. A deeply religious woman dedicated to social justice, Louise was the traveling companion of the elderly Mary Beecher, a patron of the arts, founder of several benevolent associations, and who in later years would fund the first King James Version of the Bible in Braille. What's significant about the two summers Brigham spent in Spitsbergen was how she chose to occupy her time.

The provisions and other equipment necessary for the mining camp's operation had to be transported in wooden boxes on supply ships from the mainland. The boxes came in all shapes and sizes: massive crates which contained a portable house in which Brigham and the Longyears lived, six-foot-long tool and equipment boxes, and assortments of tea caddy and dry-goods containers. When the supplies were unpacked, the boxes began to accumulate. As Louise would later note, the boxes were a rich resource on an island where lumber was unavailable and the only plant life consisted of "famine bread," the edible moss upon which the reindeer fed, and "polar willow" which grew but two inches in height.

Louise took the opportunity to explore a concept which she had conceived back at art school in New York. Seeing the wooden crates piling up, she asked her hosts if she could make something practical from the "odds and ends" to furnish the camp. "Cut off from other materials, the possibilities of the box seemed greater than ever, and the work, which daily grew in interest, was commenced," she would later write. "As I worked in that far-off marvelous land of continuous day, surrounded by mountain and glacier, I felt anew the truth, so familiar to all, that work to be of real value must be honest, useful and beautiful."

Louise requisitioned a chest of hand tools which she used to build a wide array of what came to be known as "box furniture." Among her many creations were bookcases, wardrobes, chairs, washstands, and a dining table with a sideboard. She would remove and reuse the nails, plane the rough edges, stain the wood with boot polish and whale oil, and then stencil design patterns over the surfaces. As various Arctic explorers visited the camp on their way to the Pole, they would remark on how attractive and ingenious Brigham's creations were—a civilizing influence and touch of home in the Arctic wilds. One visitor, Prince Albert of Monaco, who watched Brigham at her workbench, was so moved that he encouraged her to teach her skills to others. Boxes in those days cost mere pennies, were plentiful everywhere, and when used as Brigham did, held artistic, social, and practical value.

Prince Albert of Monaco, c. 1910.

As Brigham would later remark, "If . . . [children] could be encouraged to supplement their school work with materials found in the home, they would find near at hand a practical opportunity for creative activity and the working out of educational principles. What better opportunity for such uses can be furnished than by the box as found in or near every household? Here is an often neglected opportunity for the transformation of humble . . . material into objects of beauty and usefulness."

Louise thus launched her career teaching how recycled or repurposed materials—primarily boxes—could be fashioned to create all manner of home furnishings, and more important, how young people, regardless of whether they knew how to read or write, could use basic carpentry skills they learned from making such furniture to better their lives and the environment in which they lived. Her modular box furniture designs and teaching methods would take her on trips throughout the world where she would both educate and study the handicraft design and traditions of different countries and cultures. Her creations were exhibited in museums and galleries; books and pamphlets featuring her work became primers in youth and young adult classes taught the world over. Her work would deeply influence Frank Lloyd Wright and the American Crafts Movement, and her modular designs can reasonably be said to be the precursor to the vastly popular lines of ready-to-assemble home furnishings by IKEA.

"Waste not, want not" was her greater message and was rooted in a deeply felt conviction of what she believed Christianity was about. That infant Jesus had been born in a manger, that he worked as a lowly carpenter, and that he had fed the masses with five loaves of bread and two fish conveyed a central tenet of His ministry: simplicity of life, kindness to all, and stewardship of God's abundance.

Although Brigham didn't preach the gospel and it would not be until her senior years that she would meet Edgar Cayce and explore her own past-life biblical associations, she had long dedicated herself to ministering to the social and physical needs of society. Raised in a suburb of Boston and orphaned at age nineteen, Brigham had found her way to New York and studied at New York's Pratt Institute and the Chase School, which is today known as Parsons. During this time she became deeply involved in the international "Settlement House Move-

The cover and a page from Louise's book, *Box Furniture.*

ment" whose goal was to encourage rich and poor to live in closer proximity to one another in intentional communities. Properties in poor urban areas would be purchased, staffed by volunteers of all income and social brackets, and nutritional meals, daycare, health and legal services as well as recreational facilities would be provided. While in her early twenties, she joined a team of settlement workers in Cleveland, Ohio, and established her own settlement house, "Sunshine Cottage," which eventually became an orphanage and homeless shelter.

In 1907, after her return from Norway, she embarked upon her campaign to bring "box furniture" to the world. Over the next decade she visited nineteen countries and published a bestselling how-to book appropriately titled *Box Furniture*, which is still in print today. Illustrated with simple line drawings, her book offers dozens of different furniture plans, advice on how to select and break down crates, and instructions on basic carpentry. Complementary advice was also offered on design patterns and color schemes. It wasn't only her ingenious designs and presentation that caught on, but also the social message that accompanied it. After a successful museum exhibition of her furniture in 1910, New York City officials permitted her to use Gracie Mansion, the former home of New York's mayor, as the head-

Miss Brigham's Workshop in Gracie Mansion.

New York Times, Jan. 19, 1913 photo of Miss Brigham's Home Thrift Association woodworking "laboratory" for boys at the Gracie Mansion (the former home of New York's mayor). It began in just two rooms but quickly outgrew its space as it expanded to over 600 apprentices in its first year of operation.

All the furniture in Louise's New York apartment (63 pieces) was made from old boxes by the boys in her Home Thrift Association as a show of gratitude. Each article is original in design, intended to meet some special need, and to fill some particular space. The desk, for instance, is built around a window that's throwing light upon the writing section which is just inside.

quarters for her Home Thrift Association woodworking "laboratory" for boys. "We give each boy a set of the seven simple tools and show him the beginnings of his work," Brigham said. "Then he does the rest." Eventually the association was opened to girls as well, and the movement spread. At Boys Town, Nebraska, for example, Father Joseph Flanagan had orphans producing and shipping box furniture which was marketed throughout the country.

The showcase for Brigham's box furniture was her East 89th Street New York apartment, where she experimented with new designs and where many journalists, teachers, and fellow artists found inspiration. Among other visitors was Cleveland industrialist Henry Arnott Chisholm, whom Louise likely knew years earlier when she was an Ohio social worker. A recent widower, sixty-four-year-old Chisholm married Brigham, aged forty-one, in 1916. Their marriage was happy, although short. He died in Yokohama, Japan, in 1920 on the couple's second world tour.

No matter where Brigham traveled, she took her tool box with her. Her favorite destination was the Holy Land, which she visited twice, and on both occasions celebrated Christmas in Bethlehem. She would join other pilgrims and spend the night under the stars reimagining Jesus' birth. She also researched traditional Hebrew female clothing of that time, which consisted of an ankle-length tunic or robe made of strips of black and alternating colored cloth and a draped headdress or veil. So moved by the experience was she that each Christmas, no matter where in the world she was traveling, she would dress in traditional Hebrew garments and recount the nativity story to audiences.

Given her inclinations, it was no small wonder that, according to several Cayce readings, she had been in Bethlehem and had witnessed Jesus' birth in a previous incarnation. Initially, Brigham vehemently resisted the information that came through Cayce in the Life Readings. This wasn't because she didn't have faith in Cayce's abilities; two of her close friends had received convincing trance counsel, and she herself received medical advice that may have saved her life. For more than a decade she had been undergoing treatment for a severe gastrointestinal condition that the Cayce recommendations cleared up in a matter of weeks. The problem Brigham had with the information that came through in her Life Readings was that Cayce's account of Jesus' birth was markedly different than what church tradition had taught and which she took for gospel truth. It wasn't that Cayce's account contradicted the biblical account. Rather it was far more expansive and featured among other things, Brigham helping Mary deliver Jesus.

The first Life Reading Brigham received was conducted in New York on April 20, 1936, at David Kahn's West 77th Street apartment. Brigham had learned of Cayce from her friends Lillian Cox, who had received several health as well as spiritual readings, and New York philanthropist Irene Seiberling, with whom Brigham sat on the boards of several social welfare associations. Seiberling accompanied Brigham to the Kahn house to witness the reading in person, as she would on several subsequent occasions when Brigham received readings. Unlike many recipients of the Life Readings, the Source indicated that Brigham's previous incarnations were few in number. Fascinating and important though her incarnations were in ancient Atlantis and Egypt, it was Brigham's life in the Holy Land that drew everyone's attention and would be studied for many years to come.

In the Holy Land during the period she incarnated, described in the readings as a time of "great changes, great opportunities," which had been brought about by the "prayers of many," Brigham's name was Sarapha, and she was the daughter of Apsafar, the owner of the Bethlehem inn where Joseph and his pregnant wife Mary had sought refuge. The story of what happened was spelled out in Brigham's two Life Readings and was referenced in upwards of ten other Life Readings of other people she had known or met at that time. This is the body of material that eventually brought Brigham to Gladys' office in Virginia Beach, and it was her pioneering efforts to cross-reference the nativity readings that give Cayce students today a picture window into a far more expansive story of Jesus' birth.

According to the readings, the weather was cold on the evening that Joseph and Mary, accompanied by other family and fellow carpenters who worked with Joseph, arrived at the inn. Joseph was said to be thirty-six; Mary sixteen. At twilight, when the party arrived, Apsafar told Joseph that "there was no room at the inn." The reason, as stated in the Gospel of Luke, and confirmed by Cayce, was that the inn was already crowded with people who had come to Bethlehem for the same reason as Joseph. A census was being taken and taxes levied.

Cayce goes into considerable more detail. Laughter and jeers at the inn followed the sight of the elderly Joseph with the beautiful young wife, who was heavy with child. This was particularly upsetting to Apsafar's daughter Sarapha, who couldn't understand why her father seemed to be so cruel as to send the pregnant Mary away. What Sarapha didn't know was that her father was an Essene, the same Jewish sect as Joseph and Mary. This was why the family had gone to this particular inn. Here is just the beginning of the intrigue to come.

Apsafar kept this knowledge to himself as it was dangerous to be associated with the Essenes. Judea's Roman overlords were on the lookout for an Essene who was soon to give birth. They had been tipped off to the birth of a Jewish Messiah by visitors from Egypt, India, and Persia—those who were described in the Bible as the "Wise Men." Apsafar was thus protecting Joseph and Mary by making a show of turning them away from the inn; the plan was to keep them out of sight in a nearby stable which was built into the side of a cave or grotto. Apsafar and his family had to be careful for other reasons as well. The Roman tax collector in Bethlehem had amorous intentions on Apsafar's young daughter. Although Sarapha had rebuffed him, the tax collector had made clear his continuing interest in her. There was no telling when he might next unexpectedly appear at the inn.

Sarapha was described as a beautiful young woman only a year younger than Mary. Empathetic with the plight of the couple who had been turned away, she asked her father if she could give aid. She was given permission to visit the stable, but only after she had finished her chores in the inn.

> Then the entity, Sarapha, aided, so that all was in readiness when, in the evening—just before the sun in all its glory of the Palestine Hills gave forth almost unto the voice of nature, proclaiming the heralding of a new hope, a new birth to the earth, and the glorifying of man's hope in God—the spectacle of His Star in the evening sky brought awe and wonder to all who beheld.
>
> Then when it was known to the entity that the den, the cave, the stable had been occupied . . . oh, the rush; oh the desire to be off to see what that experience might be, held the very being of the entity! And as soon as its duties were cleared about the home—

> as the space was very near—the entity started. But as the entity walked into the open upon that Eve, the brightness of His Star came nearer and nearer. And the entity heard [the Angel], even as the Shepherds, *'Peace* on earth, *Good Will* to men.'
>
> There came again that awe, that feeling of a new creation, of a new experience, as the entity among those—only with the closer attendant of the Mother . . . [Sarapha] hastened to the quarters where the Mother lay, in all that awe of a new experience, and the light as from His Star filled the place, the entity then first beheld the *babe*. That was the crowning experience, until the plea that she—too—might hold that glorious child in her arms also! Then as this became a reality, there were those feelings, those experiences—Oh that the world might know the beauty, the joy, the glory of the experiences of His Life in their own hearts and minds and beings!
>
> There the entity also saw the shepherds gather, there the entity also saw on the morrow the Wise Men—with their ladened beasts or camels, with all their praise for those who had kept the faith, in making and preserving, in keeping and helping those that were in need, that were alone—yet *God* with them!
>
> There were those experiences of the presence as well as that expressed in those strange tongues to the entity, though the entity knew and thought and felt and experienced the reverence and awe as shown by all . . .

Sarapha and Mary grew close to one another in the twenty-nine days that Jesus and his family were said to have been under the protection of Apsafar's family in the stable. The experience of kissing Jesus and holding him in her arms would forever be written on her soul and was the reason, as Cayce in trance, would point out: "Is it any wonder that thou hast looked long into the face of those that were newly born and wondered . . . what their purpose, their hardships, their joys, their sorrows would be in the earth?"

In the years after Mary and Joseph left the inn, Sarapha desired to keep in touch with the family, but communications being difficult at

The Nativity by Jacob de Backer, (late 16th century).

the time, she heard only sporadic reports. She was especially worried when the edict was passed by King Herod to slaughter the Jewish newborns, what is described in the Bible as the "Massacre of the Innocents." As the reading stated: "Those made for days and weeks and months when the entity wondered and wondered and wondered . . . Yet often the entity in the stillness of the evening reviewed the happenings [in Bethlehem], and there was the seeking more and more as to what had become of His Star, His Light."

Cayce continued: "Throughout those experiences, then, the entity . . . sought for word as to His progress, in following that which had become almost as a story; yet the entity held to those visions, those experiences . . . during those periods when they beheld the light, when they beheld the Child in the Mother's arms—and that glorious moment when it had been placed in her own, and the entity had pressed its own lips to the brow of that Babe!"

After Apsafar's death, Sarapha moved from Bethlehem to the outskirts of Jerusalem, where she opened an inn, identified in the Cayce readings as the "Wayside." Here she heard more news of Jesus; how he had become a carpenter like his father. She desired to go out and see him, but her duties at the inn prevented her from doing so. She would not see Him again until he passed by on the road to Jerusalem, followed by a mighty crowd of people. She had doubts, as did the others. Jesus appeared to be a mere man, who "seemed to exert so little of that necessary material application of a glorious power and might."

Not until after Jesus' crucifixion would she visit with Mary again and have the opportunity to meet the Holy Women who had been around Jesus. Sarapha held fast to her faith and was among the first women to suffer martyrdom when Roman soldiers attempted to disperse a crowd of Christians. It was Sarapha's faith, which was brought forward into her incarnation as Louise Brigham, that the readings said had and would sustain her. This was presumably why she had had so few incarnations.

"Hold *fast* to that, Oh Daughter of the Inn Keeper, Oh the Beholder of His Glory," Cayce told her. "Oh the joyous, gracious feelings that fill thy soul and being with the richness of the earth poured out at His feet, with those that experienced the lowly shepherds that came to see that glorious sight, and they—too—were not hindered from beholding the face of their Savior. And ye, too, Oh Daughter, may know His face—but turn *within*! For *there* ye may meet Him, as so oft ye did in those days, those weeks, those months, those years ye recounted in thine inner self those glorious experiences, those glorious happenings of that day when the Babe, the child Jesus lay in thy arms."

Brigham had many questions which she would ask of Cayce in follow-up readings and in her studies of the other nativity-related Life Readings. Among them was a question that provided a clue as to her own karma in her present incarnation. Her question related to the Roman tax collector whom she had rebuffed in Bethlehem. Had they crossed paths again? Indeed, they had. He was one and the same as Henry Chisholm, the man she may have loved or been in a relationship with back in Cleveland, whom she met again in New York after the death of his wife. The one whom she had rejected in her previous incarnation, she had married this time around.

Besides her steadfast faith in the "Master Carpenter" and other inclinations which had come as a result of her Holy Land innkeeping experience was her innate desire to travel, to care for travelers, to provide comfort for the poor as well as to build box furniture.

Cayce—in trance—poetically told her what she felt in her heart: "It made for those feelings in the experience of each and every traveler that there was a care and a thought for their own . . . rest and harmony and beauty . . . [no matter where]. Could the entity then imagine a home, whether earthly or spiritual, without a builder or a carpenter?"

Louise Brigham with Gladys Davis, c. 1936.

George Conjar, c. 1939.

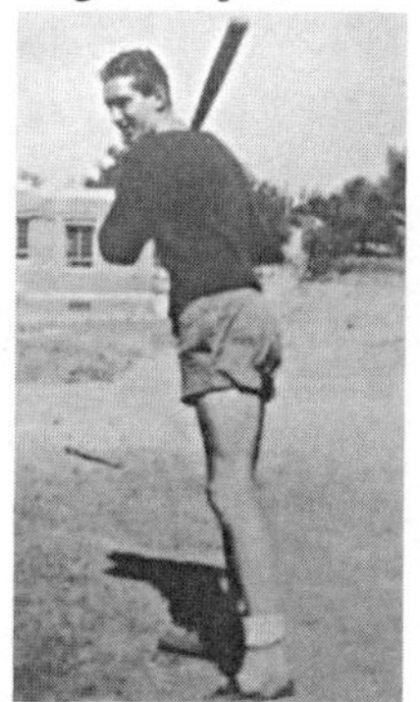

GEORGE CONJAR:

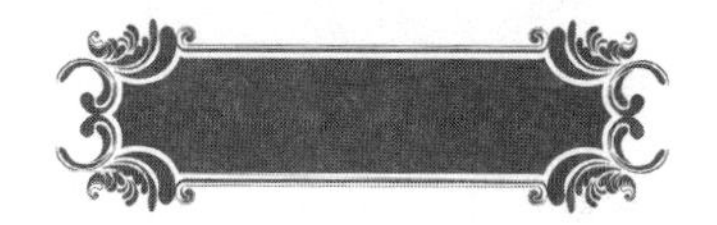

CURED!

"You're doing fine, just fine . . ." nineteen-year-old George Conjar was told.

These were the words spoken by Dr. Charles Custer, chief of medical services at the Pennsylvania State Tuberculosis Sanatorium at South Mountain, intended to comfort the young man. Only Conjar, in room 441 of the South Mountain men's ward in a building complex where he had lived for the past three years, knew he wasn't fine. Tuberculosis had destroyed his left lung and the infection had spread to his right. He was spitting up mouthfuls of bloody mucus; fever and cold sweats kept him from sleeping; and he had lost nearly twenty pounds in the last eleven weeks. But on this day, July 8, 1943, he had reason to believe his prayers would be answered. Three hundred miles away in Virginia Beach, Edgar Cayce was going into trance to try and save his life.

Four years earlier Conjar was a happy and healthy high school junior in Harrisburg, Pennsylvania—one of five children born to a family of working class Eastern European immigrants. An honors student, he

The South Mountain Restoration Center was only an unheated barn and tents until 1902 when several 8 x 10 shacks which slept 5 people each were added. By 1938 it looked more like this and it was 1 of 700 TB Sanatoriums in the United States. These were self-contained communities which became known as "waiting rooms for death."

The Children's Hospital also known as the Preventorium at South Mountain Sanatorium.

was class president and played on the football team. Then, in the late fall of 1939, while playing an away football game on a particularly cold and rainy afternoon, he was injured and later became ill with pneumonia. He spent the Christmas holidays in bed and returned to school when the next semester began. By all outward appearances he seemed to be doing well, but when his school tested him for tuberculosis, the results came back positive for "incipient stage" TB in his left lung. Since TB was a contagious disease, he was taken out of school. By state mandate he was then sent to a Preventorium, an institution designed to contain and treat children who had been exposed to tuberculosis but were not yet symptomatic.

Conjar's three-month stay at the South Mountain Preventorium was not altogether an unpleasant experience—more like a "summer camp," he later said, except that the kids—ranging in age from fifteen months to eighteen years—were rarely permitted outdoors. There was still plenty of exercise, however, mostly in the form of calisthenics and swimming in one of two indoor pools along with the occasional outdoor baseball game. In addition to the indoor pools, the massive four-floor building in which he lived contained an auditorium, a library, four classrooms where nutrition, hygiene, and a wide range of other subjects were taught. There were also lounges where patients could go to listen to the radio, play cards, and talk among themselves.

Conjar easily made friends among the approximately three hundred patients who lived in the dormitory-style sleeping quarters, and with regular visits from his family, the months passed quickly. He was sure that he had beaten the disease. He had gained weight—thanks to the generous helpings of food served three times a day—and had put on muscle, the result of the calisthenics. He was looking forward to football and starting his senior year when, as routine procedure before release, he was retested. The X-ray showed his left lung had worsened. Rather than being sent home, he was remanded to the South Mountain Sanatorium, a seven floor hospital and cottage complex directly across the street from the Preventorium. As there was no known cure for TB, this was where most patients went to die. Whether it was a few months or years, it was just a matter of time.

Where patients in the Preventorium were only children, here there were young and old alike, nearly a thousand TB sufferers in total. With the constant reminder that death was the inevitable next step—the South Mountain TB cemetery was directly behind the building—there was a sense of gloom and despondency. George experienced the same wide range of shifting emotions as the others: hope, despair, love, sorrow, happiness, and tragedy. He enjoyed playing cribbage, visiting the chapel, walking the hallways, and living in a quaint cottage where other patients with less severe cases lived. This was where he was staying when his first phrenicotomy was performed. The procedure involved making a small incision in the skin just above his collarbone and "crushing" the phrenic nerve, thereby paralyzing a portion of his diaphragm and diminishing the volume of air he could take into his

The Chapel.

The cottages in the Men's Camp.

lungs. The procedure may have been moderately effective in slowing down the progress of his infection, but it left him sick to his stomach and increasingly having to gasp for air.

By the end of the first year his disease was considered moderately advanced, and he was moved into the main hospital building. Treatment was advanced to include pneumothorax, which consisted of pumping air into the pleural cavity around his left lung and thereby collapsing the diseased area. Still his condition continued to deteriorate. In addition to coughing up blood, there were fevers and night sweats. So sensitive was his stomach to food that he could eat only breadcrumbs. As would eventually become his routine, he kept slices of bread in his bedroom drawer and throughout the day put tiny crumbs on his tongue until they dissolved. When X-rays showed that his right lung was also now infected, physicians recommended a thoracoplasty, in which several of his ribs would be removed to permanently collapse his left lung so that his right lung might be spared. This was just a nightmare for George—a former football and baseball player, once proud of his body and his strapping good looks. He had only to look across the dining room to see the thoracoplasty patients—

Thomas Sugrue's *There is a River, The Story of Edgar Cayce* was first published in 1942.

"slumped over like hunchbacks," as he said—to know his future.

Despondent, believing his life was over if he stayed at South Mountain any longer, he packed his things and telling no one, slipped out the front gates to hitchhike home. He was warmly received by his family—not so by friends and neighbors. Anyone who came into contact with him could potentially become infected. He was also too weak to even do routine chores around the house and was unwelcome at the local hospital. Physicians didn't want their patients exposed to him. Five months later, just shy of his eighteenth birthday, he returned to South Mountain, now resigned to his fate.

One of the roommates he enjoyed playing cribbage with was a young Presbyterian seminary student, Howard Roemer. Like George, he was in the critical stage of the disease. He had dropped twenty pounds, suffered nausea, and the mere sight of food made him sick. After one of their many conversations Howard gave him a new book by author Tom Sugrue, *There Is a River*, the first Cayce biography, which had been released only the month before. George liked it so much that he immediately decided write to Cayce and obtain a reading. Had he known how many unfilled demands there were already for Cayce readings—the backlog was nearly two years ahead—he might have been discouraged from even trying. But George, as he later admitted, was naive. "I had to try."

In fine but unsteady penmanship, Conjar introduced himself in a letter dated May 25, 1943, devoting more words to his inability to pay to join the A.R.E. than he did describing his condition.

> I have been told that a sum of twenty dollars is asked of members. You've probably realized by now that I am unemployed—that I

> have no money. I do get a few dollars from my mother now and then, and if need be, could fall back upon her . . . However, I'm against making this decision because I'd like to repay my own debt. After some debate I thought of the following: Mr. Cayce, if you gave me a reading that resulted in a cure, I'd offer you my services for eight hours of every day for one year in the practice of helping my fellow man. I'd do this entirely free of charge, food, or board, and any type of work assigned me would be undertaken with a glad heart. In the event that no cure occurred I would anyway try in same degree to do a little handwork that might bring in a few dollars. This money I would send to your foundation in the hopes that another would perhaps be benefited . . . You probably understand my reason for the preceding sentence is not brought on because of any lack of charity; my health would require a stoppage at this point.

In signing off, Conjar simply said: "Well, I guess I said about all there is that needs be mentioned. Closing in all sincerity, George Conjar."

Edgar responded three days later:

> Have yours of the 25th. Am enclosing a blank [A.R.E. application]. Will be glad to try and be of a service—and it will be entirely up to you, whether you pay anything or not. Just feel from past experience with this trouble that you can be helped, but do feel you will probably have to be at home, but do not think the cost for your treatments will be very much . . . Just hoping to be the means of a service.

A date of July 8 was set for the reading. To be certain that Edgar—in trance—would find him, George said that he would be in room 441 in the bed "alongside the window" and that when the reading was being given he would be in "prayer and meditation." He also expressed, as he would repeatedly do in his correspondence to come, how grateful he was that Edgar would be doing this for him. "Until then [when the reading is given]," he wrote on June 11, "I will say an inadequate thank you for the service you are so graciously rendering me. May God bless

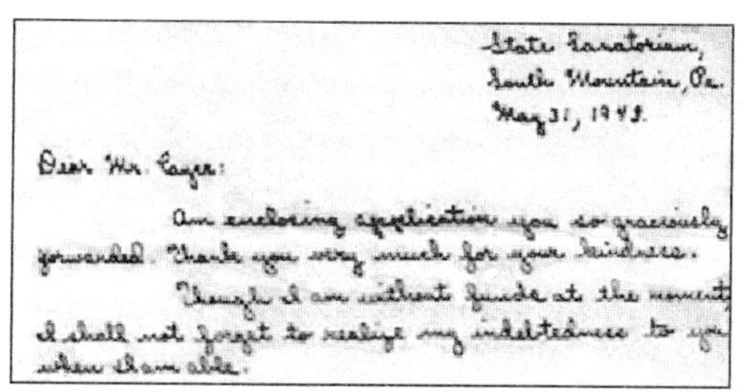

State Sanatorium,
South Mountain, Pa.
May 31, 1943.

Dear Mr. Cayce:

Am enclosing application you so graciously forwarded. Thank you very much for your kindness.

Though I am without funds at the moment I shall not forget to realize my indebtedness to you when I am able.

A snippet of George's letter to the Sleeping Prophet enclosing his application for membership in the association.

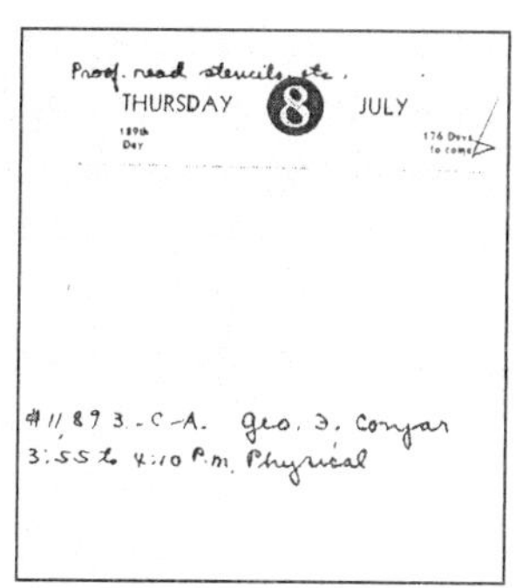

Proof. read stencils, etc.
THURSDAY 8 JULY
189th Day
176 Days to come

#11893.-C-A. Geo. J. Conjar
3:55 to 4:10 P.m. Physical

George's appointment on the Cayce Day Planner for July 8, 1943.

you always and may He reward you in some way for this kindness you have shown to me."

Conjar's month-long wait to receive the reading was difficult. He continued to steadily lose weight and twice collapsed unconscious in a state of shock and had to be revived. What pulled him through was the conviction that Cayce would provide help. Just prior to when he was to receive the Cayce reading, he wrote a letter to the chief supervising physician, Dr. Custer, to share his excitement. In the same letter he also expressed his intention to leave South Mountain the same day he received the reading and return home to begin the recommended treatments.

The following day Dr. Custer called Conjar into his office to tell him that he was making a grievous mistake. In so doing, Dr. Custer related a story about a mentally deranged young man who had put his faith in a "cult" and had foregone professional medical help which led to a tragic ending. He didn't wish George to make the same mistake. Conjar countered by telling the physician that Cayce did not want him to join a cult. He was acting out of kindness, seeking to help people who came to him by using his God-given talents.

Dr. Custer, suddenly irate, demanded to know who had told him about Cayce. Reluctant to implicate his friend Howard, George referenced popular radio show host Isabelle Manning Hewson, who had done a segment on Cayce. Instead of discussing the matter further,

Custer reached for the phone and called the radio station which broadcast her show. To George's alarm, Custer proceeded to file a grievance, claiming that Hewson was driving his patients into "hysteria" with her ridiculous notions. He then referenced Conjar's name, citing him as a patient who had become mentally unbalanced by Hewson's discussion of Cayce.

"He thought that I would be forced to forget you," Conjar later confided to Edgar by letter. "He then said he didn't want me arousing the other patients with my crackpot ideas though I don't ever remember arousing anyone in any manner. All this time he had been speaking without any apparent idea of what your work consisted of, and this even though my letter concerning your readings was plain enough."

When a nurse in the room came to Conjar's defense, Dr. Custer became all the more irritated. As George later wrote, "He then began speaking of my religion and how you were not in accordance with it. I replied that a Catholic priest, who knows much more about my religion than I, was cured by following the readings prescribed treatment. 'I'll bet his name wasn't in the book,' he said. 'No,' said I, 'but any doctor may go down and examine the various case histories and see for himself the work of the readings.' This stumped him momentarily and then he told me to go and get the [Cayce] book. When I returned, he was looking over my chart and then said to me, 'George, you're doing fine, just fine. I don't want you to go home and undo this good.' Well that certainly hit me . . . He tells me I'm doing fine. Just where did he get that information? He wanted me to put faith in the medical profession and him talking like that. I couldn't reply before he ushered me out into the hall."

Dr. Custer missed his next appointment with Conjar, which was just as well, as George had received the Cayce reading in the mail. Since Custer was too busy to see him, George's mother checked him out of the hospital and took him home. He couldn't wait to get started on a treatment plan.

The Source, speaking through Cayce, described Conjar's tubercular condition as being in "advanced stage" but was not so far gone that he wouldn't respond to treatment if he consistently followed the recommendations. "This disturbance may not only be allayed, and stayed, but the body may be capable of doing very good work, and contribute

Breathing in fumes of apple brandy from a charred oak keg was one of the same treatments Cayce used to save Gertrude Cayce's life many years earlier. The Calcios Cayce recommended is still available today and a good source of natural calcium.

to the spiritual things of life."

The recommendations, in brief, were as follows: he was to remain quiet, preferably at home, and inhale the fumes of pure apple brandy from a charred oak keg. Further, every other day he was to ingest a teaspoon full of Acigest, a commonly available type of hydrochloric acid, stirred in a glass of raw milk. He was also to take the calcium supplement Calcios, which he was to spread thinly on a whole wheat cracker as he would butter. And rather than remain indoors, as had been prescribed at the sanatorium, he was to go outside. "Keep in the open when practical . . . Stay out of the night air, yet have plenty of ventilation . . . Keep in the sunshine, but not in the noonday sunshine—rather stay in the shade but out of doors. Rest a great deal . . . A little exercise may be taken; only such as walking or the like."

Conjar was also advised to pay careful attention to his diet, which was to consist of eating seafood, bones included, twice each week. Chicken, stewed bones included, was to be eaten at other meals. No other kinds of meat should be consumed, unless it was wild game. Further, he was to drink plenty of milk and milk products. Large quantities of cooked and raw vegetables and fruit were also to be eaten, but these were to be "yellow," such as yellow squash, yellow peaches, yellow yams, and yellow carrots. The Source didn't explain how foods with this particular color figured into the treatment equation, nor did Conjar ask, but the reason, as later would be evidenced in studies of phytochemicals, show that these fruits and vegetables are extremely high in organic chemical compounds which the body converts to vitamins A and C, omega-3 fatty acids, and folate.

This, along with a recommendation that he receive a check-up reading eight weeks into his treatment, was the extent of the advice. To help put the advice to best use, enclosed with the reading was an illustration of the charred oak keg and how it should be configured so that he could best inhale the apple brandy fumes.

Conjar received the reading on a Monday, arrived home the next day, and wrote Edgar on Wednesday. "By Friday I expect to have everything in readiness and to be able to begin my cure . . . I am also enclosing four dollars which I have managed to save from my allowance. Soon I hope to send you money regularly; first to try and pay in part for what you are doing for me and secondly, in the hopes that with it you may be helped by me in the continuing of your work for your fellow man. Thank you very much for your kindness; I can't express my gratitude appropriately."

Conjar would continue writing Edgar, telling him of the progress he was making, asking questions, and invariably enclosing a dollar or two. However, hopeful and committed as he was to carrying out the recommendations, he had challenges yet to be met. Foremost among them was obtaining a charred oak keg. In a letter he wrote to a manufacturer he indicated that he wouldn't be using it for distillery purposes, but to follow health recommendations for treatment of TB. In return correspondence, the manufacturer expressed his sympathy for Conjar and his condition, but said that he wasn't licensed to sell kegs for medicinal purposes.

Conjar went to his upstairs bedroom and cried into his pillow, thinking that his treatment would have to be delayed until he could somehow obtain a keg. By then it might be too late. But the next day he was delighted to suddenly find one delivered by the same company he had initially made his request. Though the manufacturer hadn't been able to "sell" him one, the sales agent had been touched by George's letter and "given" him one. Then there was the problem of obtaining brandy. Apple brandy was not available in Harrisburg, only apple jack. George's older brother solved this problem by a making a road trip to Maryland. The other products, Acigest and Calcios—were more easily obtained. Thus, with a concerted and well-choreographed effort by his entire family—his father prepared the keg, his siblings brought the food, and his mother prepared it—his healing began.

Four days into the treatment plan Conjar reported "a queer, light-headed feeling for an entire day." Twenty-four hours later, however, the feeling was gone. He then experienced a slight fever which lingered for a week and profuse sweating. He wasn't concerned; rather, he was pleased that the treatment seemed to be having an effect. As numerous times before, he expressed his thanks in a letter to Edgar. "What you've done for me I'll never be able to repay you for. I thank God for letting me come into contact with you . . . If God is willing that my health be restored through you, it will make me, I believe, happier than anyone on this earth. I already am ecstatically happy for what has already come to me."

Conjar's correspondence continued to be upbeat. In August, little more than three weeks since acting on the recommendations, Edger received a few more dollars in the mail, along with a note: "I'm feeling fine since starting treatment, in every way. Really, a new man. The sunshine feels wonderful, too; it's the first I've been out in it for a length of time since 1940."

In reply, Edgar encouraged him to stick to the regime. "You are going to have days when you won't feel so good, but I sincerely believe from past experiences that if you will do all the readings suggested for you and don't overdo it, you are going to get real results and I know that you will be a new and a happy man and I am looking forward . . . to talk to you personally."

George, too, looked forward to that moment. This, written in early September, which accompanied his $2 a month allowance: "With your permission I'll come to Virginia Beach and thank you personally. It won't be an adequate thank you, since I can't even begin to put into speech such a great 'thanks' as I feel . . . I am in need of spiritual help as well a physical, and since I've come to know you I am, I know, much better spiritually, and feel much better physically."

Edgar was pleased that George should be thinking beyond his physical healing. He sent George a copy of a new book, *A Search for God,* which was a compilation of spiritual readings Edgar had given for the group of A.R.E. members in Virginia Beach and Norfolk who had come together out of profound desire to better understand themselves and their relationship to God.

In response to George's letter, Edgar wrote: "We need help in our spiritual lives, if we are to use our physical abilities better, and I am in hopes that you may through the offices of the Association find something worthwhile just as so many others . . . If you will stick right close to all of the suggestions indicated in your reading and be mindful of your diet, I feel that you are going to get along all right. Let us hear from you and . . . hoping to see you in the not too distant future."

Eight weeks into the treatment Conjar applied for a follow-up check reading as had been indicated in his first reading. In an accompanying note, he also expressed his profound pleasure in reading *A Search for God* book. "It was like receiving a rare pearl after having already been given a rare diamond. You're so very good. No matter what I am or ever shall be, I shall never forget the kindness you've shown me, nor the joy you've given me nor will I ever stop working to strengthen myself spiritually so that I may duplicate part of this kindness toward another . . . I want you to know that whatever the outcome, I am a much happier man for having met you and will be always."

Throughout this correspondence Edgar never alluded to difficulties he was having with his own deteriorating health, the backlog of readings still to be conducted, or the feverish pace in which he was now giving them. The Source had said that Edgar, for his own health, ought to restrict the amount of trance sessions to twice a day. Gertrude was so concerned that she pulled him aside, requesting he put the brakes on.

"You're killing yourself," Gertrude had said. But Edgar wouldn't listen. He led her to the back storage room of their house and emptied an entire mail bag of correspondence onto the floor. "How can I turn them away?" he asked. "It kills me not to do the readings. If I overdo it, that will kill me, too."

Cayce never alluded to the drama taking place behind the scenes. He merely scheduled a follow-up reading for Conjar and apologized

George Conjar on the mend.

for him having to wait until January, 1944. "I know that is a long time . . . but it is the very best we can do at the present time. I thank you very much for what you have said. Our whole purpose is to be of a service wherever and whenever it is possible. I am sure if you keep your thinking right, then act just as you think and pray the same way, you will get much better."

Edgar received no specific reports of Conjar's health in the lead up to the second reading; rather, he received a money order for $4 and a promise of $10 per month to be put toward an A.R.E. life-membership. Then, just before the January 4 date the reading was to be conducted, this letter came from Conjar in the mail:

> It has been almost five months since I began treatment as the reading suggested and I certainly must say I feel great. Since the 4th will divulge the extent of my improvement I am very much on pins and needles this day. For my entire three years spent in the sanatorium only one X-ray turned out favorable; the remainder—about 10 in number—were all rather disappointing. It has been a long while since I've felt as well as I do today. My heart owes you

> much, not only for my physical reading, but also for the spiritual help I've received through you. My life cannot help but be happy.

The follow-up reading Cayce conducted lasted a mere five minutes. The Source declared that there was no longer an infection, yet he should continue the treatments as previously outlined to more fully restore his health. He could, in fact, begin physical labor, in moderation. "Do not work under conditions where the feet get cold or damp, or where there is not proper ventilation in the working surroundings. But the body can begin with its activities. Keep continually the constructive thinking within itself and within that which it would do for others. For in the manner ye treat thy fellow man ye treat thy Maker. Take time to be holy. Ye have made promises to self, to thy Maker, to thy friends. Remember—what thou hast vowed, keep. For the Lord hath need of those who are honest with themselves."

Conjar was ecstatic. "Thank you from the bottom of my heart," he wrote on January 10. "I cannot—nor can words—express . . . the joy that fills my entire being every minute of every day. My gratitude to you is likewise inexpressible . . . my heart thanks you always . . . As soon as I can make financial arrangements for a trip to Virginia Beach, I am going to visit you so that I can thank you personally for your great kindnesses to me."

Despite the now overwhelming demands on his time, Edgar wrote back a long and heartfelt letter. This, in part, was what he said:

> I am looking forward with a great deal of pleasure and interest to the day when I may meet you in person. I believe you are going to be entirely well of this trouble. I know my own wife, whom I hope you will meet when you are here, in 1910 was in a much worse condition than yourself, and is entirely well and has little or no recurrence . . . It will be very well for you to check on your condition with an X Ray and I hope that you will get just as wonderful results as many others have. You ought to be entirely well, George, in possibly less than a year.

Conjar went ahead and had an X-ray at the Harrisburg Hospital. No evidence could be found of the disease in his right lung. His left lung

Conjar with his wife, Jacqueline, and three grandchildren on vacation in California.

was scarred, but disease free. The physician declared him healed. How, he didn't know, but George's recovery, by any measure, was miraculous.

The tragedy—as Conjar would later note—was twofold.

Physicians had let so many others die when Cayce's treatment plan was so effective, inexpensive, available to nearly everyone, and had so many added healthful benefits. His entire body had been rejuvenated. The pharmaceutical based treatment that was finally devised and used to treat TB in the 1950s, which would virtually eradicate the disease in the U.S. and is still the prescribed treatment, acts on the body as does chemotherapy. It kills the infection, but at great cost to the human body.

Conjar's other regret was that he didn't get to thank Edgar in person. In the year after getting well, while his brothers were off fighting in WW II and he had to work to support his family, Edgar's own health had deteriorated. He was critically ill with pneumonia. He would pass before Conjar could afford thc train ticket.

Conjar had no other regrets. Life was a celebration. Every morning at six a.m., he stopped at church to say a prayer for the blessing which had been given him, treated each new day as an opportunity to share his good fortune with others, and gave a third of everything he earned to charity and for the betterment of mankind. Conjar went on to receive a college business degree and would work for the same Harrisburg, Pennsylvania, wholesale product distribution company for forty-one years. When a Cayce Foundation archivist went to interview him in 1998, he had just celebrated his seventy-fourth birthday, and a party would be thrown several months later for his forty-fifth wedding anniversary, which was attended by his five children and seven grandchildren. Today he is a happy and healthy ninety-years young. He hasn't spent a night in a hospital since when, with his Cayce reading in hand, he left the South Mountain sanitarium.

Edgar in Capitol Square, Columbus, Ohio with the 13 foot bronze sculpture of the *Angel of Peace.*

In October 1930, Edgar woke up from a reading with the following report: "As I went out, I realized that I had contacted Death, as a personality, as an individual, or as a being. Realizing this, I remarked to Death: "You are not as ordinarily pictured—with a black mask or hood, or as a skeleton, or like Father Time with a sickle. Instead, you are fair, rose-cheeked, robust—and you have a pair of shears or scissors." In fact, I had to look twice at the feet or limbs, or even at the body, to see it take shape.

He replied: "Yes, Death is not what many seem to think. It is not the horrible thing which is often pictured. Just a change—just a visit. The shears or scissors are indeed the implements most representative of life and death to man. These indeed, unite by dividing—and divide by uniting. The cord does not, as usually thought, extend from the center—but is broken, from the head, the forehead—that soft portion we see pulsate in the infant. Hence we see old people, unbeknowing to themselves, gain strength from youth by kissing there; and youth gains wisdom by such kisses.

Indeed the vibrations may be raised to such an extent as to rekindle or re-connect the cord, even as the Master did with the son of the widow of Nain. For He did not take him by the hand (which was bound to the body as was the custom of the day), but rather stroked him on the head—and the body took life of Life itself! So, you see, the silver cord may be broken—but vibration . . . " Here the dream ended."

Edgar Cayce:

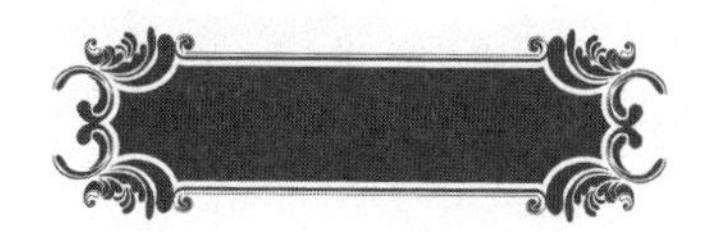

In *His* Presence

Edgar's physical condition began to seriously deteriorate in early 1944. That February, suffering from a severe cold and cough, he agreed to take a short vacation to visit Tom Sugrue in Clearwater, Florida. He enjoyed wading out into the surf with his fishing pole as Tom sat on the beach soaking up the sun in a lawn chair. But when Edgar came back to Virginia Beach ten days later, his condition hadn't noticeably improved. And despite trance counsel otherwise, he plunged back into giving readings—at times five or six in a single day—though the Source had recommended no more than two, or none at all. By the beginning of March, Edgar was in bed with pneumonia.

Despite orders from his physician and once again ignoring the advice in the readings, Edgar prescribed for himself a potent drug—a sulfa compound that he had once taken at the onset of a severe cold. The shock to his system left him in such a weakened condition that he was forced into bed and unable to give further readings until March 14, when he gave one for himself. Then, against the pleadings of Gertrude and Gladys, he began doing readings for a few friends in desperate need, and by March 20 he was giving nine readings in a single day—this in addition to trying to read or respond to the upwards of five hundred letters sent him each month. In one day alone, he received an all-time high of 750 letters. "It is hard to hear the pleas of some who phone and wire and not try to do something about it," he wrote to Edgar Evans, who was then serving in the Army Signal Corp. "But [I] can do just so much."

Edgar's office.

The Cayce home and Association for Research and Enlightenment (A.R.E.) headquarters in Virginia Beach, c. 1940.

A secretary helping Gladys with the correspondence was so upset by the "depleted" state in which Edgar frequently found himself after giving readings that she referred to his trance sessions as the "drain machine" and encouraged him to stop. "Hour by hour, day by day I could sense some vital life sustenance ebbing from the body of a man whom I had come to admire and to love in some special personal way," she later wrote.

Despite admonitions to slow down, Edgar continued to entertain visitors to Virginia Beach who came to witness trance readings or seek psychic advice and counsel. Ernest Hemingway's mother sought counsel, as did band leader Vincent Lopez, and through Harold Reilly in New York, future New York Governor and Vice President Nelson

In 1944 a phone call came in for Edgar from soon-to-be President Harry Truman, who would take office upon the death of FDR in April of 1945.

Rockefeller and labor leader George Meany.

Among several mysterious visitors to Virginia Beach around this time was an unnamed government agent who arrived from Washington, D.C. on May 30, 1944. At Edgar's request, Gladys led the visitor into the study, and the doors were closed. All that is known about the privately conducted trance session comes from a letter Edgar wrote to Edgar Evans. His father described his visitor as "one of the higher-ups," who was "an advisor to those in authority, who were the ones that formulate the patterns about the inter-relations that are to be with all of the other countries after the war." Coincidently, around this same time, divinity student, Harmon Bro, who was working as a secretary under Gladys, reported answering a telephone call, which he put through to Edgar from the office of Harry Truman.

If Truman, soon-to-become President, received a reading, it was never recorded for the official archive. However, an astonishing 1,385 readings were given between June, 1943, and June, 1944. After that the number precipitously declined along with Edgar's health. He slept longer each morning and retired earlier each night. His garden was left unattended.

In August, 1944, Edgar was stopped by a stroke that left his right

Edgar Cayce donning his "reading robe," a gift affectionately made for him by one of his four sisters, c. 1940-41.

Gardening was one of the passions that Edgar had to give up due to his illness.

side partially paralyzed, preventing him from using a pen or typing letters. On the advice of his physician, he went to recover in Roanoke, Virginia, where he was put under the care of an osteopath recommended in the readings. He and Gertrude stayed at the Meadow View Inn in Cloverdale, which was owned and operated by his physician and his wife. By this time the doctor and his wife would have closed the inn and gone to Florida, but out of courtesy to the Cayces, kept a room open to more easily check on Edgar's condition and permit friends to make daily visits.

Gladys, back in Virginia Beach, wrote cheerful letters to ease the Cayces' minds that the A.R.E. was in good hands. However, Edgar knew well the challenges placed on her shoulders. Now that he had stopped giving readings, the A.R.E. had no income. Friends and grateful recipients of the readings helped meet her and the family's daily needs, but they could no longer afford extra staff to answer the phones or update the correspondence.

The Meadow View Inn where Edgar and Gertrude stayed in Cloverdale near Roanoke. It had been originally a farmhouse built in the 1800s and in front of it was the "Sacred Tree of Cloverdale" (which went down in a windstorm in 1961). The huge black walnut tree had stood for 500 years and had a circumference of 25 feet. The tree was known through the years as the "Ancient Worship Tree of the Indians."

Among the letters arriving in Virginia Beach was one from Hugh Lynn, stationed in France with the U.S. Third Army, who wrote his father a heartfelt letter of encouragement: "I know, and it makes me glad, how easy it will be for you to slip away when you decide to do so. You must realize that you have done a magnificent job . . . It is not for any accomplishment for yourself that I ask you to continue, but for those of us who need your help a little longer here. The crystallization of our efforts lies just ahead, the molding of our work for the masses is shaping and needs your guidance, the influencing of several important individuals is needed—need I mention those close to you, your grandsons."

The last Cayce reading ever given was for Edgar himself on September 17, 1944. There was little doubt in anyone's mind that an angelic presence, the "Master of Masters," was in the room and speaking through Cayce. Those gathered at Edgar's side were counseled to be at peace. "Let not your hearts be troubled," they were counseled. Neither

. . . be afraid, for Lo, it is I, and I have promised to be with thee, even unto the end of the world."

The only recommendations that came through in this last reading were provided for Edgar's physical comfort.

A week later Cayce suffered another stroke, which resulted in complete paralysis of the entire left side of his body from his neck to his feet. Still, he was in good spirits and sufficiently strong to dictate a list of instructions for Gladys. Among other things, Gladys was to pay the car insurance, see about the heating bill, and rent the extra bedroom in the house to help offset expenses. He also left instructions for Rains, the gardener, to dig a trench and plant his tulip bulbs.

Captain Edgar Evans Cayce, temporarily home on leave, arrived in Roanoke on November 19. Edgar struggled to whisper into his ear, telling Edgar Evans that he wished to spend his final days at home surrounded by the people and things he loved most. Edgar Evans promptly bundled Edgar in blankets, checked him out of the Meadow View Inn, and took the wheel of the ambulance that returned Edgar to Virginia Beach.

In anticipation of Edgar's arrival, Gladys and the volunteers overhauled the house and did a spring cleaning. Despite their outward enthusiasm, however, they awaited Edgar's arrival with mixed feelings. The reports Gladys had received indicated that Edgar was on the mend, but she intuitively knew–as did Edgar Evans–that the end was near.

Edgar himself knew that the end was approaching, and it was perhaps for this reason that he asked that the ambulance stop in Blackstone, Virginia, on their way to Virginia Beach, to see if Beatrice—Little Anna—was home. She, too, had sensed that the end was near and had driven to Virginia Beach in hopes of seeing Edgar.

Upon arriving, Edgar had to be carried into their Arctic Crescent home on a stretcher. There were tears, but these belonged to Edgar, happy to be home after three months away. "[He was] so glad . . . " Gladys wrote, "But heartbroken to be in such a fix."

Though paralyzed from the neck down, and barely able speak above a whisper, he dictated several letters, among them to Hugh Lynn. "I really think I have improved more since I have been home than in all the time since I have been sick," Edgar wrote on December 2.

Edgar moved in and out of consciousness for the next ten days until, on December 13, he went into a coma, which lasted through the night. The next morning he looked much better and his circulation seemed improved, but he was no longer alert and couldn't sleep for more than thirty minutes at a time without waking.

Jane Williams, a friend of the Cayces' since the demise of the hospital, was sitting with Edgar when he suddenly woke up and in a whisper, told her about a dream that he'd had. She didn't understand all his words but felt certain that he had told her he would be "rejuvenated" on January 5.

Later that night Edgar also spoke to Gladys with astonishing clarity and deep insight. "Faith, hope, and love—they are real," he told her. "Faith is the substance of things hoped for, the evidence of things not seen, but it is more real than anything you can see. Love is universal, not personal. When it becomes universal, it is [a] creative [energy]. It can bring life just as surely as two bodies united become a channel for the entrance of a soul into the earth."

Christmas of 1944 was not the happy occasion it had traditionally been in the household. Edgar was again comatose. On New Year's Eve, when the midnight horns were sounded at the nearby naval station, he rallied.

"Happy New Year!" Gladys told him. "We're going places and doing things in 1945!"

Edgar replied: "Same to you . . . if the Lord is willing."

Two or three times that night, Edgar would wake up saying such things as: "This world is in an awful mess, and we've got to control it. I just hope I am worthy."

Gertrude's last conversation with Edgar was on January 2, just after sunset. He said, "You know I do love you."

Gertrude nodded, and he asked, "How do you know?"

She smiled, then said, "Oh, I just know."

Edgar looked at her with tears in his eyes. "I don't see how you can tell," he said, "but I do love you." After taking a moment to gain strength, or reflect, he continued. "You know, when you love someone you sacrifice for them. And what have I ever sacrificed because I love you?"

Gertrude broke into tears and left the room.

Gladys would vividly recall her last conversation with him, late in the evening of January, 2, 1945. As if roused from a deep sleep, he tried to raise his head and whispered to her that someone was in the room with them.

"Who is that man?" Edgar asked.

Gladys couldn't see anyone, but she suspected that the Master of Masters had come for him. She asked Edgar to describe what he saw.

"He looks like a musical conductor," Edgar said. "[He's playing] beautiful music."

Gladys asked what kind of music was being played.

"I don't know" came the reply. "I don't know much about music."

Gladys was sure that he did. "You know all about music. You know about the harmonies of the universe."

At 7:15 the next day, Edgar stopped breathing. His journey through "God's other door" had begun, not with a blinding white light, but with music and a divine conductor. Gladys and Gertrude, too, understood what had happened.

In Edgar's first prayer experience as a child back in Beverly, music had been a bridge or means of expression linking a soul to God. People praying together could create a divine harmony. It was entirely appropriate that Jesus should appear to Cayce as the Master Musician and that Gladys should remind Edgar, who didn't play an instrument nor was particularly musically inclined, that he knew all about the harmonies of the universe.

He had dedicated himself to doing God's work.

Gertrude would join Edgar 3 months later on April 1, 1945. And until her death on February 12, 1986, Gladys would carry on the work with Hugh Lynn, Edgar Evans, and many others. The Association for Research and Enlightenment has since grown around the world and continues to carry on the Cayce mantle.

". . . Death in the physical is the birth in the spiritual, see?"
Edgar Cayce (900-331)

A.R.E. Press

Edgar Cayce (1877–1945) founded the non-profit Association for Research and Enlightenment (A.R.E.) in 1931, to explore spirituality, holistic health, intuition, dream interpretation, psychic development, reincarnation, and ancient mysteries—all subjects that frequently came up in the more than 14,000 documented psychic readings given by Cayce.

Edgar Cayce's A.R.E. provides individuals from all walks of life and a variety of religious backgrounds with tools for personal transformation and healing at all levels—body, mind, and spirit.

A.R.E. Press has been publishing since 1931 as well, with the mission of furthering the work of A.R.E. by publishing books, DVDs, and CDs to support the organization's goal of helping people to change their lives for the better physically, mentally, and spiritually.

In 2009, A.R.E. Press launched its second imprint, 4th Dimension Press. While A.R.E. Press features topics directly related to the work of Edgar Cayce and often includes excerpts from the Cayce readings, 4th Dimension Press allows us to take our publishing efforts further with like-minded and expansive explorations into the mysteries and spirituality of our existence without direct reference to Cayce-specific content.

A.R.E. Press/4th Dimension Press
215 67th Street
Virginia Beach, VA 23451

Learn more at EdgarCayce.org. Visit ARECatalog.com to browse and purchase additional titles.

ARE Press.com

Edgar Cayce's A.R.E.

Who Was Edgar Cayce?
Twentieth Century Psychic and Medical Clairvoyant

Edgar Cayce (pronounced Kay-Cee, 1877-1945) has been called the "sleeping prophet," the "father of holistic medicine," and the most-documented psychic of the 20th century. For more than 40 years of his adult life, Cayce gave psychic "readings" to thousands of seekers while in an unconscious state, diagnosing illnesses and revealing lives lived in the past and prophecies yet to come. But who, exactly, was Edgar Cayce?

Cayce was born on a farm in Hopkinsville, Kentucky, in 1877, and his psychic abilities began to appear as early as his childhood. He was able to see and talk to his late grandfather's spirit, and often played with "imaginary friends" whom he said were spirits on the other side. He also displayed an uncanny ability to memorize the pages of a book simply by sleeping on it. These gifts labeled the young Cayce as strange, but all Cayce really wanted was to help others, especially children.

Later in life, Cayce would find that he had the ability to put himself into a sleep-like state by lying down on a couch, closing his eyes, and folding his hands over his stomach. In this state of relaxation and meditation, he was able to place his mind in contact with all time and space—the universal consciousness, also known as the super-conscious mind. From there, he could respond to questions as broad as, "What are the secrets of the universe?" and "What is my purpose in life?" to as specific as, "What can I do to help my arthritis?" and "How were the pyramids of Egypt built?" His responses to these questions came to be called "readings," and their insights offer practical help and advice to individuals even today.

The majority of Edgar Cayce's readings deal with holistic health and the treatment of illness. Yet, although best known for this material, the sleeping Cayce did not seem to be limited to concerns about the physical body. In fact, in their entirety, the readings discuss an astonishing 10,000 different topics. This vast array of subject matter can be narrowed down into a smaller group of topics that, when compiled together, deal with the following five categories: (1) Health-Related Information; (2) Philosophy and Reincarnation; (3) Dreams and Dream Interpretation; (4) ESP and Psychic Phenomena; and (5) Spiritual Growth, Meditation, and Prayer.

Learn more at EdgarCayce.org.

What Is A.R.E.?

Edgar Cayce founded the non-profit Association for Research and Enlightenment (A.R.E.) in 1931, to explore spirituality, holistic health, intuition, dream interpretation, psychic development, reincarnation, and ancient mysteries—all subjects that frequently came up in the more than 14,000 documented psychic readings given by Cayce.

The Mission of the A.R.E. is to help people transform their lives for the better, through research, education, and application of core concepts found in the Edgar Cayce readings and kindred materials that seek to manifest the love of God and all people and promote the purposefulness of life, the oneness of God, the spiritual nature of humankind, and the connection of body, mind, and spirit.

With an international headquarters in Virginia Beach, Va., a regional headquarters in Houston, regional representatives throughout the U.S., Edgar Cayce Centers in more than thirty countries, and individual members in more than seventy countries, the A.R.E. community is a global network of individuals.

A.R.E. conferences, international tours, camps for children and adults, regional activities, and study groups allow like-minded people to gather for educational and fellowship opportunities worldwide.

A.R.E. offers membership benefits and services that include a quarterly body-mind-spirit member magazine, *Venture Inward*, a member newsletter covering the major topics of the readings, and access to the entire set of readings in an exclusive online database.

Learn more at EdgarCayce.org.

EDGARCAYCE.ORG